The Guardian Guide to Careers

Contents

3 Go get it!   223

4 Day by day: how to find a job in a month   307

Thanks to writers, contributors and the generally helpful: Sylvia Arthur,
Tola Awogbamiye, Tash Banks, Rosie Blau, Miles Brignall, Marianne Curphey,
Lisa Darnell, Hilary Freeman, Karen Hainsworth, Andrew Haydon, Alice Hunt,
Adeline Iziren, Irene Krechowiecka, Harriet Marsh, Amy McLellan, Barbara Oaff,
Stephen Overell, Ruth Petrie, Su Quinn, Sarah Richardson, Lucy Ridout, Ben Siegle,
John Sturzaker, Fiona Thompson, Annabelle Thorpe, Louise Tickle, Jilly Welch,
David Williams, Ian Wylie, Charles Young.

And especially to Nikki, Sammy and Olivia.

Introduction

■ It's simpler than you think

I've no idea what colour my parachute is. I'm not even sure I've got one. I don't know who moved my cheese, or even if there was much left. If there's blue-sky thinking to be done, it's when I'm planning my holidays.

Management and career theories are all very well but they don't half use some daft terminology. And after a while, you start to think that this may be deliberate – to make you think that getting a job and moving on up the ladder depends on joining a rather exclusive club where they use an obscure coded language. Of course, to find the key to the code, you have to buy the book and the problem with elaborate theories is that they start to take over. People spend more time worrying about where they are in the theory that the job-hunting takes second place. It's a bit like colour-coding your revision notes when you're supposed to be revising. The notes look great, but you haven't achieved much.

This is not to say that the books and theories aren't actually very good. They contain some excellent ideas about work and how to succeed, and you'd do well to read them, but they tend to smokescreen the fact that looking for and getting a job you love is a rather practical matter. You have to decide what job you want and then go and get it. See? Simple.

Of course, there's a little more to it than that, but getting a job is a step-by-step process. You have to make sure that you know *why* you're taking each step and that you're happy with the choices you make. The first step (Part 1: Discover your niche), as you may have guessed for yourself before even picking up this book, is to decide what kind of job and lifestyle you want. Do you want to be rich? Do you want a clean conscience? Do you want to work outdoors? Now, these aren't mutually exclusive. You could, for example, be a successful cricketer who refuses to tour Zimbabwe while it's still ruled by Robert Mugabe. But they are pointers to the kind of career you should be considering, and provide clues as to where to look next. If you want to turn your hobby into a career, for example, you need to think hard about whether it's practical, whether there's a market for it and whether you're good enough at it to become successful. In Part 1, you should be asking yourself the sort of questions which could prick the bubble. Do you really want to work from home, never truly escape from the job and hardly speak to anyone all day? Are you genuinely cut out for an ethical career when what you really want is a gas-guzzling limousine outside your luxury apartment block, earned on the sort of cash that social work just doesn't generate? And could you really live with yourself, knowing that the investment funds you're working on rely heavily on an armaments industry that's blowing merry hell out of entire continents?

Once you've worked out what your priorities are, the next stage (Part 2: Find your industry) is to get specific – look at the individual industries which meet your criteria and then at the jobs within them to narrow down your search. Do you want to work with money? Then maybe try the financial sector. What tickles your fancy? What are you qualified for? And what would you be good at?

No book can make these choices for you. All we can do is prompt you to ask yourself the right questions, provide you with the information and offer hints for further research. We can try to ensure that when you are trying to come to some decisions, you do it from a position of knowledge, so that you don't dismiss a career simply because you know nothing about it or because you didn't realise you could do it. All we can ask is that you're honest with yourself. If you ask the questions inside your head, no one else is listening so don't be swayed by what others think. Don't head for a job because your ·mate is, or because your family think it's suitable – do what most appeals to you. You may get it wrong the first, or even second, time and you may find yourself in a job that doesn't suit. It may be that the role is wrong for you, or it could be that the whole industry just isn't right. Consider your options carefully but, in the end, do something. If a job is making you unhappy, you can change it.

Once you've made your choices, then the third part of the book (Part 3: Go get it!) is on the even more practical matter of how to get that job. It's all about persuading other people that they would like to work with you, and to be with you eight hours a day, five days a week, for forty-odd weeks a year. You have to persuade them that you're likeable, competent, trustworthy and hard-working enough to sit at a desk/in a tank/on a stage/wherever with them and prove that they were right to hire you all along. It's a question of learning how to sell yourself, of being confident enough in your own ability, of taking the care to present yourself in the best light and being tenacious enough to make sure that you're in the right place when the right opportunity comes up. You're an intelligent soul capable of making good decisions (you picked this book up after all), so now you just have to go ahead and prove it.

Finding the right career is a matter of planning ahead, making choices from a position of strength and working hard to achieve the goal you set yourself. And the goal itself is pretty straightforward. You want to find a job which provides enough money to fund the lifestyle you want for you and yours, and which fills forty or so hours a week in as enjoyable, stimulating and fulfilling a way as possible. It isn't rocket science, it doesn't involve parachutes and the cheese is just the one that goes with the crust you've earned. It won't always be easy and there's some hard thinking ahead and some pretty serious graft, but getting the right job is something we can all achieve and, by the end of this book, it won't be as far away as you thought.

1

Discover your niche

Before you do anything else, it would be as well to know where to start. And to do that, you need to know what your motivation is. Do you want to be rich? Fulfilled? Challenged? Yes, yes, you want to be all of those, but we don't all get to tick all the boxes with our career choices. You need to prioritise just what are the things you want most out of your career. And be honest with yourself (no one's listening). There's nothing wrong with wanting to be rich, nor is there anything wrong with wanting to be in charge or wanting to work in the sunshine. These are your choices, not anyone else's.

Another thing to remember is that none of these choices are mutually exclusive. You can be creative and rich. Ethical and outdoors. And, indeed, creative and rich *and* ethical and outdoors. This chapter, indeed this book, can't make your mind up for you: we're just raising the questions you should be considering.

■ I want to earn lots of money

What do you mean?

Flicking enviously through *Heat* magazine, who hasn't at some point reflected on the advantages of being seriously affluent? Of being in possession of smart cars and a prestigious home in a wonderful location? Is that your target, or are you prepared to settle for something more modest?

Will £30,000 do it? £50,000? More? The higher you set the financial bar, the narrower your career options. You can make a perfectly good living in almost any career, but if you want to be stinking rich then ask yourself just what you are prepared to do, what you are prepared to sacrifice. If money is seriously your sole motivation you need to select a career that attracts the cash and then make sure you're good at it. That may mean going into the financial sector or property – are you cut out for that? The rewards might be attractive but the day-to-day realities have to be faced too.

What jobs will you do?

If you have a talent, for football, music or writing fiction, for example, and fate sees that it is discovered, that's great. If you are lucky or determined to reach the top of your field there will be money eventually – even in relatively poorly paid career sectors like the NHS or acting. But the odds of obtaining a large salary – of, say, three times the national average wage of around £24,908 a year – significantly shorten if you choose to enter a money-generating profession like corporate law, strategic consultancy, investment banking or fund management. There's a logic to it: to make money, you need to work with money. So if you want a Porsche Boxster sitting on your gravel drive, you'll be interested to know that the highest salaries are to be found in investment banking, consultancy, law, oil companies, retail and commercial banks, IT and fast-moving consumer goods companies.

Another option is to be your own boss. Starting up a company direct from college or very early in your career is fraught with danger. Estimates vary, depending on which scare story you listen to, but the majority of businesses fail in the first few years. But succeed, and the rewards are yours, all yours.

For some leads, see the following sectors, but these are just suggestions for careers that can lead to cash, and there's money elsewhere too:

- ➤ **ADVERTISING, MARKETING AND PUBLIC RELATIONS:** see page 36
- ➤ **FINANCIAL SERVICES:** see page 93
- ➤ **LAW:** see page 142
- ➤ **MANAGEMENT CONSULTANCY:** see page 149
- ➤ **PROPERTY:** see page 172

What qualities do you need?

Money won't flow your way just like that. You will need commitment and the ability to keep calm under constant stress. The demand for results produces a very particular kind of pressure and you'll have to always be thinking ahead, be quick on your feet and in your mind, and committed heart and soul to your career. You'll need to be self-reliant and have management skills, technical expertise and a business brain.

To start, you'll also have to have the academic wherewithal. Employers recruiting for the really high-flying jobs will initially screen graduates on exam results. It's a given that candidates will have great A-levels and a 2:1 or first. For the financial sector, demonstrable numeracy is important but you don't necessarily need a number-crunching degree in economics, maths or statistics. Beyond that they're looking for aptitude and for someone that gets things done, can problem-solve and think for themselves.

If you fit the criteria, the recruitment process itself is pretty slick. The big consultancies, corporate law firms, banks and financial companies will be hanging round universities in your third or fourth year like flies round honey. If you've already left, it matters little as they have well-greased graduate recruitment programmes. Though these can be quite drawn out, requiring two or three interviews and the odd assessment day here and there, you will eventually be picked out if you're sufficiently clever, committed and quick-witted.

Will you like it?

You'll need stamina and dedication and this can have a knock-on effect on your personal life if you're asked to give too much of yourself to your job. But as you look around, remember that although it can be mentally punishing, it doesn't have to be. Many companies know that they have a duty of care to their employees and there are graduate recruitment schemes which are well respected but don't flog you half to death. The best way to find out about the atmosphere (which on City trading desks, for example, can be pretty macho) is to talk to people already there.

Remember too that while your vast salary might look impressive when you mention it casually in conversation ("anyone seen my Lotus keys?"), it can be less so when you work out your actual hourly rate, factoring not only the many hours you clock up in the office, but also the time spent travelling and entertaining clients. You may be being paid £60,000, but, if you're working 80 hours a week and are expected to go to America or Europe at a moment's notice, with no account taken of weekends spent travelling, then your life is not your own, and in terms of hourly rate you're being paid less than a temp.

While the financial sector has many qualities, it doesn't always have a brilliant record in selecting black, disabled or even female candidates. There's a thin line between a "cultural fit" (are you exactly like everyone else they've ever employed?) and discrimination, and the line can be blurred occasionally. However, light is filtering into even these dark corners and it's not the problem it once was. And if you are set on joining an investment bank or a corporate law firm, remember they are not all the same. Companies have different cultures and approaches: some will suit you more than others, and some will be easier to adapt to than others.

You also need to ask yourself some ethical questions. To some degree or other, most money is made off the back of another, so how much will you worry if you end up in an investment bank with big stakes in armaments or oil? If you don't give a monkey's then that's fair enough, but if it'll nag away, read the ethical questions at the end of each section in Part 2 (which starts on page 35).

More

Books

The Boardroom Entrepreneur by Mike Southon and Chris West (Random House)

Good to Great by Jim Collins (Random House)

Rich Dad, Poor Dad by Robert T Kiyosaki (Time Warner)

Online reading

Business Link www.businesslink.gov.uk

Leap to Success www.leaptosuccess.co.uk

Startups www.startups.co.uk

■ I want to do something ethical

What do you mean?

You will spend around 70,000 hours at work in your lifetime, so it makes sense to find a career that you can live with. One perhaps that makes you feel as though you are adding to, not subtracting from, the sum of human happiness.

The vast majority of job-seeking graduates rate ethical standards as imperative when seeking a new job. Obviously, some of you are lying, but for those who aren't you've got to ask yourself just what you consider to matter. Do you want to change the lives of individuals or do you want to change the world? Do you want to work with people or with the processes that affect them? And if the reality of your ethical stance means a lower salary and standard of living, will you be happy with inner warmth rather than a winter holiday in sunny climes?

What jobs will you do?

The obvious starting point for an ethical career is to look at the caring professions. There's a clear difference to be made to people's lives if you become a teacher, nurse, doctor or social worker. The entry points into these careers are well defined and the link between working and making a difference is obvious. But you don't have to be a teacher to work in an ethical way. A lawyer can work for human rights organisations, an architect can specialise in affordable housing, and a City trader can make sure his or her investments avoid arms manufacturers, tobacco companies and those firms that rely on sweatshops in the far east. In almost any job you have, you can make ethical choices somewhere along the way, by checking the provenance of the raw materials you use, by making sure you pay fair wages or by using recyclable materials.

An ethical stance is a state of mind: the skills you have are almost always transferable to a more ethical setting. Fair-trading companies still need IT; companies producing renewable energy still need someone to organise their human resources department. There are thousands of jobs in companies that were set up with ethics and making a difference in mind and it's as entrepreneurial a sector as any other. As with all ethical choices, however, you need to balance your priorities and weigh up your personal values, your practical needs and your interests. They are not always mutually exclusive.

For some potentially ethical careers, see the following sectors, but be aware that these are neither exclusively ethical nor are they the only careers that can have ethical elements:

What qualities do you need?

To enter the more obviously ethical professions of teaching, social work or healthcare you need the relevant academic and vocational training – a medical or social work degree, or a PGCE teaching qualification. Once you're in, you'll find that many ethical careers can make extraordinary demands in terms of the hours and dedication required of you. Hospitals, schools and social care departments are not noted for being over-resourced and the shortfalls in funding are usually plastered over by the willingness of staff to go the extra mile.

You will need to be patient with others (both colleagues and charges) and tolerant of the fact you may be seeing people at their most vulnerable and perhaps irrational. This might apply to a patient in a hospital, an asylum seeker desperate to stay or a bullied child in a playground. Yet you also need to be able to make logical decisions in such stressful situations. You'll need to retain enormous amounts of technical knowledge and have good communication skills – the ability to listen as well as talk. And you must inspire trust in those around you.

If you're outside those "obvious" professions, you'll still need the technical skills relevant to your job; a human resources officer in a charity needs to be just as qualified as an HR officer in a multinational. Don't think that an ethical workplace will have lower recruiting standards or that it should be grateful that you'll work for them at all. The endgame may be different, and money may not be the motivating factor for your ethical institution, but that doesn't mean they will set their sights at a lower level.

Whatever sector you end up in, you'll need to see the bigger picture, to realise that your actions make a difference beyond your workplace and that your responsibilities are correspondingly wider.

Will you like it?

There's no doubt that there's an enormous amount of satisfaction to be gained from an ethical career choice, whether it's from setting a child on the right road in life, getting a well constructed in an African village or, less dramatically, making sure your company recycles the ink canisters from its printers. Whatever difference you are making, the chances are it will help you sleep better at night. Which may be handy if that job is also a stressful one. Many ethical careers involve demanding situations, in hospitals or care homes perhaps, and that can be wearing. It's not for everyone and there's no shame in thinking "stuff that, I want an easier life".

Nor are the financial rewards always ample recompense. The caring professions don't top many salary leagues (although things have improved), and salaries often don't match the responsibility levels you have. True, they may match your reporting lines – you may get more money if you have responsibility for other staff – but they often don't reflect the responsibility you have over the lives of others. If you work in social care or for a charity, for example, then the work you do or don't do will directly affect the quality of life of a number of people. That can be deeply rewarding but also rather daunting. It's a question of balance. You may be a bit knackered and a bit skint, but isn't that a fair price for a clean conscience?

More

Books

Ethical Ambition by Derrick Bell (Bloomsbury)

The Ethical Careers Guide (New Internationalist Publications Ltd)

The Sustainable Careers Handbook by Allan Shepherd and Fiona Rowe (Centre for Alternative Technology)

Online reading

Environmental Careers www.environmentcareers.org.uk

Ethical Careers www.ethicalcareers.org

Ethical Consumer www.ethicalconsumer.org

Scientists for Global Responsibility www.sgr.org.uk/ethics.html

■ I want to make my hobby my work

What do you mean?

Imagine a working day spent doing the things you enjoy most. Not just activities that make up the best bits of your job but actually whatever it is you see as your source of relaxation or fun. By its very nature, your hobby is something you enjoy and are both good at and knowledgeable about. What would it take to turn that something into a way of earning your living?

It's a question that occurs to many, but is viable only for a few. Right from the off, you've got to be level-headed, hard-nosed, self-critical and all the other stern faces you can conjure up. The chances are that you won't be able to make a decent income from macrame. And if you want to earn a living from music, ask yourself if you really are as sweet-voiced as your mother seems to think.

But let's keep positive. It's better to have a dream you can adapt to reality than to let the difficulties prevent you from dreaming. Turning a hobby into a career is of course easier if you spend your spare time creating computer code rather than collecting mushrooms, but almost any activity has earning potential. It's easy to underestimate the knowledge, skills and contacts you develop around something you do in your spare time. You might be an expert without realising it and experts make money from sharing their insight.

What jobs will you do?

Take something that's comparatively easy to envisage as both a hobby and a job, like photography. If you're any good you can earn money simply by doing it: people will pay for what you produce. Perhaps not enough initially to provide the income you need but there are all sorts of related activities that could help keep you solvent. You could teach others to do it or sell products related to photography.

Depending on which other skills you have, you could write about it, give talks or organise photography-oriented holidays. There's no reason why you couldn't combine all of these. Many who successfully exploit the earning potential of a hobby do so through a multi-faceted approach. If the idea of taking a risk by working for yourself doesn't appeal, you could look for employment doing any one of these activities. Now substitute your hobby for photography to see if it could work for you (remembering that not every pastime will be suitable of course). Sport, art, music, drama and craft skills all have obvious potential, but you don't have to look hard to see people making a living from something that started as an interest – in good food and wine, for example, or in clothes, witchcraft, yoga, watching films, listening to music or even writing letters of complaint.

For many, turning a hobby into a profession means self-employment. It's often the logical step to move from making pottery for your friends and neighbours, for example, to selling it to strangers and building up a business from there. But if your chosen path lends itself to a more corporate way of earning cash, then some areas will be more fertile than others:

> ➤ **ARTS AND HERITAGE:** see page 47
> ➤ **FASHION:** see page 87
> ➤ **ICT:** see page 135
> ➤ **MEDIA AND JOURNALISM:** see page 158
> ➤ **SPORT AND LEISURE:** see page 197
> ➤ **TRAVEL:** see page 209

What qualities do you need?

First and foremost, you'll need some talent, or at least technical skills. It's no good trying to be a portrait artist if you can't paint for toffee or a professional footballer if you trap a ball further than you can kick it. To do something professionally you have to do it to a much higher standard than the average hobbyist. The problem lies in whether you are qualified to judge yourself. Are you being honest with yourself? You may think you are a fabulous creative writer but has anyone outside your immediate circle read what you have put to paper? And did you get an honest assessment out of them?

You almost certainly won't be the first person ever to have wondered what it would be like to do your chosen hobby professionally. Nor is it likely that you're the most talented person ever to have picked up a brush, pen or surfboard. The key will be your level of application and that could take any number of forms. It might mean you need to be dedicated to physical fitness; you may have to network like crazy; or you may just have to work harder than you ever have before. Each situation will require a different kind of commitment and stamina but success is unlikely to be instant so you'll need a great deal of stickability.

Even if you have, or are convinced you have, the talent, technical skills and determination to make a living, then that's not the end of it. To be self-employed, you'll need the business skills and application to make that work (see page 31 for more on being your own boss). Or if you find a role within a company, you'll need to learn how to adapt those funny little ways of doing things that seemed perfectly OK in your garden shed to a more corporate methodology. You won't be able go to work in your pyjamas any more.

Will you like it?

If you do get going, there's always the possibility that you suddenly find the hobby isn't so great after all. Dressmaking might be fine when you just do it every now and again, but if you're doing nothing else, the magic might start to wear off. Very few people can honestly say their work is relaxing; therefore, the reality is that once you turn your hobby into your work it brings pressure. Chances are you'll have to find yourself a new hobby.

Because you're so motivated and doing something enjoyable it's easy to work far too hard. Being overworked initially is almost inevitable, particularly if this move has also meant becoming self-employed. But not paying enough attention to the need for time away and involvement in other interests is a recipe for burnout. The big danger is losing the ability to switch off and that's not sustainable. Look at any survey on what is important to 21st-century workers and work–life balance is always near the top. Earning money from your hobby won't automatically put that right, though many assume it will. But that shouldn't stop you dreaming. Surfing every other weekend in St Ives is one thing, but just imagine – it's the world championships in Hawaii, and next up to the waves, it's you...

More

Books
Creating a Balance: Managing Stress by Stephen Palmer, Cary Cooper and Kate Thomas (British Library Publishing Division)
How to Get a Job You'll Love by John Lees (McGraw-Hill)
The Magic of Work by Mike Pegg (Management Books)

Online reading
Business Link www.businesslink.gov.uk
Prince's Trust www.princes-trust.org.uk
Shell LiveWIRE www.shell-livewire.org

■ I want to reinvent myself

What do you mean?

This one's more for those of you who've got a job. You might be on to your second or third by now and are thinking that perhaps you made a bit of a mistake. All of us at some stressful, boring or disastrous point in our careers will wish that we were elsewhere doing something more relaxing, interesting or successful. All of us, at some point, want to change.

Now at this, presumably quite early, stage in your career it might seem a little drastic to be pressing "restart" already. But, as you settle into a career in accountancy, say, you wouldn't be the first to think "I'd rather be a carpenter". How realistic is it to down your old tools and pick up a new set? Well, it's far from simple, but it is possible.

What jobs will you do?

Clearly, your first task is to decide what it is you really want to do. Knowing what you don't want to do is only about 5% of the journey. Choosing the next step is far harder. You should start with a self-audit. Look at yourself and try to understand what it is you see. List your strengths, skills and interests. Then write down what you like and dislike about your current position and what you want from any future position. Finally, note your values, what is important to you personally. Be honest. Be thorough.

Now do a careers brainstorm. Think of jobs or business opportunities that complement your abilities, enthusiasms and expectations. Use whatever you need for inspiration, perhaps a business directory, a recruitment website, the employment section of a newspaper, or some type of specialist careers counsellor. You may find you come up with lots of ideas. Possibly too many. Here is the agony and ecstasy of choice. The solution is to rank your options.

Go on now to investigate your top preferences. For a job, find out what it really involves, how much it actually pays, what type of vacancies are currently advertised and what type of training you would need. For a business, determine what you would offer, the demand for your product or service, the mechanism for bringing it to the marketplace and the funding required to put it all into practice. Even if you think you are fairly well informed, do a reality check anyway. Read books, scan the papers, look at industry websites and flick through industry journals. Also, go to networking occasions where you can talk to people in the job or business itself. Perhaps even arrange to shadow them for a day or two. Or offer to do some voluntary work.

Afterwards, compare your real view of the job or business opportunity with your imagined view. Expect to be surprised. Maybe shocked. Hopefully also excited and enthused. At the end of it all you should know which job or business is most suited to you and your future.

What qualities do you need?

Figuring out how to realise that future is the next challenge. This can take more time and be more complicated than you might imagine. Changing careers is not fast. It takes months and years rather than days and weeks. Consider how long it will take you, how much it will cost you, and what impact it will have on those closest to you. Stay realistic. Next, identify which steps to do in which order. Bear in mind the one that is the easiest, the quickest, the least risky, the least expensive. Factor in items such as retraining (or, more fundamentally, taking a whole new degree course) and relocation and note the change in earnings, career structure and long-term prospects that any new direction might bring.

When it comes to funding all this, you have various possibilities:

- See if you can take a break from making your monthly rent or mortgage repayments. Alternatively, find out if you can reduce them by extending the life of your mortgage or by switching to a cheaper interest rate. Or consider simply renting a cheaper flat.

- Reduce your overheads: shop for cheaper insurance, look for more competitive utility providers and cut back on luxuries.

- Apply for a grant. The Educational Grants Advisory Service can outline what is available for job-shifters. For business start-ups, talk to your local Business Link centre.

- Get a career development loan or a professional development loan to cover tuition fees and some living expenses.

- Cash in some investments or dip into some savings. This may be the rainy day you have been waiting for.

The best way to get that first break is to network. Networking can get you to where you want to be much quicker. It can give you vital information about upcoming vacancies and introduce you to the people who do the hiring. It can also give you invaluable intelligence on what the market is doing and where the dangers and chances lie. So, contact the relevant professional bodies and go to their meetings, seminars, dinners and lunches. Mix and mingle at other events where you are likely to meet people of interest and influence.

Of course, even if you do make good contacts that lead to interviews, that doesn't guarantee you'll be chosen for the job. Be sure your CV has been brought up to date and modified to suit the career you want to take on, not the one you want to leave behind. Also, ensure you use each interview to confidently convey why you are up for the job; in the absence of any substantial experience always highlight your potential and your energy.

Will you like it?

It will be impossible to always be positive during this rigorous reinvention process. Changing your career can effectively mean changing your life and that is bound to present difficulties. At some point, you will feel overwhelmed by your decision. In moments of despair, try to remember why you wanted to change careers in the first place. Then see yourself in that role and imagine how much happier you'll feel. If your self-confidence is taking a bit of a knock revisit your list of capabilities and competencies. Read over it. Know it to be true. Also, talk to friends and family who are supportive of you and will help rebuild your inner faith. To overcome a sense of impatience at how slow everything seems to be going look at what you have already achieved. Then celebrate it. Remind yourself that the longer it takes, the more rewarding it will be. Finally, be inspired by the actions and achievements of others.

But one small word of caution. Be courteous and correct in leaving your old job. And thank everyone who assisted you. Don't be tempted to be anything other than scrupulous in all your words and deeds as you never know when you are likely to cross paths with people again. Or when you'll want your old job back.

More

Books

The Career Change Handbook by Graham Green (How To Books)

Dare to Change Your Job and Your Life by Carole Kanchier (Jist Publishing)

Planning a Career Change by Judith Johnstone (How To Books)

Online reading

Business Link www.businesslink.gov.uk

Career development loans www.lifelonglearning.co.uk

Community Service Volunteers www.csv.org.uk

Educational Grants Advisory Service www.egas-online.org

■ I want to work from home

What do you mean?

So you love the idea of defining your own working day? You delight in daydreams of dumping your boss (even if you haven't got one yet), having friends over for lunch and finishing at four? Clearly, working from home is the only way forward. But it's not all sushi and green tea for people who take this appealing-looking career option.

Temptations abound and the variety of extra-office activities are limitless. Friends and family know you're at home and often expect you to be ready to play. And then there are those duvet days that can so easily slip into duvet vacations without anybody knowing the difference. Dress-down Friday becomes dressing-gown Monday and the only thing that can get you moving is you. Naturally you need to work out whether you can keep temptation at bay. If you've got what it takes, however, the benefits will ensure you remain a homeworker forever.

The flexibility and not having to commute are the two things that most tempt people to work from home. We all, at some point, get sick of fighting through the traffic and having to be at our desk at a certain time. You might also want more freedom, more of a work–family balance and less stress, all of which could be achieved by spending more time in the home environment. But if the idea of working from home is appealing because you want to avoid work, then maybe, just maybe, this isn't going to work.

What jobs will you do?

Gradually, more of us are taking the plunge. According to the Office for National Statistics in 2004, more than 2.1 million people work from home, and 8 million spend part of their week in the house, hooked up to the outside world via a computer, telephone line and fax. Occupations include those you might expect, like web design and freelance journalism, but solicitors, radio presenters, audio typists, architects and travel agents can also fulfil their role outside of the office as long as they've got the right equipment – generally a computer, broadband access, and a nice little cubbyhole away from everyone else.

You're in the strongest position if you are in work already. If you are the parent of a child of six or under and/or if you're the parent of a disabled child, then you can make use of legislation that creates a framework for homeworking. This enables you to make an application to your employer in a very formal way. They have to respond within a certain number of weeks and if they don't let you do it they have to come up with a good reason why not. Ultimately there is an employment tribunal if they can't justify their refusal but usually it's a matter of working out a practical way forward with the employer.

If you're looking to go down the self-employment route, then only you know if you have the talent, contacts, motivation and self-promotion skills to make it happen. If the preparation is done right and things run smoothly, you'll be able to work to your own schedule. And if you're at home opening a bottle at 6pm instead of waiting for the delayed 18.03 out of Cannon Street, then who's to say you haven't cracked it?

In the end, there's any number of jobs that can be done from home even in industries that don't seem too promising to start with. Want to work in healthcare? Certain complementary practices can be run from home – osteopathy or physiotherapy for example – if you have a big enough house. Only you can know if your work and your desired work practices can really be married up, but some areas may be more promising than others:

> **ARTS AND HERITAGE:** see page 47
> **EDUCATION:** see page 56
> **FASHION:** see page 87
> **HEALTHCARE:** see page 114
> **MANAGEMENT CONSULTANCY:** see page 149
> **MEDIA AND JOURNALISM:** see page 158
> **PROPERTY:** see page 172

What qualities do you need?

Consider your style of interaction. Think about how you like to work and the type of communication you enjoy. Do you prefer having conversations face to face or on the telephone? Do you like working things out on your own or swapping ideas with a team? And how do you deal with problems or decisions – alone or with input from others? It's still possible to get others involved in your work when you're based at home, but it requires organisation.

One of the key factors that could influence your success or failure as a home- or teleworker is your level of competency at the outset. A lack of expert knowledge in your chosen field can be stressful. Asking a question of the colleague sitting next to you can feel very different from telephoning someone for an answer, particularly if you don't really know them. It's far better to learn the job thoroughly first and then take the plunge and start doing it from home.

If you're still determined, if you reckon you've got the right personality, the right type of home and the right type of family set-up, then there are a few practicalities to sort out:

- Check your mortgage and lease details to see if there are any restrictions on running a business from home.

- Work out what equipment you need and get expert advice before you decide to purchase.

- Keep yourself safe by downloading a copy of the homeworkers' health and safety booklet from the Health and Safety Executive's website (www.hse.gov.uk).

Will you like it?

Have you really got the self-discipline to make a success of this way of doing things? It's important to know yourself very well. You need to know if you can maintain your self-motivation, and as importantly, what de-motivates you.

It can all add up to a big lifestyle change. If you do switch to working in your slippers, you'll enjoy a honeymoon period when everything is hunky-dory and your only thoughts are as to why you didn't do this earlier. Then you'll start to get friends popping round for a chat. There's still a notion that unless you go out to work, preferably in a suit, you're not actually gainfully employed, so you're fair game for those on the hunt for a witter and a biscuit. And how good are you at self-motivation? Perhaps you won't have any problems getting your work done but you might discover hidden aspects of your personality – like the cookie monster for example. It is, after all, far easier to eat a whole packet of choccy biscuits when there's nobody to watch you nibbling.

Whether you're a nibbler or not, homeworkers do tend to be more productive and work longer hours than those in the office. You'll be trying to prove to yourself and to your clients or bosses that you are just as good as, if not better than, you were in the old days. Of course, that hard work creates a level of expectation in those you work with and for. What? You're ill? But you're at home – you can still get to your computer...

Happily, most of these challenges can be overcome. You can limit your chances of overdoing it, for example, by making a distinction between your home and your business, both physically and psychologically. It's very important to have a separate place of work. Otherwise you could be sat at your desk all the time, always working because work is always there. Some people are very fortunate and can convert a garage or a bedroom.

And then there's the rest of the household to consider. Conflicts happen when a spouse or family has a different idea of when the homeworker's working day should end. A successful homeworker is one who can stand back and assess themselves, their personality and their family needs – and discuss and agree a working model that suits everyone.

And there's one definite no-no. Homeworking and childcare do not mix: both are full-time jobs and they simply can't be combined. So set up childcare arrangements just the same as if you were going to the office, and as your children get older, make sure your nippers have an understanding of what work and your workspace mean. A child wailing in the background does not give your client confidence that the work will be done on time.

More

Books

The Quick Guide to Working from Home by Hugh Williams (Lawpack Publishing)

The Which Guide to Working from Home by Lynn Brittney (Which Books)

Working from Home by Peter Hingston and Alastair Balfour (Dorling Kinderlsey)

Online reading

Health and Safety Executive's PDF file on homeworking www.hse.gov.uk

Telework Association www.tca.org.uk

■ I want to work outdoors

What do you mean?

You might want to feel the wind on your face and the ground beneath your feet; you might yearn to be close to nature and in touch with the seasons; you might long for the sheer invigoration of a more physical and more organic existence; or perhaps you just can't stand sitting in an open-plan office opposite some pasty-faced dullard all day. All perfectly legitimate reasons for wanting the outdoor life. But don't go thinking that the outdoor life is somehow simpler. Forget those patronising city thoughts right now. An outdoor life, even a rural existence, can be every bit as complex as a city-based career, so don't, for a second, think this is an easy option.

You need to be sure you know what you mean by working outdoors. Do you mean in a rural environment or just work that doesn't involve sitting at a desk all day? Are you after escaping the rat race or just the 11am race for the coffee machine? There's a world of difference between industrial engineering and running your own organic farm, so just a breezy desire for fresh air is not a real career decision. Will your skills translate out of doors? There's not much call for open-air software engineering but construction engineering does cut it. You need to translate vague notions into career realities. And you need to be ready for the rain.

What jobs will you do?

We can divide "outdoors" into rural and urban and there are opportunities aplenty in both. Rural industries are an increasingly sophisticated and competitive area in which to work, as well as being pretty big business. Agricultural work has been in some measure of decline over decades and indeed centuries. But that doesn't mean you shouldn't consider it. For one, it can be a very agreeable option and for another, there are new opportunities as agribusiness finds new ways to diversify. The increase in demand for organic produce for example produces new challenges and opportunities, while genetically modified crops, on the other hand, present both a moral quandary and an economic opportunity, with trials still taking place, even if some have to be in secret.

On the environmental side of countryside work, there are not just opportunities but clear skills shortages. Environmental organisations have a much broader role than many people realise. Where once they might have just been a pressure group involved in merely drawing public and government attention to a problem, they are now much more occupied with advising on and providing solutions. This means they require people who are both concerned and have the skills to act. Yet there are not enough people coming through from the universities and it is becoming more of a challenge to fill vacancies in both government and the charity sector, as well as in the commercial consultancies advising organisations on their environmental commitments.

Although there are already more than 2 million people employed in maintaining and developing the built environment, there is still a skills shortfall. The construction industry calculates that it is going to need an additional 83,000 people a year for the foreseeable future, whether that be in civil engineering or in the follow-on trades such as electricians and plasterers. The price of labour in the UK has doubled since the start of the millennium, while the starting salary for civil engineers has risen steadily and graduates are being tempted with golden hellos and sponsorship deals. The skills shortage is particularly noticeable in the south of England but it does extend throughout the UK.

Anyone deciding today to train in construction or engineering is likely to have their investment rewarded. Another advantage of working in construction is that it is very easy to find small firms who might be prepared to train you up; it's also straightforward to set up on your own as start-up costs are very low. Over 97% of the construction industry workforce is employed in companies that have fewer than 50 employees and there are over 60,000 sole traders.

For outdoor work, you can consider:

➤ **ENGINEERING:** see page 66
➤ **ENVIRONMENTAL, FOOD CHAIN AND RURAL:** see page 73

What qualities do you need?

Most people working outdoors will need to develop the ability to manage themselves for part or all of the time. There are downsides to self-determination. While some jobs such as building-site work can be very social, others such as farming and conservation work can require spending a lot of time in your own company and not everyone thrives in this situation. Equally, while a lack of immediate supervision can bring a new sense of personal responsibility, it can sometimes mean that there is no one to turn to when things go wrong and that there is no defined career path to follow.

And you can forget the idea that outdoor jobs are all about age-old skills and values. While this may be the case for some kinds of organic farming and outdoor crafts, working under the sky does not mean you can get by without developing sound business and IT skills. You also need to be flexible. Rain, snow, temperature, livestock, insects and ground conditions are all unpredictable, and anyone working outdoors quickly learns that sometimes they cannot do what they intended to do at a certain time. People who like to control their environment and their time are less likely to thrive in the open air.

Will you like it?

Working outdoors is not only about living like Hugh Fearnley-Whittingstall or hand-rearing your own Gloucester Old Spot. Outdoor jobs can also be urban and industrial, so the air may not be so fresh nor the landscape quite so appealing. And that might be a problem. But if the ephemera of new technology palls and the idea of real horny-handed graft appeals, then the outdoors will offer opportunities as wide as the horizon.

For large parts of the rural and food industries, it is less a job and more a way of life. Farmers and conservation workers often live and work within the same environment and the job can, therefore, be all-consuming. Commitment is everything. For others it will be 9–5 in the lab or the office, although you may work shift patterns if you're in a 24-hour food production unit for example. In construction or engineering, normal working hours are more likely to apply, but even there you can be expected to do a lot more when rain delays, for example, have pushed you right to your deadlines.

Since you're never entirely in control outdoors, this necessarily means that you will be entailing more risk. There is considerable variation across industries. Large-scale construction is now very risk-aware, but smaller owner-managed businesses sometimes cut corners and expose their workforces to situations that are only rarely tolerated indoors. We're not saying you're putting your life on the line every time you put your workboots on, but a higher threshold to acceptable levels of risk can come in handy.

More

Books

Careers Working Outdoors by Judith Humphries and Allan Shepherd (Kogan Page)

Working Outdoors by Mark Hillsdon (Department for Education and Skills)

Real Life Guides: Working Outdoors by Margaret McAlpine (Trotman)

Online reading

Construction Industry Training Board-ConstructionSkills
www.citb.org.uk

National Farmers' Union www.nfuonline.com

Naturenet www.naturenet.net

■ I want to work abroad

What do you mean?

Can you imagine yourself spending lunch-breaks seeking out the best bistro that Paris has to offer? How about lazing beside the river Arno in Florence, or nipping out to do a bit of shopping on New York's Fifth Avenue? Of course you can, and that is because most people have at one time or another wondered what it would be like to live and work abroad.

The huge growth in international business and the tearing down of trade barriers have both conspired to produce a world in which people routinely move around continents as part of their careers. It is no longer unusual to come across executives who have worked in each of the major continents, and even those who simply spend a year in another country almost always benefit from it.

Working abroad can mean a number of different things. Does it entail a permanent move or is it a short-term posting? Do you want to pursue a chosen career in another location or are the career and travel intertwined? Do you understand the level of commitment involved in making such a huge change in your lifestyle? For some, the idea of working abroad is a delaying tactic, a chance to try out new challenges, sometimes half-heartedly, while waiting for their real career to reveal itself. They may do fairly mundane jobs such as bar work or fruit-picking just for the sheer joy of being in another country. But the decision we're considering here is a longer-term one.

What jobs will you do?

Any number of careers can take you abroad. A journalist might, for example, be posted to Washington as a special correspondent. Sales staff might be sent to exploit new markets in the far east. IT staff could be flown out to set up online banking and call centres in India. The possibilities are vast. And then there are the professions that lend themselves more obviously to travel, like the travel industry, or the armed forces.

But there are two obvious ways to make sure you get to travel for your work. The first is to choose a career path or organisation that offers the possibility of moving overseas, and then carefully manoeuvre yourself into a position where you are sent abroad. So if you're in banking, you'll begin by jockeying for a position with a multinational, before looking at the international section of the internal vacancies. And if working abroad is your game plan don't get a job in local government, for example. Pick an industry that translates across national boundaries and start plotting from there.

The other angle is to decide where and when you want to go, and then set about finding the position that will enable that to happen. If you want to work in Japan, then perhaps a Tefl (teaching English as a foreign language) role would suit, or maybe something in electronic engineering?

But remember that working abroad will be just as rubbish as working at home if you can't do the job. You will need the skills for the industry you choose and all other rules apply. All you're doing is changing the setting.

If you're set on heading for the airport, then you could try:

> **EDUCATION (TEFL):** see page 61
> **ENGINEERING:** see page 66
> **FINANCIAL SERVICES:** see page 93
> **ICT:** see page 135
> **MEDIA AND JOURNALISM:** see page 158
> **TRANSPORT:** see page 203
> **TRAVEL:** see page 209
> **UNIFORMED (ARMED) SERVICES:** see page 216

What qualities do you need?

Just as the secret of buying property is all about location, the secret of getting a good job abroad is languages, languages, languages. Unless you are going to work in the English-speaking world, your prospects will be greatly enhanced by, and in some cases will stand or fall on, your knowledge of the local language. How much of it you're going to require depends on where you're going and what sort of company you are joining. For example, it is relatively easy to work in Holland without any Dutch, but quite difficult to work in France without very good French. That said, plenty of multi-national companies now use English as the language of business and it's quite common to find groups of, say, designers from all around the world working in France but communicating in English. It's worth noting, though, that even if you find yourself in such a position, it is quite difficult to integrate into a place without being able to communicate about issues more complicated than the weather. In short, any time you spend learning the language of the country in which you want to work will not be wasted. It is not by chance that those who are able to speak the local language seem to get the most out of working and living abroad.

To live abroad, away from your family and friends, takes a good deal of commitment. Many try it and come back after months of homesickness. And there's nothing wrong with that. Before you sign up to a year or two abroad, make sure it's what you want and check the details around the job just as much as the job itself. Will the company help you find somewhere to live? If you have a partner or family, what are the arrangements for them to come with you? And what's the support network like, once you get there?

From the company's point of view, your most important quality is that you can do the job. The qualities you need to fill that foreign posting are largely those of experience, skill and aptitude and only you and they know if you've got those.

Will you like it?

Whatever your route, it is unlikely that you will regret it. George Orwell famously said that the best way to get to know a people was to go and work amongst them, and he was right. Working abroad is stimulating for a number of reasons. It is incredibly challenging to work in an entirely new environment, perhaps in another language, not least because it should cause you to question many of your preconceptions, and introduce you to a few new ideas. Culturally it may be very different; if you move to Europe you may have to learn to stop and take two hours off for lunch no matter what, and if you go to the US the opposite ethos generally applies. Even on a basic level, mundane things like food shopping suddenly become interesting again. Getting a phone connected is a battle just waiting to be won, and your weekends off are suddenly spent skiing, going out into the desert, trekking, whatever...

You also walk into a network of sorts provided by your new work colleagues, and someone will usually be on hand to explain the local customs and deal with any bureaucracy. Even if it isn't your dream job, it will enable you to get into the country or city of your choice, and to start moving in the right circles. It's now considered quite reasonable to say at an interview for a new job that you would like to be sent abroad at some point, as long as that fits in with their future plans for you. It also shows you've got ambition and a bit of balls.

More

Books

The Back Door Guide to Short-Term Job Adventures by Michael Landes (Ten Speed Press)

The Guardian Guide to Working Abroad by Nick Clayton (A&C Black Publishers)

Working Abroad: The Complete Guide to Overseas Employment by Jonathan Reuvid (Kogan Page)

Online reading

Eurograduate www.eurograduate.com

Foreign & Commonwealth Office www.fco.gov.uk

Study and Work Abroad www.independentliving.org/studyworkabroad

---

■ I want to be a leader

What do you mean?

You have a burning desire to become the next Anita Roddick, Bill Gates or Tony Blair, but do you want to be admired and recognised or do you want to make a difference? Do you want glory or do you want to be the person who changes things?

The first thing you're going to have to learn is a little patience. Unless you're self-employed, leadership does not come straight away. Just as you won't be made captain of your football team on your first day, so management and leadership roles are something you earn and move on to. But if it is such a role you want, you have to plan ahead and make sure you have the skills and experience to take on the grown-ups' roles when they become available.

Exactly what you do doesn't make much difference if it's leadership you're interested in. You can be the top bod in almost any field. What matters more is the attitude you take to the job you do. The higher the level to which you aspire, the broader your focus will need to be. This means being able to think across a range of different business areas or functions and, importantly, being effective at thinking about longer-term developments across industries and markets. As you progress to higher-level leadership positions, you are likely to become more distanced from your technical specialism. So, if you passionately enjoy your current technical area, whether this be in science, finance, marketing or human resources, it is worth considering whether you would be happier following a "senior specialist" route instead.

What jobs will you do?

Every field needs its leader. You can be the headmaster of a school, a captain of industry, the head of a primary care trust in the health service. Your task, should you choose to accept it, is to focus on the top of the mountain, not the foothills.

The key to your future lies in the fact of your management, not necessarily what, or who, you are managing. While you'll need core skills to understand the business you work in and to gain the respect of your colleagues, these are merely the tools to a different end. Look at the structure of the industry you're about to enter and see if it opens up the possibilities you're looking for. A chance for promotion? For training and development? And how important is speed? Do you want to rise quickly or are you content to emerge slowly at the top of a very large pack? Know yourself, your capabilities and the extent of your ambition and then all you need do is choose a horizon to aim for.

What qualities do you need?

A careful process of self-examination won't be wasted. Arguably the most crucial leadership quality is self-awareness. To be a successful leader, you'll need to have a clear understanding of your strengths and capacities, together with a well-tuned ability to find opportunities to deploy these to the full. You'll be able to manage the downsides associated with your strengths (does your self-confidence spill into over-confidence?) and min-imise your weaknesses. And the best way to do that is to hire people who are good at what you can't do. Bad at the financial side? Hire the best accounts department you can afford.

You'll also need to be an excellent communicator: socially adept and good at influencing people, particularly from a distance for those who don't report directly to you. The people who make up teams in organisations may have different reporting lines, and a leader needs to be politically astute in understanding all the different lines and agendas.

And what you're communicating is rather important too. To be success-ful in your leadership role, you'll need a strong vision for the future and you'll need to be able to plan ahead and react quickly and decisively when those plans go awry. The best way to be adaptable is to be a good learner. Those who rise to the top are very good learners. They will actually seek out situations, roles and tasks which are slightly beyond their present comfort zone so that they can give themselves development "stretch". Those who tend to stay predominantly within the realm of familiar situations or stick to tasks that they can handle easily are less likely to progress their development or their career prospects.

You'll also need high levels of "emotional intelligence". This means being very good at reading what is required to get on and be effective in your organisation, then adapting your approach and behaviour in response – while still remaining authentic to your own principles and values.

Will you like it?

It's really important to give serious thought to your overall life plan and where work fits in with that. Think carefully about what you want to do with your life in general, and whether your chosen career direction will either add to that or make it more difficult to achieve. Sometimes people come to the decision that a big leadership role would not be satisfying for them and that they would be better off being more flexible by working freelance or in a consulting role. It's easy to be blinded by the glamour of leadership roles, but there are a lot of onerous aspects too.

The rewards of pursuing a leadership role are recognition, success, money (usually) and a job that constantly challenges you. You will be in charge of leading the business or institution to sustainable financial and non-financial performance, helping people learn and grow and grooming your successors.

The drawbacks are that many leaders end up living for their work, putting in long hours and neglecting home and social life. They can find it difficult to build and maintain close relationships, and it can be lonely at the top, particularly if you are in an executive-level role. There is constant pressure, and if you joined an industry because you loved your subject, you will have to let go of being a technical expert.

And not least, remember that if you're at the top, you're there to be sniped at. Many a comedian has noted that it's a shame that all the people best qualified to run the country are too busy driving taxis or cutting hair. And it's the same in any organisation – everyone knows that, whatever it is the boss is doing, they could do it better. Being top of the pile opens you up to all the criticism and all the whining from those below, none of whose skills have been properly recognised, none of whom are properly paid and all of whom want your job.

More

Books

The First 90 Days: Critical Success Strategies for New Leaders at All Levels by Michael Watkins (Harvard Business School Press)

Funky Business by Jonas Ridderstrale and Kjell Nordstrom (FT Prentice Hall)

Leadership and the One Minute Manager by Ken Blanchard, Patricia Zigarmi and Drea Zigarmi (HarperCollins Business)

Online reading

Department of Trade and Industry www.dti.gov.uk

Mind Tools www.mindtools.com

Secrets of Success www.secretsofsuccess.com

■ I want to work for myself

What do you mean?

Working for yourself is always an attractive option. At least you know the boss isn't an idiot. You can roll in late if you fancy it, you don't have to sit in meetings wondering what the sales director just asked you, and you don't have to barter with anyone else about when to take your holidays.

By working for yourself, do you mean freelance work or do you mean setting up your own business? Working as a freelancer isn't really working for yourself, it's a form of serial monogamy – you have to work for a series of different bosses. The difference is that if you don't like them you can, providing you've got enough other options, just not work for them again. And the freelance life also offers you the chance to work at your own pace and pursue the sort of projects that interest you most, whether that's working on particular gaming software, writing solely about financial issues or designing costumes for TV dramas.

However, working for yourself can, and frequently does, mean setting up your own business. Is this your game plan? Have you the bottle, the backing and the brilliant idea to make it a success? You may have always wanted your own chutney emporium, but is the rest of the world ready for it? The world of the small business is fraught with danger, and a little realism never hurt. Around 310 businesses a week went bust in 2004. Many fail within the first year as poor planning, cash-flow problems and over-ambitious expansion kick in. But don't let that put you off. What's worse: fear of failure or everlasting regret? It could even be that you're just the kind of person cut out for business success.

What jobs will you do?

The first step on the road to a successful business is to have a good idea. Begin by looking at jobs you've had and the skills you've already acquired. Ask yourself how you can use these skills to start a business. Think about your hobbies: can these be transformed into a viable business? Also, look at the products and services you use. Can you improve them? Are there products and services you need that don't exist?

Inspiring stories abound of go-getting individuals who have improved existing services or products or created new ones, whether it's producing fat-free muffins or running a nanny agency. The only way you'll know for sure if your idea will fly is by doing your research. Find out if people will buy your product or service and if they have other related needs you could meet. If you want to provide a product or service that already exists, look at the competition. Consider the competition's strengths and weaknesses and ask yourself how you could provide a better service or product. Consider the impact your product or service will have on the environment. What waste will it produce? What can be done with the waste? Is any of it recyclable?

The next step is to write a business plan. A business plan is more than just a tool to help you get funding, it's like a roadmap to get you where you want to be. Developing it requires a lot of time and energy, but it's invaluable for one primary reason – it forces you to come to terms with your business idea. Your written business plan should cover how you will generate income, what your expenses will be and what your business does. It may seem obvious what your business does, but you need to think about it and consider what sets your business apart, what service you offer that is unique and what is going to put you ahead of the competition.

You can be your own boss in almost any industry, but the following are particularly common:

> **ADVERTISING, MARKETING AND PUBLIC RELATIONS:** see page 36

> **FASHION:** see page 87

> **HEALTHCARE:** see page 114

> **HOSPITALITY:** see page 125

> **MANAGEMENT CONSULTANCY:** see page 149

> **PROPERTY:** see page 172

> **RETAIL:** see page 178

What qualities do you need?

To reduce your career to the banalities of a teen magazine: if you can answer "yes" to six or more of the following questions, then you probably have what it takes.

• Are you willing to take risks?

• Do you have one or more goals that you want to achieve?

• Are you an optimist?

• Do you make the most of opportunities?

• Are you motivated and willing to work long hours?

• Do you believe in yourself?

• Can you bounce back after a setback?

• Can you stand by your actions in spite of criticism?

• Can you make your own decisions?

• Do you have the potential to lead people?

Most of you will have either lied or fallen short on one or two points. Some of these are fundamental: if you aren't motivated and see self-employment as a way to cut down your working hours, then you won't last long. But if you know that you're easily wounded by criticism then at least you're self-aware and you can work on thickening your hide a little.

Depending on the industry you are in, you'll need the technical skills to survive. Whatever your idea, you are, at some level, selling a skill or a product which you want people to believe is better than the skills or products of the bloke down the road. You'll need to either produce something special or be able to do something special and you'll need that quality from the start. You can, and will, learn a lot on the way, but if you open that chutney shop before you know how to make chutney, then there's trouble ahead.

The other side of all this is the ability to run a business. Much of that comes with experience, but the good news is that you don't have to walk alone. There are many organisations just waiting to give you the advice and support you need. They can give you advice on how to do your research and write a business plan, they can suggest an accountant for your business, and they can connect you with a network of like-minded people. Some organisations even give you a grant. Organisations like the New Entrepreneur Scholarships (NES), Business Link and the Prince's Trust are likely to be more proactive and more generous with grants than banks (who don't offer them) and softer on any loans (they're less likely to try and repossess your house). They also offer great guidance to start-up businesses. For more suggestions, see below.

Will you like it?

If you don't try it, you'll never know. A life forever shadowed by wondering what could have been if you'd strode out alone. If you never tire of the cliche that it is better to regret what you've done than what you've not done, then this might be for you. You can fulfil your ambitions, do it on your own terms and be beholden to no other. You're not a wage slave creeping in after your train was delayed hoping that your boss doesn't see you. The confident stride of the self-made success, that's you.

Of course, you're also always haunted by the fear of failure. Those statistics which highlight the failure rate of start-ups, the resounding echo of the dotcom crash – they can mark a person. Overnight success stories are few and the road to any level of success is a tricky one. The question of whether you like any job is always dependent, in some part, on whether you're actually successful at it. Here though, more than anywhere, the question of whether you'll like it is summed up by another little question – will it work?

More

Books

Forming a Limited Company by Patricia Clayton (Kogan Page)

A Guide to Working for Yourself by Godfrey Golzen and Jonathan Reuvid (Kogan Page)

Small Business Websites that Work: Get On Line to Grow Your Company by Sean McManus (Prentice Hall)

Online reading

Business Link www.businesslink.gov.uk

My Own Business www.myownbusiness.org

National Federation of Enterprise Agencies www.nfea.com

New Entrepreneur Scholarships www.nesprogramme.org

Prince's Trust www.princes-trust.org.uk

Shell LiveWIRE www.shell-livewire.org

2

Find your industry

So, you've worked your way through Part 1 and you know what sort of person you want to be for 8–10 hours a day. But we all want to be a rich good person who is also a creative leader. The trick is not to find out what you want to be, but to work out what you can be, to match your daydreams with your skills and aptitudes and find the profession best suited to you. It's not an exact science and it may involve a few compromises, be they moral, financial or practical. But by now you should have some idea of what sort of industry you see yourself in, so this is the time to revive those idle images of you standing in front of a class or a marketing conference and to see if that role would really suit you – and if you would suit it.

The information in this section is intended to give a broad-brush introduction to the careers you could end up in, explaining what sort of thing you would be doing, how to get qualified to do it and where to find out more about it. After that you'll need to talk to people already in the jobs, read the trade magazines and get in touch with the groups and authorities who run your chosen professions.

The jobs included are intended to be roles specific to that industry. The army has human resources managers and IT specialists for example, but you won't find them in the uniformed services section. There are many careers which can be translated into many different industries and the roles outlined below can apply in any number of sometimes surprising situations, so keep an open mind about where you can apply them.

NB: The salary details are taken from a survey done by the Higher Education Statistics Agency and are the average salaries of full-time first degree leavers entering full-time paid employment in 2006. Although they are startlingly precise, treat them as ballpark figures for the sort of job you're going for. Or, if you're feeling cocky, treat them as a starting point in negotiations.

Advertising, marketing and public relations

Those who work in advertising, marketing and PR are the shock troops in the battle to make you spend your money. They make you think you can't live without their products, make you feel all warm and cosy about them, and give you every opportunity to buy them. It's a fast-moving, exciting industry, sometimes glamorous, but always hard work. You'll need people skills, stamina, creativity, strategic nous, the ability to think on your feet and, just occasionally, the morals of a rattlesnake. You'll have an original imagination, the ability to put those ideas across to your bosses and your clients, as well as the diplomacy and flexibility to change in mid-flow if the client isn't happy or it simply isn't working.

■ Advertising

Advertising has been around longer than you might think. The Industrial Revolution spawned mass production which, in turn, created the need for manufacturers to differentiate between their products and make you think what they had was better. Hence the need for advertising. But nowadays, it's unlikely that you'll find yourself placing an ad in *What Bobbin?* magazine. Instead, you'll be helping a client company create an image for their product and a way of promoting that image through different media, and you'll be using a wide range of creative and organisational skills.

For all the impact the advertising industry makes, it is a relatively small sector. There are around 20,000 people working in large and small agencies across the UK, and the buzz is in London. Though few in number, UK advertisers are widely regarded as world leaders in innovation and technical skills, contributing to an industry worth over £19bn in 2006. Agencies differ in approach and philosophy so, while getting your foot in the door in such a competitive world is a priority, you'd be advised to research the agencies before you approach them, noting who their clients are and what sort of work they specialise in.

Most of the bigger household-name agencies do full-service work. In other words, they develop a campaign from start to finish with the client, turning the basic ideas into full press, TV, radio or web ads and then placing the ads on the client's behalf; this process involves a wide range of roles from account executives to creatives to media buyers. Other agencies may specialise in media planning or market research, doing more strategic work with their client. Still others might specialise in direct marketing: creating campaigns and printing up the mailshots, buying the lists of addresses and getting mailing houses to send them out.

Roles

- Account executive/Account planner

The **account executive** is the link between the client and the agency staff, and is likely to get it in the ear from all parties. As several teams within an agency work on an individual client's accounts, it is your responsibility to make sure all goes smoothly. You must interpret the client's wishes, through meetings with them, through intimate knowledge of the product (so pray you get the Porsche account) and through separate research. You've got to make sure the creatives, media planners and anyone else who is to be involved know what is expected of them; you must also ensure that they deliver on time and, of course, on budget.

Account planners perform a not dissimilar role, but usually take a longer-term view. You will draw up plans for the client's next campaign and will also make strategic decisions for the agency as a whole, perhaps regarding the kind of work your company specialises in.

Both planners and executives tend to work on a number of accounts at a time, so you'll have to juggle tasks and prioritise. You'll need to be a strategic thinker with the ability to work through problems logically and keep an eye on the bigger picture. You'll need to know the industry (both yours and, often, your client's) inside out so that the oh-so-witty, imaginative thoughts you have are backed up by extensive knowledge and research, rather than guesswork. You'll need drive and stamina (meeting those deadlines is never fun) as well as the ability to sell your idea to a sceptical client.

- Creatives

Once the account execs have had their say, it's time to get down to the hard work of translating the germ of an idea into a successful ad campaign. This is where the **creatives** come in. Usually working in a team of two – copywriter and art director – you'll use whatever medium you think best, or has been agreed on, to combine words, music, graphics and images to put over the desired message.

Copywriters need a literate imagination but must work within considerable limits in terms of the space available, the nature of the brief and the confines of the advertising industry's code of practice (see page 45). You can no longer claim, for example, that alcohol will make you more attractive to the opposite sex, even if you regularly drink yourself to that conclusion. The **art director** settles on the visual appearance of the advert, deciding whether to use photography, illustration, video, animation or computer graphics and which fonts to go for – whatever suits the medium best, and whichever most successfully reflects the message you're trying to put across.

Generally, the roles are pretty collaborative, with copywriters chipping in ideas on the visuals and art directors putting forward thoughts on the words, so that the two work in harmony. Once you're established as a team, agencies often hire in couples. The relationship between the two is often quite intense and the chemistry of a successful partnership can be difficult to recreate with a new person, although it's also common for companies to employ singles and play matchmaker.

It's the kind of job where originality needs to meet the discipline of the brief, so you'll need to be clever and creative (they don't think up these job titles for nothing), but with more than half an eye on the commercial message you're working on. This is business, not art.

■ Media buyers/planners/researchers

It's all very well, these highly strung creative types having lots of ideas, but without actually getting these adverts in front of the public, it's all a bit point-less. This is where the media buyers, planners and researchers come in. The **researchers** are the ones upon whose work many of the decisions are based. You provide the information and statistics to help both the client and the agency understand the market (it may be as basic as chocolate = women, but is likely to be a mite more sophisticated than that). It's a researcher's job to know all there is to know about the perception and image of a product so that decisions can be made about how to change or exploit that. Researchers can also often find work in marketing departments and may jump from one job to the other.

Media planners take this information and work with the account executives and the creatives to decide which media are likely to reach the target audience unearthed by the researchers. It might be that radio ads work better than posters, or TV is more suitable than cinema, but you calculate the costs of the various methods and media available and decide which would, strategically and financially, be the optimum outlets. **Media buyers** are the last link in the chain: you purchase space in the media – TV, newspapers, radio, web – so that your client can advertise there. There's a lot of wheeler-dealing going on in trying to win the best price and it's not unlike trading in the City.

To work in the media end of agencies you need business acumen and an ability to understand a client's needs. Planners need strategic minds, buyers need quick minds. Researchers need to be aware of social and economic trends, but must also have technical skills in statistics and number crunching. You all need to understand teamwork and you'll all require persistence, an understanding of the wider media and popular culture and, often, thick skins.

QUALIFICATIONS AND TRAINING A number of universities and further education colleges run degrees or HND courses in advertising but while these may be useful, they are not essential for **account executives and planners** to gain entry into the industry. There's a great deal of competition for admission to this oh so glamorous world so you need to be of graduate calibre, even if you can sometimes get away with not having an actual degree to wave in people's faces. Larger agencies run in-house training schemes and some operate graduate training schemes for management positions.

Contacts

Advertising Association
7th Floor North
Artillery House
11-19 Artillery Row
London SW1P 1RT
(t) 020 7340 1100
(↗) www.adassoc.org.uk

Advertising Standards Authority (and Committee of Advertising Practice)
Mid City Place
71 High Holborn
London WC1V 6QT
(t) 020 7492 2222
(↗) www.asa.org.uk

Communications, Advertising and Marketing Education Foundation
Moor Hall, Cookham
Maidenhead
Berks SL6 9QH
(t) 01628 427120
(↗) www.camfoundation.com

Institute of Practitioners in Advertising
44 Belgrave Square
London SW1X 8QS
(t) 020 7235 7020
(↗) www.ipa.co.uk

Market Research Society
15 Northburgh Street
London EC1V 0JR
(t) 020 7490 4911
(↗) www.mrs.org.uk

Online reading
BrandRepublic www.brandrepublic.com
MediaGuardian www.MediaGuardian.co.uk
Mad.co.uk www.mad.co.uk

Both the Institute of Practitioners in Advertising and the Communications, Advertising and Marketing Education Foundation run courses to help those already in the business to progress either through continuous professional development (CPD) or through diplomas and certificates, which you *can* wave in people's faces.

Agencies are quite happy to recruit **creatives** from broad backgrounds if they think you have the mindset. You're likely to be hired on the basis of your wit and new ideas, so whatever evidence you can bring to bear from an arts or design course (for the art director roles) or from literate degrees (for the copywriters) will be useful. Either way, a portfolio of campaign ideas, either coursework or your own doodlings, is much more likely to win you an interview.

To enter the world of **media planning or buying** you will need to demonstrate a deep knowledge of the advertising and media industries. Again, a graduate-level intelligence is as important as the degree itself, but you'll be expected to show a sharp mind and commercial acumen. **Researchers** have to be numerate. Training is often on the job and CPD is either not always embraced by agencies or is simply swamped by the pressure of work (you'd love to do that course, but it clashes with a deadline).

SALARY The average graduate starting salary in sales and related professions is £18,352.

■ Marketing

Marketing is not unrelated to the advertising world and the two departments often work in close proximity. The difference is that marketing is all about creating the mechanisms by which people can buy the products they feel they so desperately need (which is where the advertisers came in). If you're in marketing, you'll be about creating, pricing, promoting and distributing products so that consumers can buy them in the optimum amounts to make your company profitable. You'll tap into market research to understand and exploit people's purchasing habits.

Ever wondered why supermarkets are set up the way they are? They are carefully designed to make the most of the fact that you are horribly predictable in the way you potter round them, with goods presented in the ways that will most tempt you. That's just good marketing.

Roles

■ Marketing executive
In a world of constant rebranding you won't be surprised to learn that the job title can also be **assistant brand manager/product manager** or similar.

The exact responsibilities vary from company to company and may partly depend on the size of the company and the share of the market it already possesses, but for the most part the job involves researching ways to persuade and enable people to buy more of your product, whether it be soap powder or a charity (the "purchase" then being donations). You need to research the market you're aiming at and be able to understand and analyse what you see, which may mean changing the product, the packaging, the advertising, the point of sale, the after-sales service... a whole range of things.

Plenty of different organisations have marketing departments. It's not just about moving FMCGs (fast-moving consumer goods... come on, keep up), it's also about making people want to buy insurance, visit the zoo, eat more apples and so on. Or you may specialise in business-to-business marketing: the industrial marketing of tools to engineers, photocopiers to offices, that sort of thing, which is a whole different exercise.

You can also specialise in marketing methods. The growth in databases and database management means that direct marketing, whether by post, email, telephone or text message, is an ever-expanding area. Or you can opt for e-marketing, exploiting a whole new medium via websites, digital TV and SMS.

Wherever you land and whatever you're flogging, you'll need a high degree of business acumen, you'll be good with numbers and statistics, you'll be hip to economic and social trends and you'll know how those trends translate into your field. You're unlikely to lack confidence and you'll have the ability to sell ideas to clients and colleagues and to take the criticism if and when, after all that, it bombs.

QUALIFICATIONS AND TRAINING The entry level qualifications for **marketing executives** can vary considerably according to the size and nature of the company, but the bigger companies will want a good degree at the very least for admission to their graduate recruitment schemes. Some prefer business studies or marketing degrees, while industrial companies may prefer science degrees for their marketeers. The big firms may settle for a good humanities degree from a top university. For the smaller or more specialised companies, a diploma, such as one of those awarded by the Chartered Institute of Marketing, is the minimum (there are four levels of CIM qualifications and your entry point depends on your academic qualifications or experience). For graduate trainees, there will be a set pattern of experience and training, while other firms will be happy to send you out for training as and when appropriate but may be more reliant on on-the-job knowledge.

SALARY The average graduate starting salary for sales and marketing is £20,741.

■ Public relations

Public relations is the attempt to mould public opinion and win over a possibly sceptical public. But such brainwashing doesn't (necessarily) make you Joseph Goebbels. You'll be using the tools of the media, hopefully in a benign way, to build and maintain a good reputation for companies or products, trying to establish the sort of goodwill that means we will buy your butter or tolerate your nuclear power station on our doorstep.

Roles

■ Public relations officer/executive

A **public relations officer's** job is not about pure publicity, it's about creating, preserving and promoting a company or institution's reputation. PR executives use a variety of strategic, creative and people skills as they busy themselves with project planning, advising clients, media liaison, pestering journalists, organising conferences and events, writing and producing press releases, brochures and websites, producing multimedia promotion programmes, public speaking and organising photo shoots.

Some bigger companies have their own PR departments and may even divide the press and PR responsibilities, but you're just as likely to be part of an agency, which could be either a dedicated PR agency or one that covers marketing and advertising as well. An agency is set up like an ad agency in that you'll look after a number of clients on a project-by-project basis.

Companies are your clients, but their target audiences can differ. If it's corporate PR, you will be concerned with selling a policy or a series of ideas to opinion formers: you could be lobbying MPs, government departments, shareholders or stakeholders, directors or employees as you "sell" the prospect of an expansion or closure or the acceptance or denial of responsibility for something. The stakes can be high and you can work for the public sector as well as commercial companies (though in the publicly owned or run set-ups your title may be "information/press officer").

You may want to specialise in conferences and events, setting up and running events for single clients or whole industries, in places ranging from meeting rooms in office blocks to Earls Court in London or the NEC in Birmingham. You'll need impeccable organisational skills and no little motivational ability as you cajole clients, support-staff, media and your audience into spending days in each other's company while ensuring they still come away thinking it was all worthwhile.

Whatever your specialisation, you won't be surprised to know that to work in PR you need exceptional people skills to woo embittered professionals, jaded journalists and a sceptical public. You'll need initiative, a good knowledge of the media and what makes it sit up and take notice of you, excellent literacy talents and razor-sharp skills in persuasion and diplomacy.

QUALIFICATIONS AND TRAINING Traditionally, the move to **PR executive** was a switch to a friendlier environment for many a jaded journalist and it's still an accepted entry point. But for those just starting, rather than switching careers, the safest way in is via a degree. The Chartered Institute of Public Relations lists on its website the institutions and courses (around 15 of them) which it regards as worthy of associate membership of the organisation, so that's a good measure of the copper-bottomed ways in. Business studies or economics degrees are also able to smooth the approach. The IPR also has its own postgraduate and diploma courses, which are run by a number of colleges and universities (around 20 at the last count). The Chartered Institute of Marketing also runs a number of full- and part-time PR courses. Training is otherwise dependent on the company you join and is likely to be in the nature of experience at the coalface.

SALARY The average graduate starting salary for public relations executives is £17,489.

Contacts

Chartered Institute of Public Relations
CIPR Centre
32 St. James's Square
London SW1Y 4JR
(t) 020 7766 3333
(↗) www.ipr.org.uk

Public Relations Consultants Association
Willow House
Willow Place
London SW1P 1JH
(t) 020 7233 6026
(↗) www.prca.org.uk

Online reading
MediaGuardian www.MediaGuardian.co.uk
PR Week www.prweek.com
YoungPRpros www.youngprpros.com

CORPORATE CULTURE

Advertising, marketing and PR is a pretty broad church for generalisations about the culture – but such niceties won't stop us. Obviously it depends on the company and your role within it, but generally it's an industry with more front than Selfridges. People whose job it is to sell strong, confident images of their clients are often inclined to present themselves in that way too, so if you're likely to blush and become flustered when people challenge you and put you on the spot, then maybe think again. Some areas, such as media buying, can be very competitive and the atmosphere not unlike a trading desk in the City, with lots of bullish machismo and, sometimes, a rather patronising attitude to women who don't fancy being one of the lads.

The dress code tends to depend on what your job is and how much time you spend with clients. In PR, for example, image is all, so you're not likely to enjoy much time out of your suit. Advertising creatives on the other hand are, well, creative, which gives them licence to dress like teenagers while pretending it's because they're in tune with the zeitgeist.

Normal office hours are just the starting point. Before a big campaign or event you'll work all the hours necessary, weekends included, although sometimes you'll be able to make this up when things aren't quite so frantic. Holidays usually need to be fitted around campaigns and events, but much depends on the size of your team. If you're the account executive or lead organiser, jetting off to Ibiza during the run-up to a major campaign won't be such a brilliant idea.

If you want to be sociable, you're in the right place. These are very sociable careers – the relationships that need to be maintained with clients and contacts are central to the work. You're most likely to need to wine and dine if you're an account executive, a creative director, a PR executive or an event organiser as these are the roles that involve most frontline work with the client. The hours you'll be working will be demanding and irregular and it can be exhausting, especially with peer-group pressure to hit the alcohol when you'd prefer not to. And if you want to see your real mates (the ones you made before you hit the treadmill), socialising out of work is likely to be all about scheduling ("how about a week Tuesday") rather than a regular pint on quiz night at the Dog and Duck.

Men, white men mostly, still dominate advertising in the UK, particularly in creative jobs (despite the fact that women account for the majority of arts graduates). Ethnic minorities make up a tiny percentage of the work-force. On the bright side, the number of female account handlers and agency directors is increasing and women tend to be more prominent in PR and conference organising, but you're not entering a sector that wins any diversity awards. It is also a young industry – the majority are under 40, which is great when you're a whippersnapper but you might find yourself sidetracked at 39 even though you feel as young as ever.

If it's job security that you're after, remember that these industries are particularly susceptible to the whim of economic cycles. During boom times, when consumers are spending money, your advertising job will be safest. During economic downturn, however, advertising budgets get slashed and clients become more PR- and marketing-dependent; PR and marketing is cheaper than large advertising campaigns and target the customer more directly. Conferences are also on the list of nice-but-not-essential during a downturn, so those jobs can be vulnerable too. Either way, this remains a ruthless world – if you don't achieve your targets, you'll be shown the door. Equally, you're working in a meritocracy. Hit the targets and, assuming you don't annoy the wrong people on the way, you can expect good rewards.

ETHICAL QUESTIONS

The industry is, perhaps ironically, subject to a bad press and many people consider advertising and PR to have questionable ethics. Yet all advertising is regulated by the Advertising Standards Authority, an independent body set up by the industry to police compliance with advertising codes. The overriding concern of the ASA is to protect consumers by ensuring that advertisements are honest, decent and truthful, and individual advertisers must be able to prove that the claims they make in marketing their products and services are true.

To make an informed judgement about a particular company or agency you need to know what products or services the firm advertises, or which companies they represent. What are the ethics of the products that are being marketed (oil, cars, tobacco, etc), where are they produced (repressive regime?), by whom (child labour?) and under what conditions (sweat shops?)? Are you happy with that? Or is your paypacket more of a priority?

Are the methods used by the agency responsible, who do they target and how? For example, do you consider it acceptable to advertise unhealthy food on television targeted at children, or to include toys as part of a meal package?

Is the company involved in "greenwashing" (glossing over a firm's nefarious activities for the sake of its image) on behalf of their client? In an industry where image is everything this might not be easy to discern, and a cynic might say this is a central reason for the existence of a large and growing PR industry.

Some high-profile organisations have moved away from the traditional model of what it is to be a company (employing staff and making products) and towards a new model based on managing a brand to allow more effective marketing. On the surface this does not appear to be an ethical problem, but one of its effects is to allow companies to subcontract labour-intensive areas of their business like manufacturing or call-centres to companies operating in countries which may have questionable records on human and workers' rights. Is the company involved in this sort of outsourcing, and if so what steps does it take to ensure their subcontractors' workers are treated fairly?

Arts and heritage

Unless you are a performer or creative artist (and let's face it, you'll be so taken with your muse that there's not much chance of you picking up a careers guide), the arts and heritage industries may apply more to the subject matter you are working with than to the mechanics of the job. So, while you may be in an office, you're working for a theatre company. While you may be estimating the financial value of something, it might be a priceless painting.

To get on in the arts and heritage world, you'll need commitment since the hours can be long, you'll need creativity since the chances are you won't be working for a company that can throw money at a problem, and you'll need technical skills, whether in typing, prop-making, sound engineering or film-making. The likelihood is that you'll feel intellectually rather than financially rewarded, as both industries are likely to exist on grants and handouts.

■ Arts

"The arts" is a vast catch-all term for a huge variety of jobs, careers, professions, vocations and callings. For the purposes of this book, there is little point in telling you how to be an actor (go to drama school), a film director (go to film school) or a theatre designer (have you thought of a theatre design course?). The chances are that, if these are viable options, you will have thought about it long and hard already.

There is a long and well-established theatrical tradition in this country and these theatres need administrators and publicists to work alongside the more obviously creative roles such as wardrobe, prop-making, stage management and lighting and sound engineering. Likewise, fine art also doesn't have to mean a paint-spattered smock. You can buy and sell it, restore it or value it. You can dabble in it as a freelance or you could try joining a fine art and antiques auction house. Britain has two of the world's oldest and largest fine art auctioneers, Sotheby's and Christie's, and a whole host of independents across the country.

Which links nicely into the heritage industry. There are relatively few large, well-resourced and high-profile organisations in the heritage industry and a great deal of very small and medium-sized businesses. Over 50% of the people working for them are self-employed, and many of those have "portfolio" careers – that is, they are holding down more than one job at the same time. You'll often need your creativity in balancing your work between jobs as well as within them.

Roles

■ Administrator

Administrators are needed by galleries, theatres, museums, arts festivals, regional arts boards and local authorities. There may be one administrator or several, depending on the size of the organisation, but arts administration can cover fund-raising, accountancy, publicity, organising exhibitions and the management of people, buildings and financial resources. Those working for buildings – such as in an arts centre or theatre – may also have to tackle managing programmes of events, dealing with visiting and resident companies and general office work.

■ Craftsmanship and technical roles

This is probably the area (other than acting or fine art) that you were thinking of when you thought of the arts and the possibilities are endless. Your **craft** could be costume design, stage management, sound engineering, lighting, filming, video editing, directing or prop-making. Often, with this sort of job, you will either fall into the job because you have developed the technical know-how elsewhere or you will do a specific vocational course (in studio engineering for example) which leads directly to a job in that field. Unless you are attached to a particular studio or theatre, the work is likely to be piecemeal – a recording here, a production there, leading to a patchwork career. It can be hand to mouth, but it can also be an invigorating series of fresh challenges.

■ Performing/Creative artists

Actors, dancers, musicians, painters, sculptors... If this is your bag, then you need talent and drive, and the technical skills to translate both into a performance or piece of art that people are willing to pay for. So you may go to a conservatoire to hone your musical skills, art school to iron out the kinks in your artistic bent, or drama school... you get the idea. After that, you'll need a mixture of luck, contacts and hard graft to succeed.

■ Teaching

Before the Training and Development Agency for Schools got their hands on it, the phrase used to be "those who can't, teach", but there are many people who find that **teaching** the arts is as rewarding as practising them. It doesn't have to mean teaching in schools or colleges (perfectly good choice though that is), it can also mean using the arts or music for therapy in hospitals, or providing opportunities in underprivileged areas or, at the other end of the scale, teaching privately to school-age children or adult enthusiasts. You'll need formal training of some kind, if not necessarily PGCE, just to prove that you know what on earth you're talking about.

QUALIFICATIONS AND TRAINING Whatever type of **artist** you want to be, doing a foundation course, fine art degree with specialism or drama school course or studying at a conservatoire will give you not only technical knowledge but the beginnings of a portfolio of work and a fledgling network of contacts to build on. These will give you an in for arts council grants to develop your work, and for speculative or direct applications to theatre companies, orchestras and commissioning bodies. Above all it's about being motivated and constantly building on your achievements.

Administrators will find that employers are looking for graduate-level thinking as well as enthusiasm and knowledge of the area. Often training will be given on the job or as you rise through the ranks, but it may also be an advantage to gain qualifications in areas such as fundraising, marketing and general or arts administration from professional bodies or colleges such as the Institute of Fundraising (see page 170), the Chartered Institute of Marketing (see page 42) or ISPAL (The Institute for Sport, Parks and Leisure) (see page 201). Work placements are also a very good introduction to administration roles; try to get as much work experience as possible. In fact, that advice goes for every role in this highly competitive sector.

Technical roles will need qualifications. Technicians, stage managers, camera operators, directors, sound recordists and everyone else involved in technical and creative roles can train at drama schools, universities or technical colleges. This will lead to qualifications such as degrees, BTECs and HNDs in technical theatre/theatre and production arts, film and television production and related subjects, although on-the-job training is also usual. Expect periods of training and constant development throughout your career, as technology, particularly in film and television production changes.

If you're looking to **teach** an arts subject the level of qualification you need will depend on the level you wish to teach at. To teach in a school, see page 59. **Private tutors** don't necessarily need a teaching qualification but to qualify as a teacher through the Associated Board of the Royal Schools of Music the very least you will need is a grade 6 in theory and a grade 8 practical in your instrument of choice (including voice), plus passes in their written, spoken and recital exams. This will give you the first of their three stages of qualification. Teaching at a drama school or Saturday class might simply be based on your experience and your prospective employers will specify what it is they want from you in terms of paper qualifications and experience. An increasing fear for children's safety also means that in addition to professional qualifications you will probably also need to be cleared by the disclosure services if you are going to work with children.

Contacts

Associated Board of the Royal Schools of Music
24 Portland Place
London W1B 1LU
(t) 020 7636 5400
(↗) www.abrsm.org

Association of British Theatre Technicians
55 Farringdon Road
London EC1M 3JB
(t) 020 7242 9200
(↗) www.abtt.org.uk

Association of Illustrators
2nd Floor
Back Building
150 Curtain Road
London EC2A 3AR
(t) 0207 613 4328
(↗) www.theaoi.com

Incorporated Society of Musicians
10 Stratford Place
London W1C 1AA
(t) 020 7629 4413
(↗) www.ism.org

EQ
Suite 229
Dean Clough
Halifax HX3 5AX
(t) 01422 381618
(↗) www.thinkeq.org.uk

Musicians' Union
33 Palfrey Place
London SW8 1PE
(t) 020 7840 5504
(↗) www.musiciansunion.org.uk

National Council for Drama Training
1–7 Woburn Walk
London WC1H 0JJ
(t) 020 7387 3650
(↗) www.ncdt.co.uk

Stage Management Association
55 Farringdon Road
London EC1M 3JB
(t) 020 7242 9250
(↗) www.stagemanagement association.co.uk

Online reading
Your Creative Future www.yourcreativefuture.org
Guardian Arts and Entertainment arts.guardian.co.uk
Arts and Letters Daily www.aldaily.com

■ Heritage

Britain is a nation in love with its heritage. It is a country stuffed with museums, galleries and conservation centres, and a career in those areas holds a certain level of responsibility. This isn't soap powder you're dealing with, this is a nation's history you're managing and interpreting. So you'll need a genuine interest in the subject matter, since you'll be entering an area where there are plenty of highly qualified and motivated people, and where your audience or market (ie the British public) can be remarkably well informed.

Although there are vocational courses in conservation and management, there is no single route into the heritage sector – many of those who work in it have backgrounds in other industries and are simply transferring their IT, marketing, fund-raising or HR skills to a different sector. For the purposes of this section, we'll ignore them, vital though they are to the success of the whole gig. You'll find more on those sectors in the relevant chapters of this book.

Being a specialist in museums or galleries is not easy. Even if you have the vocational qualifications, there is some pretty intense competition for jobs, pay is often fairly low (with some top-level exceptions) and career progression can be tricky – it helps if you are willing to relocate across the country. The key to entry can come with volunteer work and experience in local museums and galleries but, as in most industries, determination and hard work will take you a long way.

Roles

■ Conservator/Restorer

A **conservator** uses scientific methods to preserve, restore and care for paintings and objects in collections. Though conservators are often attached to particular galleries or museums, it is also possible to work exclusively in a laboratory and/or be involved in developing new ways of treating objects. The job requires a scientific knowledge of the materials you'll be working with and of the ways in which they deteriorate.

■ Curator

As a **curator** you are responsible for acquiring objects, researching, identifying and cataloguing them, storing them and providing information about the collection to visitors. You also ensure they are stored correctly, monitor the lighting and atmospheric conditions and arrange for any necessary conservation. You may also be involved in arranging exhibitions in your museum or gallery or on tour. In larger museums and galleries you might get to specialise and become an expert in, say, 16th-century French painting, while in a smaller operation you may have responsibilities stretching from acquisition to organising school groups and tracking down sponsors.

■ Education officer

Many museums and galleries rely on their links with schools to keep visitor levels up. **Education officers** liaise with schools and colleges to make those links as rewarding as possible for all concerned. You may also be concerned with adult education.

■ Publications officer

Many galleries put a lot of store by the brochures they create for exhibitions and the extra educational material which they use to put the exhibits into context. A **publications officer** could be in charge of anything from a multimedia website or a glossy catalogue to an A4 piece of folded paper – whatever is the optimum way to get the information across. Essentially it's a branch of journalism (see page 158).

QUALIFICATIONS AND TRAINING This is a competitive area, so degrees tend to be important. Apart from anything else, these roles often require a certain amount of research work, so further study indicates dedication as well as the requisite study skills. To be a **curator** you'll need at least a degree, and although for some positions the subject won't matter, it's probably advantageous for it to be in a relevant subject such as art history or something that relates specifically to the collection you would be curating. Working towards membership of the Museums Association and following their Continuing Professional Development (CPD) programme is also advantageous. Sotheby's and Christie's also run training schemes, and any work or training experience is a huge advantage.

Conservators also usually require both qualifications and periods of CPD to gain entry to the best jobs. You'll probably need a relevant degree, BTEC or HND (trade associations such as the British Antique Furniture Restorers' Association list those that they approve) as well as a good portfolio of work.

Education officers will also usually need a degree or relevant qualification plus experience in the area you'll be working in. You may well be given training on the job, particularly to keep up to date with things like national curriculum requirements if you'll be dealing with school-age visitors. Your communication skills will be of paramount importance, as will your enthusiasm for your subject.

For the role of **publications officer** it stands to reason that the basic requirements would include a relevant degree such as English, or one dealing specifically with the subject you would be publishing. In addition, any relevant qualifications gained will always be useful: these might include copy-editing or more in-depth qualifications as outlined in the section on the media (see page 158).

SALARY The average graduate starting salary for general administration roles is £14,411. For a curator, that figure is £16,438. For craftsmen and women, the average is £14,183, for an education officer, £17,436 and for publications officer, £14,906.

Contacts

British Antique Dealers' Association
20 Rutland Gate
London SW7 1BD

(t) 020 7589 4128

(↗) www.bada.org

British Antique Furniture Restorers' Association
The Old Rectory
Warmwell
Dorchester
Dorset DT2 8HQ

(t) 01305 854822

(↗) www.bafra.org.uk

British Association of Paintings Conservator–Restorers
Po Box 258
Blofield
Norwich NR13 4WY

(t) 01603 858129

(↗) www.bapcr.org.uk

Cultural Heritage National Training Organisation
7 Burnett Street
Little Germany
Bradford BD1 5BJ

(t) 01274 391056

(↗) www.chnto.co.uk

Department for Culture, Media and Sport
2–4 Cockspur Street
London SW1Y 5DH

(t) 020 7211 6200

(↗) www.culture.gov.uk

ICON Institute of Conservation
3rd Floor
Downstream Building
1 London Bridge
London SE1 9BG

(t) 020 7785 3807

(↗) www.icon.org.uk

Institute of Field Archaeologists
SHES
Whiteknights
University of Reading
PO Box 227
Reading RG6 6AB

(t) 0118 378 6446

(↗) www.archaeologists.net

International Council of Museums
Maison de l'Unesco
1 rue Miollis
75732 Paris Cedex 15
France

(t) +33 1 47 34 05 00

(↗) icom.museum

Museums Association
24 Calvin Street
London E1 6NW

(t) 020 7426 6970

(↗) www.museumsassociation.org

Publishing Training Centre at Book House
45 East Hill
London SW18 2QZ

(t) 020 8874 2718

(↗) www.train4publishing.co.uk

CORPORATE CULTURE

The arts industry can often be predominantly a freelance existence with all that that entails: working hours tend to be seasonal, flexible, sometimes antisocial and large numbers of people who work in the industry work in other industries as well (either by choice or need). The heritage industry can be a little more straight-laced and jobs in the administration and marketing areas are as likely to be suit-bound as in all other industries.

Job titles can appear confusing, and it is important to consider the size and staff structure of an organisation when trying to define the actual role of a particular job. In a large organisation, jobs can be tightly defined whilst in small organisations the job of **curator** for example could mean anything from developing the organisation's acquisition policy or working with school groups and managing volunteers, to harassing philanthropists and writing press releases. The heritage industry also has a clique of academics attached to it, but we'll deal with those in the education section (see page 60).

In both industries, the pay for the very few can be very high but it's a triangular shape and there's not much room at the top. For the most part, it's an under-funded industry and pay tends to be below comparable jobs in other industries. Since working patterns, outside of those in the office, can often be freelance, part time or short term, there can also be a lack of job security.

The idea of promotion is not entirely alien but this is an industry where you will often find yourself moving from project to project. The concept of a vertical career path applies mainly to those in the office-based jobs – in IT, admin and marketing roles – where the more normal career structures are replicated. But, as with most jobs, if you are seen to put the time in, you will be noticed and the jobs you are offered will be better, more lucrative and more ambitious. In the early days, it's a question of going where the contracts and the enthusiasm take you. And while you're working on these separate contracts, you'll find yourself doing long hours with people who have remarkably similar interests to yourself. So the bonds tend to be strong but impermanent and the social life within the group follows the same pattern.

Arts and heritage can tend towards the white and middle class and while women are strongly represented in the industry as a whole, the "technical" jobs can often be male domains – photography, craft and technical trades such as sound engineering and lighting are still over 80% male. But in an industry reliant on local authority and lottery funding for its existence, that state of affairs is being noted and addressed.

As these are sectors that rely heavily on specialist skills and knowledge, there's a good chance that once you're established you might find yourself in demand all over. There's no general pattern though, so don't set your sights on Broadway quite yet. Most of these professions work on a short-term basis, apart from administrative jobs or curatorships, so there's always the possibility of a change of scene every couple of months, or even every couple of weeks. Even the administrative jobs tend to involve getting out and about in the never-ending quest for funding as well as to track down the specialists needed to keep the projects going.

ETHICAL QUESTIONS

In the UK the government body responsible for the sector is the Department for Culture, Media and Sport. The International Council of Museums is an international organisation of museums and museum professionals which publishes ethical standards.

Consider whether the company's cultural activities are open to all members of the company. Elitist opera company versus grassroots theatre workshop, say. Does it offer encouragement to members of society who wouldn't necessarily use its facilities or be involved in a particular cultural activity in the form of grants, scholarships or subsidies?

How does the institution resolve conflicts of interest between its cultural and commercial activities? In the case of museums, does the organisation take extra care not to purchase items illegally imported from abroad? What is the attitude to "culture stripping" from other countries? Is consideration given to whether it is ethically acceptable to keep and display certain items or human remains, and to the possibility of returning them to their original location or surviving family? Are artefacts lent to other institutions to allow more people to see them? Does the institution respect the wishes of donors who bequeath items in their wills?

Education

Whether you work in schools or in further or higher education, you can rest assured that you're at the core of the nation's future prosperity. You may be helping young minds on the road to great things, sending future leaders on their way, or researching at the cutting edge of science. The feelgood factor can be huge, just like in the movies: Goodbye Mr Chips, Dead Poet's Society, and Good Will Hunting are all in here. If it's school teaching you're after, then now is a pretty good time. The teaching profession is slowly regaining the status it deserves and the financial incentives are quite impressive if you're teaching one of the "priority" subjects such as maths, science, English, modern languages, information and communications technology, design and technology and, in Wales, Welsh. But remember, it's not the easy option to go for just because you can't think of anything else to do. Despite the long holidays, teaching requires dedication and commitment both inside and outside the classroom and, while it may not have seemed that way when you were at school, teachers have to love kids.

Tertiary or adult education in further education colleges or private language schools is a specialist form of teaching. You may work with adults who need to learn what normal schooling failed to teach them or you may be teaching in particular circumstances – to guests of Her Majesty perhaps, or to young people on day release from apprenticeship schemes. There is huge variety within this field and while the basic skills involved in passing on information to others may be similar, the approach you take will be governed by the circumstances. There's a world of difference between eager sixth-formers studying for A-levels and, say, Japanese executives wanting to learn business English, or prisoners reading Molière as a way of escaping their cells.

If it's higher education that you're after, you'll have to do postgraduate study, for which you'll need a decent degree. You will need a dedication to your subject that can withstand the fact that you'll be working in often under-funded institutions and paid accordingly. But you'll be at the forefront of your specialisation, leading your subject into new areas. In the sciences especially there may be chances to cross to the private sector, working in pharmaceuticals or the biochemical industries perhaps, where the money is likely to be better. Wherever you are, you'll need to be self-motivated to keep yourself up to date with what's happening in your field as well as imaginative enough to make the leaps necessary to make progress in your research. If you're teaching it helps if you can convey your enthusiasm for your subject, but many universities don't pay much attention to the standard of teaching of their staff, just to their academic ability, although that is changing.

■ Schools

If you decide that you want to work in a school, there's quite a variety to choose from, ranging from the academies established in 2000 to drive up standards, church schools, grammars and ordinary comprehensives to independent and private schools and those in the "alternative sector" such as Montessori and Steiner Waldorf schools. State-maintained schools follow the national curriculum; specialist schools also follow the national curriculum but have one area of special emphasis such as technology, sports, arts, languages, engineering, science, maths and computing, or business and enterprise. Fee-paying independent schools and those in the alternative sector are not compelled to follow the national curriculum or government-set education targets, and may have different qualification requirements for their teachers than maintained schools.

That said, teaching isn't limited to nursery, primary or secondary teaching, or even necessarily to schools. Teaching school-age students is also possible in pupil referral units, which cater for students such as teenage mothers, pupils excluded from school, school-phobics and the like until they are ready to go back into mainstream education. There are also the privately run secure training units, which provide formal education 25 hours a week, 52 weeks of the year for 10–17 year olds. Local authority secure units are similar, but run by local authorities.

Roles

■ Pre-school/Nursery teacher

Pre-school and nursery teachers teach children from the age of three until they are ready for school around the age of five. In England, Wales and Northern Ireland there is a curriculum for nursery teaching called the foundation stage. You'll also be expected to meet certain educational targets, called early-learning goals.

■ Primary school teacher

Primary school teachers focus on children between the ages of five and 11, working out lessons that fit in with the national curriculum and assessing students' progress in the lead-up to them taking their SATs (standard assessment tasks) at the ages of seven and 11.

■ Secondary school teacher

As a **secondary school teacher** you will teach one or more subjects from the national curriculum to students between the ages of 11 and 18, preparing them for exams such as GCSEs and A-levels.

■ Special educational needs (SEN) teacher

SEN teachers teach children with emotional, behavioural or learning difficulties and may also teach gifted children, helping to identify each child's needs and deciding on teaching strategies and support. Sometimes SEN teachers work with class teachers, sometimes on their own with groups or individuals; it depends on the institution and the students' needs. As an SEN teacher you might work in any type of institution.

■ Learning mentor

This is essentially a facilitating post, using one-on-one contact time to help children overcome social, behavioural and emotional problems so they can learn effectively. **Learning mentors** aren't teachers, classroom assistants or counsellors – an important distinction. Officially you "facilitate cooperation between the pupil and the school".

■ Music teacher

As a **music teacher** in a school you will teach children general music skills, theory and appreciation. Alternatively, you might teach children or adults the theory and practical side of playing an individual instrument or singing, either at a school or privately at your home or at a pupil's home. This might involve training them to an assessment stage.

Online Reading
EducationGuardian education.guardian.co.uk/schools
Fast Track Teaching www.ncsl.org.uk/programmes/fasttrack
SEN Teacher Resources www.senteacher.org

QUALIFICATIONS AND TRAINING **Teaching** is a graduate profession and to teach anything in a state (maintained) school or special school, teachers must have qualified teacher status (QTS). To get on to an initial teacher training (ITT) course you need to have a standard equivalent to a grade C GCSE in English and maths. If you were born on or after 1 September 1979 and want to do primary or key stage 2/3 training you also need a standard equivalent to a grade C GCSE in a science subject. You also need to be able to read effectively, and communicate clearly and accurately in spoken and written standard English. If you're doing a postgraduate ITT course you need to have a degree from a UK higher education institution or an equivalent qualification. If you've got a foundation degree you need to also have at least 60 credits at HE level 3.

Basically, **primary teachers** need to be able to teach the core subjects of English, maths and science, and do a range of work in history or geography, physical education, information and communications technology, art and design, design and technology, performing arts, and religious education. **Secondary** teachers need subject knowledge at degree level in the subject(s) they want to teach. Independent schools can choose who they like as teachers, but these qualifications are usually the least of what they'll be looking for.

Music teachers need the qualifications appropriate to all teachers at their level of teaching – primary or secondary – and to get on to any sort of degree or diploma course you will probably have to hold at least grade 6 in a musical instrument. For other music teaching qualifications see the arts and heritage section (page 49).

To be an **SEN** teacher you'll need to have all the above: QTS plus at least two years' mainstream teaching experience, then additional training at either diploma, masters or postgraduate certificate level in the area in which you wish to teach. On top of that come any additional qualifications, such as sign-language, that might be necessary in the particular special needs area in which you wish to teach.

Learning mentors don't necessarily need specific qualifications, and schools may well give training in the sort of mediation and teaching tasks you'll be required to assist with, or they may specify certain qualifications.

There are quite a few ways to get into teaching, whether you're just leaving school, have already done a degree or want to change careers. You can take an undergraduate course at university or do a one-year postgraduate course. Courses can be full time or part time and there are special graduate fast-track courses as well as flexible courses, which allow you to train at times that suit you. If you're 24 or older, it's sometimes possible to learn on the job and get paid while you train through the graduate teacher programme and the registered teacher programme.

Obviously teaching is a profession in which "life experience" can be particularly valuable, and a lot of courses and employers will take this into account with older applicants who don't necessarily have as many academic qualifications.

SALARY The average graduate starting salary in the teaching professions is £18,753.

Contacts

Department of Education, Northern Ireland

Rathgael House
43 Balloo Road
Bangor
County Down BT19 7PR

(t) 028 9127 9279

(↗) www.deni.gov.uk

General Teaching Council for England

Whittington House
19–30 Alfred Place
London WC1E 7EA

(t) 0870 001 0308

(↗) www.gtce.org.uk

General Teaching Council for Scotland

Clerwood House
96 Clermiston Road
Edinburgh EH12 6UT

(t) 0131 314 6000

(↗) www.gtcs.org.uk

Music Teachers UK

15 St Brendans Road North
Withington
Manchester M20 3FE

(t) 07951 536810

(↗) www.musicteachers.co.uk

Training and Development Agency for Schools

151 Buckingham Palace Road
London SW1W 9SZ

(t) 020 7023 8001

(↗) www.tda.gov.uk

■ Tertiary and adult education

Teaching adults in the tertiary or higher education sector is an option that can leave you room to develop your own studies either in combination with, or instead of, lecturing, pastoral care or tutoring. Academic research roles are highly competitive, so not only will your intellect have to be top-notch, but you'll need to be driven and committed. It is also possible to become an adult tutor for the prisons service, which runs adult-education programmes, or to teach adult learners in local colleges and higher education institutions. Special needs teaching and teaching English, either as a foreign language or a second language, are additional options that can lead to work in private institutions, mainstream schools or special schools.

Roles

■ Prisons instructor or tutor

The **prison service** is now very keen on offering education and training to inmates, so quite a wide variety of teaching is offered in prisons and secure units, from vocational skills, basic numeracy and literacy through to Open University qualifications. The conditions can be a lot harsher than in a school or university class and attitudes towards learning can vary wildly.

■ Teaching English as a foreign language (Tefl)

As a **teacher of English as a foreign language** you will, you'll be surprised to learn, be teaching English to students whose first language is different. The type of work depends on why the students have decided to learn, but usually the focus of lessons is on four main areas: understanding, speaking writing and reading.

■ Teaching English as a second language (Tesol and Tesl)

Teaching English to speakers of other languages and **teaching English as a second language** entails working with adults and/or children whose first language is not English and who live either in the UK or in countries where English is used as the official or semi-official language. This can mean working with children and adults individually or in classes in schools or community education centres, helping with the language as well as giving them an understanding of the British educational system, culture or working environment.

■ Teacher of English for specific purposes (ESP)

Teachers of English for specific purposes focus on a particular area, for example medicine, business, law or tourism. This usually involves a lot of general, functional, language teaching but with a bit more attention to skills such as letter or report writing and making and taking telephone calls.

■ Adult education lecturer/tutor

Adult education involves teaching a wide age range of students over compulsory school age. There's an enormous variety of subjects in this field, ranging from IT to drama for fun and adult literacy, and qualifications from certificates to A-levels and GCSEs. There are hundreds of colleges in the UK and over 4 million people study at them each year. Courses can be part time, full time or in the evenings – again, lots of variety in the teaching commitments.

■ Higher education lecturer/researcher

As a **higher education lecturer** you will teach seminars, give practical demonstrations, lecture and carry out your own specialist research at a university or university college. The work you do and the balance between research and teaching will depend greatly on the university you work for (some see themselves as research institutions and some as teaching universities). Many combine both, although not always at the same time. A lecturer may be given a year off to do his or her own research work for example. At best, you'll be doing cutting-edge work and passing on your brand-new knowledge to eager students. At worst, you'll find you never have time to do both jobs properly. In some subjects, particularly the sciences, the private sector might enable you to do better-funded research, for an agrichemical company perhaps, or in pharmaceuticals.

QUALIFICATIONS AND TRAINING Some of the qualifications necessary for this part of the sector are the same as those listed in the teaching section (see page 59). For example, if you want to be a **prisons tutor** QTS may be appropriate. It really depends on what you want to teach – vocational subjects such as building or mechanics, or literacy and numeracy subjects. You need either an appropriate industry qualification or QTS and experience of teaching or training before entering the prisons service, although different prisons will specify for each post. There's no age limit for applying to be a prisons tutor, and it tends to attract those who fancy a change of direction.

Adult education tutors can find themselves in a similar situation: qualification requirements vary depending on the type of course you want to teach and whether it leads to a qualification itself. Generally you'll need a degree or qualification in your subject plus a relevant adult teaching qualification from somewhere like City and Guilds, although sometimes professional experience will replace an academic qualification.

EFL teachers will need at least a Tefl certificate from a recognised provider such as the British Council. To do a course you need to be at least 18 (sometimes 20), and have at least two A-levels or equivalent; it's a qualification that many people choose to gain straight from school in preparation for a gap year, or after a degree, although there's no age limit. The requirements are similar for ESP, Tesol and Tesl teachers, who need at least a Tefl certificate, and if you want to teach in a school you'll need QTS as well.

HE lecturers and researchers are entering a fiendishly competitive and highly qualified profession – a lot of people want to stay put in their ivory towers, so you need to know your onions and have the certificates to prove it. You must have an undergraduate and possibly doctoral degree, plus evidence of your own research and academic publications, as well as some experience of teaching. Additional teaching training may be given by your institution. This is a path that generally follows straight from undergraduate degree through postgraduate or doctoral work, where you start teaching then moving on to looking for a full lecturing post once you've gained your PhD. Training for research isn't a realistic prospect – you are, after all, supposed to be breaking new ground.

SALARY The average graduate starting salary in the teaching profession is £18,753. In higher education research, that figure is £18,208.

Contacts

British Council
10 Spring Gardens
London SW1A 2BN

(t) 020 7930 8466

(↗) www.britishcouncil.org/
learning-elt-teach-english.htm

**British Educational
Research Association**
Association House
South Park Road
Macclesfield
Cheshire SK11 6SH

(t) 01625 504 062

(↗) www.bera.ac.uk

City and Guilds
1 Giltspur Street
London EC1A 9DD

(t) 020 7294 2800

(↗) www.city-and-guilds.co.uk

HM Prison Service Headquarters
Cleland House
Page Street
London SW1P 4LN

(↗) www.hmprisonservice.gov.uk
/careersandjobs

University and College Union
27 Britannia Street
London WC1X 9JP

(t) 020 7837 3636

(↗) www.ucu.org.uk

VSO
Head Office
317 Putney Bridge Road
London SW15 2PN

(t) 020 8780 7200

Information Centre
Carlton House
85 Upper Richmond Road
London SW15 2BZ

(t) 020 8780 7600

(↗) www.vso.org.uk

Online reading
EducationGuardian education.guardian.co.uk/higher
education.guardian.co.uk/further
education.guardian.co.uk/tefl

CORPORATE CULTURE

You might think that once you become a **teacher** you'll be stuck in front of a blackboard for the rest of your natural life, but today's teaching includes more high-level management roles than ever before, plus the government's new fast-track scheme which aims to put the most able teachers into "leadership" roles as quickly as possible, giving them extra support and training (not to mention pay) in order to achieve this. That said, even if the fast track isn't for you, schools vary a lot in their attitudes and ability to support their teachers, so check that the school you do your induction year in is committed to giving you the backing and resources you're supposed to get as part of your training. When applying for posts after you're fully qualified, make sure you investigate resources and support available for you to continue your professional development. The Training and Development Agency for Schools has a programme that gives funding for certain types of professional development, but your employer has to be flexible enough for you to be able to take up such opportunities.

Caveats aside, it's down to what you want. If you're seeking more than a front-of-class role then there are certainly opportunities available that you won't have to wait decades for. Equally, once you have developed your teaching skills you may find that you are able to become an educational consultant for a youth programme or thinktank. Essentially, it's a profession in which experience and innovation are important and can open up both opportunities for promotion and career moves beyond the bog-standard teaching image.

And you don't necessarily have to be stuck in front of class 4B in the perpetual British winter: **EFL** teachers often work abroad, and **ESL** teachers also sometimes find jobs overseas in countries such as Kenya, Nigeria and Singapore, where English is used as an official or semi-official language. Teachers also have opportunities to travel through the Voluntary Service Overseas (VSO) or similar organisations, as their skills tend to be valuable as well as transferable.

Not that travel is the only way to keep you from doing the school bell shuffle. If you want to escape routine then tutoring pupils privately is probably the best way to go. However, teachers have such a wide range of activity that it's unlikely things are going to be too claustrophobic – what with field and school trips (back in fashion), practical demonstrations and the like, teachers don't necessarily spend all their time locked in the classroom.

In **further and higher education**, you are slightly more isolated: you have your classes to teach and, perhaps, your research to do, and that is regarded as largely your own work. You'll be expected to work pretty much office hours, even if your office is a lecture theatre, library or laboratory. Travelling to and speaking at conferences will be increasingly the norm as you progress in your field. The atmosphere in the common room is generally supportive, although you may find that you are your institution's only expert on Vichy France so no one quite understands what you're on about till you meet other experts from other universities – and there is always an element of competition in those meetings.

ETHICAL QUESTIONS

Firstly, it sounds obvious but what are you teaching? An agricultural college lecturer teaching about using pesticides, or a primary school teacher teaching literacy? Inspiring children to be responsible citizens and to be world- and environment-aware is about as ethical a career as you can get. Clearly the largest single employer in the field of education is the state, but there are many others: private schools, specialist and technical colleges, universities, private and specialist tutors and so on. Regulation of the sector is by the Department for Children, Schools and Families and the Department for Innovation, Universities and Skills.

Each employer will have their own approach, but you may want to ask how an institution benefits the community in which it is based. Almost all privately run educational establishments are registered charities. What is the justification for this status? Are there any night-school opportunities, or subsidised training or bursaries to allow working people to further their education? Is the education offered prescriptive in any way, for example is just evolutionary theory taught, or creationism? Alternatively are students given as much information as possible and taught to analyse it so they can make up their own minds?

Engineering

Although almost every profession makes claims about its diversity and the wide range of potential careers available to those starting out, engineering is one profession that is almost ridiculously wide-ranging. And yet there's an urban myth that engineering is all about oily rags and spanners and men in overalls tinkering in sheds. Which is weird because most engineers work at the forefront of design technology and never use a spanner.

Today's engineers are likely to be designing more efficient car engines, more productive wind turbines, finding ways to increase computer-processing speeds or decrease flood damage along Britain's waterways – you won't find them next to an industrial-sized sink looking for the Swarfega. The Royal Academy of Engineering has estimated that up to 2 million people in the UK could be classified as engineers in some form or another. That will include the oily rag brigade – there'll always be an element of that – but the industry is an intensely modern one with engineering jobs available in new areas such as nanotechnology and medical engineering.

Engineering is a sector of rapid change and developments, so you'll need to be able to keep up with the latest developments in your field and be continually learning new skills. You'll be practical, an excellent problem-solver and will, on occasion, need to be able to think laterally as well as logically. You'll probably have something of a scientific bent, but will also need communication skills to explain to laypeople (who may well be paying for your project) just what's going on. You'll also have to budget effectively, show sound business sense (is the project worth the hassle and the money?), and be able to work in a multi-disciplinary team.

Roles

Engineering branches off into many different specialisations: there are over 30 professional institutions representing them all so we're about to be brief and will just cover the major areas. Within those areas, opportunities to specialise will come as you progress.

▪ Civil engineer

This is arguably the most practical of the engineering professions. As a **civil engineer** you are responsible for the design, building and maintenance of bridges, roads, railway lines, water supply or sewage systems – facing up to the practical challenges involved in creating and using the infrastructure of a modern country. As well as the practical side, there are also opportunities in design, management and the environment. You'll need to be a numerate problem-solver in any capacity.

Strangely, **civil engineers** seem to be held in rather low regard in the UK, despite being essential to our daily life. But at least you'll be pretty much guaranteed a job, either with a consulting or contracting engineering company, a local authority or central government, or in banking, law or the City.

▪ Chemical engineer

Almost without exception, university engineering departments report that this discipline offers one of the best career potentials, with some of the best salaries. Chemists and biochemists often need to stay on for a PhD if they're going to get the decent jobs, but **chemical engineers** are straight in there, earning the cash.

The jobs – of which there are plenty – could involve working in the chemical, process, food or pharmaceutical industries or in those areas of the City that deal with the large chemical engineering industry. The job is about the practical application of chemistry on a large scale, involving the creation and efficient operation of facilities relating to the manufacture of almost anything, from plastic gizmos to cleaning products, from drugs to toothpaste. It's about building a process, one that's economically viable and environmentally responsible. Some shy away from working in an industry with a rather poor environmental image, but a big part of the subject is learning how to manage risks properly. It's worth remembering how much of our everyday life has been brought to us through chemical engineering – from food testing to medicines to printer's ink.

- Electrical and electronic engineer

Electrical and electronic engineering have a very close link with computers, so it'll help if you're familiar and comfortable with this sort of technology. The work itself can cover a range of areas and skills. You could be involved in electricity generation, supply and distribution, software engineering, signal processing, control engineering, computer architecture, communications technology, networking, databases or e-commerce engineering. You'll have a grasp of both the theory and the practical mechanics of electrical and electronic systems, microelectronics, silicon devices and nanotechnology. You'll find work in electronics companies, telecommunications of every kind, small systems houses, satellite businesses and finance companies – and the City will be keen on your expertise too. In fact, there are very few areas of the economy where your skills will not be useful.

- Materials engineer

Materials engineering is really at the junction of chemistry, physics and engineering and you'll be taking a multi-disciplinary approach to your work. It's all about what everything is made of – the properties of materials, how to make them lighter, stronger, more heat-resistant and cheaper than before – and spans a huge range from metallurgy to textiles, working from the atomic level upwards. It's currently big on recycling, but you can be working in a wide variety of industries.

- Mechanical engineer

Mechanical engineering is also a multi-disciplinary kind of job and covers aeronautical, automotive and manufacturing engineering, so you could work across a variety of sectors. Wherever you work, you'll first need to be versed in the basics, including solid mechanics, fluid dynamics, thermodynamics, design, materials, propulsion, electrical drives, control systems, computer modelling and applied engineering. After that you can specialise in a chosen area, such as the car, boat, construction, oil and gas, renewable energy resources and biomedical industries, or you could move to areas where your expertise and transferable skills will come in handy – IT or the City, perhaps. Either way, the chances are that you won't be on the dole.

QUALIFICATIONS AND TRAINING There is no single way to qualify as an engineer, though almost all routes into the profession involve a mixture of study and on-the-job training. In the UK there are three grades of professional qualification: chartered engineer, incorporated engineer and engineering technician. The Engineering Council UK (ECUK) regulates the engineering profession through 36 engineering institutions, which are licensed to put qualified members on the ECUK's register of engineers.

To become a **chartered engineer** (CEng), you should have an accredited BEng and MSc degree or an accredited four-year MEng degree. **Incorporated engineers** (IEng) typically need an accredited degree in engineering or technology or an HND or foundation degree in engineering or technology, plus appropriate further learning to degree level.

If you don't have these qualifications there are a number of other ways to demonstrate that you have the requisite knowledge and understanding. These may include: writing a technical report, based upon your experience, and demonstrating your knowledge and understanding of engineering principles; taking Engineering Council exams; following an assessed work-based learning programme; and taking an academic programme specified by the institution to which you are applying. Both chartered and incorporated engineers also need to complete a period of professional development (training plus professional experience), a record of which must be kept, to prove that you are competent. This can either be done through schemes attached to potential employers or independently. You also have to show that you have a plan for maintaining your skills and competence.

To become an **engineering technician** (EngTech), you should have approved engineering qualifications such as an NC, advanced GNVQ or equivalent. You also need to do a period of initial professional development (which usually takes at least three years) and an IPD assessment, followed by more practical experience with some responsibility. This leads to the technician professional review, and then to EngTech status. If you're a mature candidate without academic qualifications you can still qualify through a work-based assessment.

A lot of employers offer graduate training schemes, often aimed at helping new engineers gain chartered or incorporated status. There are opportunities to start as a mature entrant, but this is very much a graduate profession, so unless your previous experience is in a related field such as building or physics, engineering is hard to get into. If you want to stand a chance of getting on to a good graduate scheme or having your pick of the companies, then work experience is an important factor on top of a good engineering degree. Most of the big companies offer internships and placements that fit in with your penultimate year's holiday periods. The engineering professional bodies detailed below have lists of companies with industrial training programmes that they approve.

SALARY The average graduate starting salary in the engineering professions is £22,185.

CORPORATE CULTURE

This is a profession that often involves a certain amount of hands-on attention, for which dress needs to be appropriate, be it safety gear or just something that you don't mind getting dirty. However, there are often clients involved, so smart dressing is frequently called for, although it's not as formal as, say, banking. Your real questions are going to be about the attitude of your company. For example, what sort of size of company or practice do you want to work for? How will it influence your development and access to promotion and development? Will your employer support you in working towards those all-important professional qualifications and gaining other skills to broaden out your knowledge?

This is obviously a profession with many potential avenues to explore, so if you want to travel, choosing a company that might have involvement in international projects is the way forward. A lot of younger civil engineers take the opportunity to work overseas on projects improving the infrastructure of countries that have suffered war or natural disasters. However, travel is possible for almost any qualified engineer as the skills are both extremely sought after and eminently transferable.

In terms of getting on and moving up, this is a sector where experience is highly valued and indeed, a requirement, as professional qualifications are the minimum for any sort of high-flying engineering job. If you're talented

Online reading

This is a Russian doll of a profession, so here's a bundle of urls to browse.

Royal Aeronautical Society www.raes.org.uk

Institution of Agricultural Engineers www.iagre.org

Chartered Institution of Building Services Engineers www.cibse.org

Institution of Chemical Engineers www.icheme.org

Institution of Civil Engineers www.ice.org.uk

Institution of Engineering and Technology www.theiet.org

Energy Institute www.energyinst.org.uk

Institution of Engineering Designers www.ied.org.uk

Institution of Fire Engineers www.ife.org.uk

Institute of Healthcare Engineering and Estate Management
  www.iheem.org.uk

Society of Environmental Engineers www.environmental.org.uk

Institution of Highways and Transportation www.iht.org

Institute of Marine Engineering, Science and Technology
  www.imarest.org

Institute of Materials, Minerals and Mining www.iom3.org

Institution of Mechanical Engineers www.imeche.org.uk

Institute of Physics and Engineering in Medicine www.ipem.ac.uk

Institution of Structural Engineers www.istructe.org.uk

Chartered Institution of Water and Environmental Management
  www.ciwem.org.uk

Institution of Water Officers www.iwo.org.uk

you might be able to spend less time doing your professional development when you're qualifying for professional status, but on the whole, it's unlikely that you'll fly up the ranks without doing your time. Obviously, once you've gained experience and the necessary qualifications, the world is your oyster and promotion goes to the most talented and innovative.

Lots of these jobs have a practical element as well as the obvious desk-based design and report work. Civil and structural engineers often work on the building sites of projects that they have also designed. It's such a multi-faceted business, with so much variation in the jobs themselves, that you'd probably be hard pressed to find any sort of engineer who spent all their time in one place.

ETHICAL QUESTIONS

The nature of engineering and the sheer quantity of materials used by the sector make it an industry where companies' approaches to the environment make a huge difference.

Does the firm go the extra mile to take into account best environmental practice? It's one thing just meeting the minimum standard required by law and another for a firm to make environmental best practice part of its core objectives. What materials does it favour? Does it build things to last? Does it think through the energy and resources used through a structure's life cycle? What are the firm's interests abroad? A number of firms have been criticised in recent years for being involved in controversial dam projects in India, Turkey and China, with concerns raised about environmental and human rights abuses. If there is tension between cost and safety, how is the matter resolved?

Environmental, food chain and rural

Despite the continuing urbanisation of the landscape, what might be (very loosely) termed rural industries are an increasingly sophisticated and competitive area in which to work, as well as being pretty big business, contributing around £24 billion to the economy annually. Historically agriculture has always been an important and major employer. And as for cultural impact, the countryside is an enormous part of our heritage and national consciousness – the National Trust is a testament to this, caring for over 248,000 hectares of countryside in England, Wales and Northern Ireland, plus almost 600 miles of coastline and more than 300 buildings and gardens of outstanding interest and importance. Domestic horticulture, meanwhile, is almost as big a growth industry as home improvement. And that's just the plants: as a nation we're notoriously potty about animals, evidenced by the fact that every year applications to veterinary science courses far exceed the number of places available, while the number of animal charities supported by the public is staggering. Far from being a "nation of shopkeepers" as Napoleon rather dismissively put it, it seems that we are a nation of dedicated ramblers, dog-walkers and enthusiastic gardeners. Not to mention eaters.

And those eaters, your potential customers, are increasingly demanding better standards of food production, as shown by the growth in the demand for organic produce and calls for supermarkets to start stocking more traditional breeds of fruit and vegetables which are in danger of dying out due to cheap imports of blander, generic foods. Genetically modified crops, on the other hand, are both a moral quandary and an economic opportunity, with trials still taking place, even if some have to be in secret.

In the rapidly changing rural (employment) landscape, you may find that the ability to remember what "red sky at night" signifies is less helpful than sound business management and IT skills. A love of the countryside and an understanding of how humanity can harness nature is one thing, but management skills and adaptability to the demands of the unexpected are equally essential. As issues such as the ban on hunting, GM foods and the environment shuffle up the ladder of public concern, you may need to deal with people vehemently opposed to what you do (or don't).

In the more strictly scientific areas, you will need both technical skills and the ability to explain the concepts to the layperson. Across much of the industry, commitment and a love for rural matters is likely to have to come ahead of a love of money. But remember, it's important work.

■ Farming and animal care

In agriculture, the average age of landowners and managers is high so there is a need for the younger generation to move in and provide fresh lifeblood. The sector needs people with skills in, for example, engineering and scientific research to sit alongside traditional agricultural skills, especially as agribusiness takes over from old-fashioned farming and provides more and more graduate employment. There is a growing diversification of courses and qualifications available as employment moves away from straightforward production and towards a more varied use of land. As for animal care, it's one of the most competitive and popular areas of this sector, but there are nevertheless options that involve working with animals without necessarily going down the veterinary route.

Roles

■ Farm manager

A **farm manager** is employed by a farm owner to plan and run all the day-to-day aspects of the farm estate. This includes accounts and office work as well as staff and work scheduling, maintaining buildings and machinery and being responsible for livestock and crops.

■ Soil scientist

Not surprisingly this job involves studying and analysing soil – not just its chemical contents and distribution but also microbiological activity and how best to exploit and conserve it. This involves helping landowners and managers to find the best crops to plant and the best ways to maintain the soil so that it remains fertile, including irrigation and drainage. It can also help to identify different problems such as salination, acidification and pollution of soil, which might affect its agricultural potential, cause contamination of the water table or compromise biodiversity. **Soil scientists** work in a number of different areas: land-use planning, agriculture, horticulture, forestry, environmental management and protection, education and research as well as advising on national and international policy.

- Animal nutritionist

This is very similar to being a human nutritionist (see page 81), and in fact the Nutrition Society is the professional body for **animal nutritionists** as well. Nutritionists advise on the best way to feed animals – it sounds obvious but it can have economic implications for farmers or feed companies. The job can involve analysing the contents of feed or working out feeding plans to enhance wellbeing and performance.

- Veterinary surgeon

This can mean working in private practice, research or industry. Some vets choose to specialise, either working with particular types of animals such as farm animals, zoo animals or racehorses, or focusing on the treatment of small animals including pets. The Department for Environment, Food and Rural Affairs (Defra) employs vets for areas such as disease control, where potential and actual animal health problems and epidemics (such as foot and mouth) are monitored. Research and industry posts can be in such areas as animal welfare organisations or even in the food processing industry, ensuring that animal welfare standards remain high (for further aspects of medical research the sections on healthcare and science on pages 114 and 184 might prove useful). While job prospects for graduates from all the veterinary schools are strong, the working life of a vet can be very stressful indeed. You should also remember that the aftermath of the foot and mouth crisis and the subsequent downturn in farmers' fortunes means that there is less likelihood that you'll be making a living treating mainly farm animals.

QUALIFICATIONS AND TRAINING The public perception of agricultural courses is that they are finishing schools for simple-minded, ruddy-faced toffs who will then drive off in the Range Rover to manage the family estate. Some places may still be like that, but the subject now involves the increasingly complex scientific issues that characterise modern farming and forestry, from genetically modified produce and the use of pesticides to conservation issues, organic farming strategies and environmental science.

Although farm management can come with the family farm, you'll find that in general to be a **farm manager** you'll need a BTEC/SQA higher national certificate or diploma (HNC/HND), a degree or postgraduate qualification, plus lashings of experience – several years' work in farming, as a supervisor or unit manager, is also generally required. It's a hands-on career, so expect to learn a lot on the job.

Soil scientists will need at least a degree, if not in purely soil science then at least with a large soil science element. For any sort of soil science research work a PhD is the qualification employers will be looking for. Big companies are your most likely employers, and some of these may have graduate recruitment schemes and internships which will fit you with further skills and training.

To be a fully qualified **veterinary surgeon** and operate on animals you need to get a degree in veterinary science, which takes five or six years depending on the university. There are additional postgraduate specialism certificates you can also study and sit for. But with up to 18 applicants chasing each place at each school, competition for entry to veterinary degrees remains fierce.

For **animal nutrition**, you'll need a degree in equine studies, animal or veterinary science, medical sciences, agriculture, horticulture or crop or plant science. If you have a degree in a different discipline such as biology you may also need a relevant postgraduate qualification to supplement your knowledge. To become an accredited nutritionist, registration with the Institute of Biology (see page 77), British Nutrition Foundation or Institute of Food Science and Technology (see page 82) usually requires a relevant degree and a minimum of three years' experience.

SALARY The average graduate starting salary in the agricultural trades is £14,265. For veterinarians, that figure is £25,355.

Contacts

British Safety Council
70 Chancellors Road
London W6 9RS
(t) 020 8741 1231
(↗) www.britishsafetycouncil.co.uk

British Small Animal Veterinary Association
Woodrow House
1 Telford Way
Waterwells Business Park
Quedgeley
Glos GL2 2AB
(t) 01452 726700
(↗) www.bsava.com

British Society of Soil Science
BSSS Administration Office
Cunningham Building
Macaulay Institute
Craigiebuckler
Aberdeen AB15 8QH
(t) 01224 498200
(↗) www.soils.org.uk

British Veterinary Association
7 Mansfield Street
London W1G 9NQ
(t) 020 7636 6541
(↗) www.bva.co.uk

Department for Environment, Food and Rural Affairs (Defra)
Nobel House
17 Smith Square
London SW1P 3JR
(t) 020 7238 6000
(↗) www.defra.gov.uk

Environmental Services Association
154 Buckingham Palace Road
London SW1W 9TR
(t) 020 7824 8882
(↗) www.esauk.org

Institute of Biology
9 Red Lion Court
London EC4A 3EF

(t) 020 7936 5900

(↗) www.iob.org

**Institute of Professional
Soil Scientists**
Administrative Centre
Macaulay Land Use Research
    Institute
Craigiebuckler
Aberdeen AB15 8QH

(t) 01224 318611

(↗) www.soilscientist.org

The Nutrition Society
10 Cambridge Court
210 Shepherds Bush Road
London W6 7NJ

(t) 020 76020228

(↗) www.nutritionsociety.org

Pesticide Action Network UK
Development House
56–64 Leonard Street
London EC2A 4JX

(t) 020 7065 0905

(↗) www.pan-uk.org

Pesticides Safety Directorate
Mallard House
Kings Pool
3 Peasholme Green
York YO1 7PX

(t) 01904 455775

(↗) www.pesticides.gov.uk

**Royal College of
Veterinary Surgeons**
Belgravia House
62–64 Horseferry Road
London SW1P 2AF

(t) 020 7222 2001

(↗) www.rcvs.org.uk

RSPCA
Enquiries service RSPCA
Wilberforce Way
Southwater
Horsham
West Sussex RH13 9RS

(t) 0870 33 35 999

(↗) www.rspca.org.uk

Soil Association
South Plaza
Marlborough Street
Bristol BS1 3NX

(t) 0117 314 5000

(↗) www.soilassociation.org

Soil Association Scotland
18 Liberton Brae
Tower Mains
Edinburgh EH16 6AE

(t) 0131 666 2474

(↗) www.sascotland.org

Online reading

Farmers Weekly www.fwi.co.uk

**Lantra: the Sector Skills Council for the Environmental and
    Land-based Sector** www.lantra.co.uk

Growing careers www.growing-careers.com

■ Gardens and horticulture

Roles here can be part of the leisure sector – in garden centres or National Trust properties perhaps – or might be concerned with the macro-economics of the agribusiness side of the rural idyll. In other words, you could be dealing with anything from GM crops to the flower banks on roundabouts.

Roles

■ Amenity horticulturist
This is horticulture for public spaces and involves designing, constructing and maintaining parks, cemeteries, sports facilities, botanic gardens etc. **Amenity horticulturists** work under different titles, as landscape architects, landscape gardeners, grounds attendants and parks directors.

■ Commercial horticulturist
In the world of **commercial horticulture**, you are concerned with how to grow food crops in greenhouses and on open land, and how to produce flowers and plants for nurseries and florists. You might be working in a hands-on way to cultivate crops and protect them from disease or you might be supervising the maintenance, harvesting and distribution of the crops.

■ Plant breeder/geneticist
You would research plant- and crop-based agriculture in order to improve breeding techniques and create new varieties of crops to satisfy changes in growing conditions or consumer demand. **Plant breeders** can work for research institutes, government agencies, seed companies, commercial plant breeders or genetic engineering and biotechnology firms.

QUALIFICATIONS AND TRAINING Qualifications in this area tend to be at least HND and above, with possible further qualifications from professional bodies such as the Royal Horticultural Society. Aspiring plant breeders and geneticists need a degree, MSc or PhD and possibly Royal Horticultural Society qualifications. This is the higher end of the qualifications spectrum, however: amenity and commercial horticulturalists need HND/NVQs to appropriate level depending on employer and exact role; RHS certificates and diplomas and training are often given on the job or encouraged by employers.

SALARY The average graduate starting salary in the horticultural trades is £17,526.

Contacts

British Ecological Society
26 Blades Court
London SW15 2NU

(t) 020 8871 9797

(↗) www.britishecologicalsociety.org

British Society of Plant Breeders
Woolpack Chambers
16 Market Street
Ely
Cambs CB7 4ND

(t) 01353 653200

(↗) www.bspb.co.uk

Institute of Horticulture
14–15 Belgrave Square
London SW1X 8PS

(t) 020 7245 6943

(↗) www.horticulture.org.uk

Royal Botanic Garden Edinburgh
20a Inverleith Row
Edinburgh EH3 5LR

(t) 0131 552 7171

(↗) www.rbge.org.uk

Royal Botanic Gardens, Kew
Richmond
Surrey TW9 3AB

(↗) www.kew.org

Royal Horticultural Society
80 Vincent Square
London SW1P 2PE

(t) 0845 260 5000

(↗) www.rhs.org.uk

Online reading

Lantra: the Sector Skills Council for the Environmental and Land-based Sector www.lantra.co.uk

The Ecologist www.theecologist.org

Horticulture Week www.hortweek.com

■ Food production

Production and distribution of food is the largest and most important economic activity in the world, and each year over 70 billion items of food are produced in the UK. Nearly a fifth of the top 100 British companies are in food manufacturing and our expenditure on food continues to increase. As our appetite for new products continues to grow our concern about the safety of products and the conditions in which they are produced has never been higher. But the outlook for jobs in this sector is pretty good. The government at all levels, locally and nationally, is employing scientific advisers to monitor food producers and suppliers, as well as people qualified to promote healthy eating and nutritional education to help spread better eating practices.

Meanwhile food producers are looking for those with the skill to develop products and processes, to ensure quality control and safety, and to explore the many other aspects that will keep consumers interested and spending.

This is the joining point between science and people so you'll need to be able to put over quite complex scientific matters in lay terms. Your communication skills will be underpinned by a love of food and drink, or at least up to the point where it's not life-threatening. You will be applying the theoretical to the practical so patience, teamwork and the willingness to soak up knowledge will all help.

Roles

■ Dietician

This is a job that combines food, science and medicine: it's all about the scientific application of nutrition. "**Dietician**" is what's known as a protected title, so you can't call yourself one unless you're properly qualified and you can't work for the NHS unless you're on the Health Professions Council register. These guys are not peddlers of trendy diets. Rather, state-registered dieticians are advisers on nutrition and health, either in an educational sense to promote healthier eating, or in a clinical sense, giving advice about food-related problems or helping people with specific health needs such as an illness or eating disorder to plan what sort of foods to eat and in what quantities. The NHS is a major employer, and you can choose to specialise – in diabetes, for example, or in children's health or cancer – but equally you could work in the food industry, sports, scientific research or journalism.

■ Food scientist/technologist

The increased interest in what we put in our mouths and how we generate it brings us naturally to the arena of food science and technology. **Food scientists** study the properties of food from the field (or laboratory) through the processing stage to the final product. It is, as you might imagine, very science-based with particular emphasis on chemistry and biology. You'll find employment in food manufacturing, packaging and the machinery of both. You'll be helping develop new products and new technologies, or you could be involved in the research side, working for government agencies or universities. **Food technologists** work to make new forms of food and drink and to improve and modify existing products and the processes that create them.

■ Food toxicologist/microbiologist

A **food toxicologist** is concerned with food safety, examining food for chemicals – those that occur naturally and those added during manufacture

– and deciding what levels are safe for consumption. This is a joint desk and lab kind of role, combining research into the effects of different chemicals with the actual testing of products. As a **microbiologist** you use your knowledge of micro-organisms to prevent food spoilage and poisoning of consumers and to promote safe handling of food in appropriately hygienic settings. The not unrelated role of **food safety advisor** works with manufacturers, shops, cafes, restaurants and other food retailers advising on the safe handling and processing of food.

■ Home economist/Consumer scientist

A **home economist** is sometimes known as a **consumer scientist**, though neither job title is very revealing. Basically it's about assessing the needs of consumers, giving advice on goods and services to consumers or on behalf of consumers to manufacturers. If this sounds a bit vague, that's because home economists tend to specialise in a particular area. One role is product development, where conducting research about consumer taste leads to the design and production of new dishes, products or services. Quality assurance is another possibility as are marketing, consumer advice or even working for government bodies such as the Trading Standards department, the Food Standards Agency or the Environment Agency, making sure that consumer rights aren't breached and safety standards are upheld. You could also work in education, either in a school or with companies or individuals who provide catering and services to different institutions.

■ Nutritionist

This role is often confused with the dietician's. Basically as a **nutritionist** you apply your scientific knowledge of food and nutrition in much the same way as a dietician, for education, health and wellbeing, but you work primarily with people who are healthy, in a preventive role, rather than with those already suffering from ill health and food problems. Although nutritionists are still waiting to have their title protected, you can register as a nutritionist with the Nutrition Society (see page 77), which proves that you have obtained a degree in nutrition or an equivalent subject and have at least three years' relevant experience.

QUALIFICATIONS AND TRAINING There's an entry point for most of these jobs with related A-levels (ie science ones) and, initially, NVQs, BTECs, HNDs and HNCs, as well as the relevant, rather specialised degree courses. Once you're in, the relevant professional bodies will be able to advise on the relevant training for membership, which may be essential if you are to practise your craft. To work as a dietician within the NHS, for example, you need to register with the Health Professions Council. You will need to keep up with scientific developments to make sure you stay on top of the subject, some of which will come through CPD-style training and some of which will come simply from making sure you subscribe to the right magazines. Maxim doesn't cut it, I'm afraid.

SALARY The average graduate starting salary in the food science trades is £18,972.

Contacts

British Dietetic Association
5th Floor
Charles House
148–149 Great Charles Street
Queensway
Birmingham B3 3HT
(t) 0121 200 8031
(↗) www.bdacareerchoices.com

British Nutrition Foundation
High Holborn House
52–54 High Holborn
London WC1V 6RQ
(t) 020 7404 6504
(↗) www.nutrition.org.uk

Fairtrade Foundation
Room 204
16 Baldwin's Gardens
London EC1N 7RJ
(t) 020 7405 5942
(↗) www.fairtrade.org.uk

Food Standards Agency
Aviation House
125 Kingsway
London WC2B 6NH
(t) 020 7276 8000
(↗) www.food.gov.uk

Health Professions Council
Park House
184 Kennington Park Road
London SE11 4BU
(t) 020 7582 0866
(↗) www.hpc-uk.org

Institute of Food Research
Norwich Research Park
Colney
Norwich NR4 7UA
(t) 01603 255000
(↗) www.ifr.bbsrc.ac.uk

Institute of Food Science and Technology
5 Cambridge Court
210 Shepherds Bush Road
London W6 7NJ
(t) 020 7603 6316
(↗) www.ifst.org.uk

Online reading
The Grocer www.thegrocer.co.uk
The Food Commission www.foodcomm.org.uk

■ Environmental conservation and maintenance

It helps if you're a bit of an optimist if you are an environmentalist. Everyone tells you that the world is going to hell in a deep-fried handbasket, as global warming, the hole in the ozone layer, GM foods and pollution take an increasingly fevered hold on the public imagination and the end of the world gets more and more nigh. Environmental conservationists are generally the ones who think they can do something about it, saving us from ourselves.

The issues facing environmental science have a variety of causes and, therefore, a variety of solutions. Hence, the work is increasingly multi-disciplinary. You'll be engaged with the principles of... (deep breath) ecology, population biology, environmental chemistry, physiology, physical geography, statistics, sociology, law, economics, microbial ecology, energy, biological survey, assessment and conservation (breathe out). In addition, you'll need to be able to produce concise accounts of complex problems and communicate them effectively to others, both in writing and verbally. You'll need analysis and presentation skills.

Job opportunities are increasing in environmental sectors, reflecting the growing importance of sustainability and environmental awareness in industry, leisure and agriculture. There is also an educational aspect as conservation for environmental and leisure purposes has become a Defra priority as well as an element in the national curriculum.

Roles

■ Environmental consultant
This is a job that involves working with commercial clients to asses and advise on issues such as environmental impact, waste management, water pollution, and air and land contamination. **Environmental consultants** also carry out environmental audits, work with clients on environmental policy and produce reports, research and policy on the impact of developments on wildlife, the water table and geology, among other things.

■ Environmental monitoring officer
This might be a specialist role, for example monitoring water quality in particular, or air quality, or it might be an integrated post. It's a job that occurs in other sectors too: many local councils have an **environmental monitoring officer** for example. In rural areas water quality is of primary concern and as a monitoring officer you will be making sure that it meets stringent

legislation-inspired targets. You would usually specialise in analysing a type of water – ground water, drinking water or waste water – and checking that the microbial and chemical content is within target limits. Depending on the type of water you specialise in you'll be looking for different types of pollutants and advising on different problems and how to manage them (see also the role of environmental health officer on page 106).

■ Forest manager/Forester

The role of **forest manager** can be varied but it basically revolves around looking after a particular area of woodland, managing habitats within it, overseeing staff and planning and supervising the felling and planting of different sections.

■ Nature conservation officer

As a **nature conservation officer** you work to promote awareness in local communities as well as protecting and managing areas of environmental importance. It's a job in which you not only need to know about ecology and wildlife but you also need to understand nature conservation legislation.

QUALIFICATIONS AND TRAINING These roles tend to need both paper qualifications and experience to back them up. Forestry is a very competitive area: for a position as a **forest manager or forester** the Forestry Commission requires at least a BTEC or Scotvec HND in forestry; a BSc degree in forestry; or a City and Guilds level 4 certificate in forestry or its Scotvec equivalent. The Institute of Chartered Foresters gives chartered status through exams to those with two or more years of experience and the Forestry Commission sees this as a good qualification to have. Less exact are the qualifications required to be a nature conservation officer. For this you'll need a degree or postgraduate qualification in environmental or life sciences, or in urban or land studies, and work experience is often necessary.

Consultancy is obviously an option for those with a bit more experience or special knowledge of the area. An **environmental consultant** would be expected to have at least a degree in something like social/economic/business studies, urban and land studies, physical/mathematical/applied science, engineering, life and medical science or agricultural and horticultural sciences. For an **environmental monitoring** post most local authorities will require at least a science/environmental monitoring degree and some companies prefer to employ staff with postgraduate qualifications. For environmental professionals in both these fields, further environmental training courses are available from organisations such as the British Standards Institution, the British Safety Council and the Environmental Services Association. Trainee schemes may well include such courses or stepping stones to qualifications.

SALARY The average graduate starting salary in the conservation trades is £17,443.

Contacts

Association of Independent Crop Consultants
Agriculture Place
Drayton Farm
East Meon
Petersfield
Hampshire GU32 1PN

(t) 01730 823881

(↗) www.aicc.org.uk

British Ecological Society
26 Blades Court
London SW15 2NU

(t) 020 8871 9797

(↗) www.britishecologicalsociety.org

British Standards Institution
389 Chiswick High Road
London W4 4AL

(t) 020 8996 9001

(↗) www.bsi-global.com

Chartered Institution of Water and Environmental Management
15 John Street
London WC1N 2EB

(t) 020 7831 3110

(↗) www.ciwem.org.uk

Environment Agency
Rio House
Waterside Drive
Almondsbury
Bristol BS32 4UD

(t) 08708 506 506

(↗) www.environment-agency.gov.uk

Forestry Commission
Silvan House
231 Corstorphine Road
Edinburgh EH12 7AT

(t) 0131 334 0303

(↗) www.forestry.gov.uk

Institute of Chartered Foresters
7a St Colme Street
Edinburgh EH3 6AA

(t) 0131 225 2705

(↗) www.charteredforesters.org

Natural England
Northminster House
Peterborough PE1 1UA

(t) 0845 600 3078

(↗) www.naturalengland.org.uk

Royal Forestry Society
102 High Street
Tring
Herts HP23 4AF

(t) 01442 822028

(↗) www.rfs.org.uk

Online reading

Sustain www.sustainweb.org

UNEP World Conservation Monitoring Centre www.unep-wcmc.org

Greenpeace www.greenpeace.org.uk

CORPORATE CULTURE

There's no unifying corporate culture since it depends on what area of the industry you work in. If you're doing pure research, then the end product of your work is less tangible and less profit-motivated than someone trying to develop new foods to sell in supermarkets, which again is completely different to someone working in nutrition in the NHS. The culture you work in is therefore determined much more by your employer than by your job. You need to look at the motivation of the company to help gauge the kind of employer it is. Is it trying to exploit, conserve or develop? From that, you can draw your own conclusions.

For large parts of the rural and food industries, it is less a job and more a way of life. Farmers and conservation workers often live and work within the same environment and the job can, therefore, be more than a little all-consuming. Commitment is everything. For others it can be simply 9–5 in the lab or in the office, although you may work shift patterns if you're involved with a 24-hour food production unit for example.

ETHICAL QUESTIONS

The production of food is currently at the heart of many ethical concerns about modern living. The legacy of food processing, in particular the pressures it places all the way down the food chain as well as on the health of the consumer, are big issues in the national debate. The Food Standards Agency is an independent watchdog set up by an act of parliament to protect public health and consumer interests in relation to food, but there are many ethical issues surrounding what we eat which lie outside its remit.

Consider first what it is that the firm produces. Processed readymeals? Frozen pizzas? Or fresh, organic foods? What are the firm's attitudes to additives such as salt, fat, sugar, flavourings and colourings? What is its approach to labelling? Does it reduce packaging, a big cause of domestic waste sent to landfill, where possible?

Where and how does it source its ingredients? Does it look locally first or does it just opt for the cheapest available ingredients regardless of production methods? Is there an awareness of the operation of the markets in various foodstuffs? Sugar production for example is subject to huge government subsidies in the developed world, making it impossible for producers in developing nations to compete. Do these market inequalities affect the firm's purchasing decisions? Is the company a member of any fair trade associations? Does it have a commitment to ensuring farmers are able to earn a living wage?

Fashion

Although you wouldn't know it from its portrayal in the media, fashion is about far more than flashbulbs popping off in the faces of temperamental supermodels.

The UK is seen as a leading fashion centre, and design, marketing, sourcing and distribution have become the main areas of employment. Meanwhile, manufacturing is increasingly outsourced, often to cheaper labour overseas, due to the increasing globalisation of companies. Clothes and fabrics are still made within the UK, especially in areas that have long been associated with textiles and weaving, such as the East Midlands and the north-west of England, but retail and design are mainly where it's at (see the retail section for more details of retail and merchandising jobs). London is the design hub as it's closely associated with the major cultural movements, trends and moods that influence style. In addition, the practice of using textiles for furnishing homes continues to be big business in the ever-expanding home-improvement market (where would we be without Ikea rugs and curtains?).

You'll need a passion for fashion (and for alliteration), since it can become the sort of job that's all-consuming. You'll need great visual imagination to succeed, allied with a sense of the possible and the practical. You'll need to be flexible and able to adapt to the different needs of a market you know and understand; you'll also have sound business sense, particularly in budgeting and costing. And you'll be happy to work in a team: despite what you may think, this is no time to be a diva – unless you're in haute couture of course, in which case you're going to need all the other skills in abundance, as well as a hefty dose of creative and business genius. For other areas of the industry, you'll need technical skills.

Altogether it's a very competitive business and when you're starting out the pay can be low and the hours long. You'll need lots of drive and may have to work in very junior roles in order to be on the scene when the breaks come. However, there are jobs out there and the fashion industry continues to grow.

Roles

■ Clothing and textile technologist

The role of the **textile technologist** doesn't necessarily have to involve clothes: basically it entails dealing with every aspect of the design, development and manufacture of natural and synthetic fabrics, fibres, yarns and textiles. These might be used for furnishings, clothes, medical supplies, all sort of things, so the design and development work needs to take into account possible usage.

■ Colourist/Dyeing technician

This is a technical, specialist role. You'd think that awareness of and sensitivity to colour were shared by pretty much everyone who works in the fashion industry, and this is undoubtedly true. But if you have an exceptionally good eye for colour – and perhaps a technical understanding of the chemicals and scientific principles involved in creating colour as well – this is the job for you. **Colourists** are used to make minute adjustments to the colours of dyes being created. You also advise on and select colour ranges for new products, help designers source potential colours, and may also work alongside fashion predictors, determining colour trends. As a **dyeing technician** you'll decide how to create a designer's chosen colour and how to apply it to the selected fabric, yarn or fibre. Technicians also ensure that the dyed material is colourfast, so it won't run or fade.

■ Designer

You shouldn't be surprised to know that a **designer** designs clothing and/ or accessories for haute couture, designer ready-to-wear or high-street companies. Be warned, however, that very few designers make it in haute couture – it's a very difficult world to break into. Although the glitzy high-profile fashion shows give us images of highly imaginative clothes, generally you'll find that most fashion design jobs aren't so much about artistic expression as the translation of ideas into solid, wearable form. Mostly it's about using market research and consumer need to create a saleable product. You'll be creating a product which fits your employer's brand and pricing strategy, and whether that's affordable clothes for high-street stores, upmarket eveningwear or workers' overalls, you still need to be able to produce sketches, translate them into flat patterns and understand the time and materials costings of making those clothes commercially.

■ Fashion illustrator

A **fashion illustrator** sketches out detailed pictures from ideas. These will eventually become designs for new clothes or accessories and may be used for marketing purposes or to replace photographs when new trends are being predicted rather than realised.

■ Fashion stylist

Like a photographic stylist, a **fashion stylist** creates visual images that will be featured in magazines, music videos, promotional videos and so on. You work from a design brief drawn up by a company or a magazine, putting together the setting, featured accessories and garments, and liaising with photographers, PR companies, manufacturers and the designers and technicians doing the lighting and set-building.

■ Fashion predictor

A **fashion predictor** forecasts the colours and styles that will determine new fashion and buying trends. This is an important design and/or retail role – buyers for major chains often have to decide what their shops will stock up to two seasons ahead of it actually appearing on the shelves. If predictors get it wrong, credibility in their brand or firm will drop and there will be an awful lot of unsold, unfashionable stock hanging about. This isn't just a case of deciding what you think should be on the rails, but a research job that involves looking at major trends in music and even politics, going to fashion shows and observing the directions different designers are exploring or going to trade fairs and looking at what is being bought and displayed. It's a diverse job – you might be doing long-range predictions or just updating clients on current moods and trends.

■ Pattern cutter/grader

This can be two jobs or one, depending on the size of the company you're working for. **Pattern cutters** take designs and create the patterns that will be used to make them into a finished product. This involves working with the designer to tweak the pattern to get the best final result. **Pattern graders** then step in, working from the original pattern to create copies so that different sizes can be made.

Online reading
Vogue www.vogue.co.uk
Drapers Record www.drapersrecord.co.uk
Fashist! www.fashist-online.com

Contacts

Chartered Society of Designers

1 Cedar Court
Royal Oak Yard
Bermondsey Street
London SE1 3GA

(t) 020 7357 8088

(↗) www.csd.org.uk

Design Council

34 Bow Street
London WC2E 7DL

(t) 020 7420 5200

(↗) www.design-council.org.uk

The Fashion Retail Academy

15 Gresse Street
London W1T 1QL

(t) 0207 307 2345

(↗) www.fashionretailacademy.ac.uk

London College of Fashion

20 John Prince's Street
London W1G 0BJ

(t) 020 7514 7344

(↗) www.lcf.linst.ac.uk

No Sweat

PO Box 36707
London SW9 8YA

(↗) www.nosweat.org.uk

Register of Apparel and Textile Designers

UK Fashion Exports
5 Portland Place
London W1B 1PB

(t) 020 7636 5577

(↗) www.ukfashionexports.com

Skillfast-UK: the Sector Skills Council for Apparel, Footwear, Textiles and Related Businesses

Richmond House
Lawnswood Business Park
Redvers Close
Leeds LS16 6RD

(t) 0113 2399 600

(↗) www.skillfast-uk.org

Society of Dyers and Colourists

PO Box 244
Perkin House
82 Grattan Road
Bradford BD1 2JB

(t) 01274 725138

(↗) www.sdc.org.uk

Textile Institute

1st Floor
St James's Buildings
Oxford Street
Manchester M1 6FQ

(t) 0161 237 1188

(↗) www.textileinstitute.org

QUALIFICATIONS AND TRAINING There's plenty of degree, foundation and HND-level fashion courses which can ease a wannabe **designer** into the industry, but make sure you check the course details, rather than just the title, as the word "fashion" can hide a multitude of specialisms, and you need to make sure the course suits the direction you want to go. Check too the progress of past students to see if you're following in the footsteps of the successful. Remember that most jobs in the industry aren't done by McQueens or Westwoods but are located at the popular end of the high street. Those companies will tend to hire from colleges with good reputations. Once qualified, you may have to do a level of skivvying you thought your degree made unnecessary, but experience, reputation and a willingness to muck in can get you a long way in this very competitive industry. Some larger companies have graduate training schemes, but for the majority, further training is of the on-the-job kind.

For the other roles you'll need an HND or degree in a relevant fashion, chemical engineering or business course, or you'll have practical experience from the shopfloor of a fashion house and be looking to change. The reflected glamour of the industry illuminates even these backstage roles, so it can be pretty competitive, which, in turn, means you'll have to prove your commitment.

SALARY The average graduate starting salary in the clothing and textile design industry is £16,800.

CORPORATE CULTURE

This is, as previously mentioned, a highly competitive industry, so to get on you may have to swallow a little pride and do as much work experience as possible. Most of it may be unpaid, but do it anyway, and be prepared to do everything and do it well. There are people kicking the door down to be there and you will be watched for potential. Once you're in there, network like hell and always seek to gain skills, understanding and experience, while taking time to maintain a portfolio of your outstanding work. Fashion is a meritocracy but you have to make sure that your merits are noticed.

While due deference may have to be given to the egos of the designers and models at the top of the tree, it is in general a pretty informal industry. In terms of your day-to-day work clothes for example that means that your dyed hair, piercings and taffeta outfits will just be dismissed as the outward trappings of an eccentric, creative mind. That shouldn't divert you, though, from the realities of the hard graft needed to keep the industry running, especially as you head towards product launch dates or fashion shows – points which remind you that, however creative you are being, you are still working in an industry looking for profit just as much as applause.

ETHICAL QUESTIONS

The textile industry has in the past had one of the worst environmental records of any industry due to the use of highly toxic and otherwise hazardous chemicals in the production and dyeing processes. Much progress has been made to eradicate the use of these substances, and the environmental impact of the sector has been reduced considerably. There are still ethical issues surrounding the sector, however.

Where does the company source its materials and labour? This is a sector notoriously linked to sweatshop labour in developing nations. What efforts does the firm make to avoid using this system? There are many campaign groups and organisations dedicated to raising the profile of and eradicating sweatshop labour: is the company a member of one of these groups? Have its procurement and labour policies been accredited by any such organisation?

Cotton production is notoriously polluting as it requires intensive use of fertilisers; does the firm use organic cotton, or even alternatives such as hemp or flax? What is its attitude towards using animal fur and even leather? Fashion based on constant seasonal changes is by nature wasteful of resources: what does the firm think about this? And what is the company's attitude towards responsible fashion – fashion that takes seriously, say, its effect through the use of models on body-image problems among teenage girls?

Financial services

Even for those of us whose financial arrangements only amount to regular threatening letters from the bank manager, money and those who keep track of it, invest it and move it about are an everyday part of life. Accounting and finance are no longer just about bookkeeping and auditing in the manner of a Dickensian clerk. Today's world of financial services may seem to be dominated by well-heeled young men in suits, but it offers an enormous range of careers and is starting to attract more women and people from diverse ethnic backgrounds.

There's a variety of roles in the financial world and you'll need different skills to succeed in each, but common to all is the fact that you must be numerate (this is money we're talking about and if you can't add the stuff up, don't expect to be making much). You'll need to have an analytical mind and a persuasive turn of phrase – more often than not, it's not your money you are having to account for so if you are persuading a client to spend money on a particular course of action, then you're asking them to part with their favourite possession. Accuracy and attention to detail ("now, where did I put that £10m..?") are essentials, as is having a businesslike manner. You'll also need sufficient IT skills to tinker with the various counting and accounting packages most institutions use.

■ Accountancy

Accountants work on a broad canvas that includes tax, auditing, analysis, trusteeships, liquidation, annual accounts, financial planning and a whole range of other financial services, right down to the minutiae of daily expenditure records, salaries and national insurance contributions as well as flagging up the warnings when it all seems about to go wrong. You may work for individuals, companies or institutions – local authorities for example – and you'll develop specialist knowledge to match. The one unvarying factor is that your level of qualification and the work that you do will be watched over by the all-seeing eyes of the industry's self-regulatory bodies, an important part of the modern financial industry.

You'll need to be bright, logical and numerate with good business sense and the ability to negotiate at all levels within a firm or with individuals.

You won't mind being chained to a desk all day and you'll have mental stamina and an eye for detail.

Roles

■ Accounting technician

As an **accounting technician** you would work alongside a fully fledged chartered accountant, doing the day-to-day practical work such as managing the payroll perhaps or preparing accounts. It has a lower entry level than the rest of the accountancy world: the Association of Accounting Technicians has an open-door policy, assuming some degree of numeracy, and offers training and accreditation at NVQ level. Many accounting technicians use it as a springboard to qualification as a chartered accountant.

■ Certified accountant

Being a **certified accountant** shows that you've completed a course and have been awarded a qualification – by a body such as the Association of Chartered Certified Accountants (ACCA) – that allows you to practice. The job often combines managerial and accounting work and certified accountants are employed across the spectrum, by public and private sector organisations. The job can include preparing budgets, financial reports and business plans, auditing, administering the payroll, dealing with tax, making sure the company is complying with all tax requirements, and controlling the income and expenditure of the company.

■ Chartered accountant

This is a higher professional qualification, showing that not only have you completed the ACCA certificate stage but you've also done a three- to five-year training contract and passed exams set by the Institute of Chartered Accountants in England and Wales. As a **chartered accountant** you may be employed by an accounting firm and sent to work for different types of client such as charities and industrial or commercial businesses, giving them financial and management advice. Or you could work in the public sector or for a particular organisation. Whoever you're working for your job will probably include auditing, sorting out accounts and tax returns, dealing with insolvency and giving financial advice.

As a chartered accountant, you could specialise in tax, covering everything pertaining to your company's dealings with HM Revenue and Customs. This involves providing advice and guidance to your employer about issues to do with tax, including keeping up to date with legislation as well as finding (legal) ways to minimise the amount of tax they have to hand over (tax avoidance, not tax evasion). You'll sort out returns, liaise with the

Revenue and sometimes Customs and Excise, audit the company's financial information and prepare and submit accounts for inspections. In some businesses you'll also be involved in the creation of business plans, giving advice on investments or perhaps mergers and takeovers.

■ Chartered management accountant

This is all about providing financial information that will allow companies to plan and control their organisations. Usually **chartered management consultants** work for a particular organisation (rather than being contracted in from a firm) and deal with setting up financial policies and strategies and delivering financial information and analysis. You might say that chartered management accountants are involved with the financial future of a company: rather than auditing and preparing tax returns which deal with the financial past, you're looking at ways of developing the business, analysing its performance in order to develop long-term strategies.

■ Chartered certified accountant

Again this is a title that shows you've achieved a high professional standard. **Chartered certified accountants** not only provide accountancy services such as corporate finance, dealing with insolvency and tax matters, but also sometimes work as management consultants. This is perhaps because their work also often involves controlling the company's funds and administering the payroll as well as producing business plans and detailed financial reports.

■ Chartered public finance accountant

Yes, it's accounting like the others, but this title means that you've qualified through the Chartered Institute of Public Finance and Accountancy to work with public money and have the requisite training to deal with it sensibly. As a **chartered public finance accountant** you deal with all the financial issues and tax requirements for a range of public bodies such as government departments, health service providers and local authorities.

■ Corporate treasurer

The role of the **corporate treasurer** incorporates some of what accountants do, but is more wide-ranging and responsible, combining elements of several financial disciplines. These include corporate financial management (making sure the financial activities of a company fit with the organisation's business strategy), capital markets and funding (discovering the best borrowing rates available and building relationships with people who can help you find the right investors), money management (trying to "free up" the company's cash so the business can avoid borrowing and can make the money it has work harder), and risk management (identifying where risks could damage your company's financial health and putting in place systems to prevent harmful events or, if this can't be done, trying to limit any negative impact). It's a big job, and the Association of Corporate Treasurers runs a qualification scheme to ensure that members have the requisite skills. Usually only large and medium-sized businesses have corporate treasurers, so it's not small amounts of money being dealt with.

■ Financial manager

Financial managers are usually qualified accountants, and can work for almost any company, institution or public body – anyone with money, basically. You'll deal with budgetary planning, risk assessment, financial analysis, preparing accounts, monitoring cash flow and allocating resources among other things.

QUALIFICATIONS AND TRAINING The vast majority of **accountants** have degrees, although the actual subject doesn't always matter. All accountants must be members of one of the professional bodies (see below) and the entry points for those vary depending on your specialisation and the body you want to join. You will need at least two A-levels and probably a degree and a period of practical training, plus a set of professional exams. The early years will certainly test your commitment. Once in work, the process of continuous professional development (CPD) will top up training and keep you in line with changes in legislation.

SALARY The average graduate starting salary in the accountancy profession is £21,601.

Contacts

Association of Accounting Technicians

154 Clerkenwell Road
London EC1R 5AD

(t) 020 7415 7500

(↗) www.aat.co.uk

Association of Chartered Certified Accountants (ACCA)

2 Central Quay
89 Hydepark Street
Glasgow G3 8BW

(t) 0141 582 2000

(↗) www.acca.org.uk

Association of Corporate Treasurers

51 Moorgate
London EC2R 6BH

(t) 020 7847 2540

(↗) www.treasurers.org

Association of International Accountants

Staithes 3
The Watermark
Metro Riverside
Newcastle upon Tyne NE11 9SN

(t) 0191 493 0277

(↗) www.aia.org.uk

Chartered Institute of Management Accountants

22 Chapter Street
London SW1P 4NP

(t) 020 7663 5441

(↗) www.cimaglobal.com

Chartered Institute of Public Finance and Accountancy

3 Robert Street
London WC2N 6RL

(t) 020 7543 5600

(↗) www.cipfa.org.uk

Institute of Chartered Accountants in England and Wales

Chartered Accountants' Hall
PO Box 433
London EC2P 2BJ

(t) 020 7920 8100

(↗) www.icaew.co.uk

Institute of Chartered Accountants of Scotland

CA House
21 Haymarket Yards
Edinburgh EH12 5BH

(t) 0131 347 0100

(↗) www.icas.org.uk

Institute of Chartered Accountants in Ireland

Dublin:
CA House
83 Pembroke Road
Dublin 4

(t) + 353 1 637 7200

Belfast:
The Linenhall
32-38 Linenhall Street
Belfast BT2 8BG

(t) 028 9032 1600

(↗) www.icai.ie

Online reading

Accountancy Age www.accountancyage.com

Student Accountant www.accaglobal.com/publications/studentaccountant

Accountancy magazine www.accountancymagazine.co.uk

■ Banking and investment

The world of banking and investment has been transformed by technology. If you think about the ways you access and spend your own money – via the internet or your phone for example – and how you would have done that even ten years ago (writing cheques, pottering into your local branch), then you get some idea of how the world of the high-street bank has changed, and the same is true for the investment and City institutions too. The basics remain constant though: you are still playing with other people's money, and with the profit you can make with that, there comes enormous responsibility. This is a high-stakes sector, even in the high-street banks. While the sums of money you're dealing with there might be relatively small, it's still taken someone all their lives to build up those savings.

So you'll have integrity and a sense of responsibility and you'll need to be accurate, backed with high levels of concentration. It's also a team game, and you'll need to be good with colleagues as well as clients.

Roles

■ Actuary

As an **actuary** you are trying to make sense of the financial future. You might work either in consultancy, advising firms on matters such as pension funds or investment, or you may be employed by an insurance company. You will use statistics, research and data-analysis to assess risks, determine possible outcomes and advise on courses of action. You might advise a company on how much it should invest in its pension fund or forecast how high insurance premiums should be to be attractive to buy but still cover a company's risk.

■ Commercial/High-street banking

In **commercial banking** you are at the public face of banking. Working for the big-name high-street and internet banks or building societies, you'll be serving the ordinary punter with banking services, maintaining accounts, setting up loans and mortgages, and arranging overdrafts, as well as acting as executor and trustee for wills and looking after safety-deposit services. There's a lot of administration and office work: fielding telephone enquiries, running computer systems, dealing with customers at the counter and selling the bank's many services. It's very much the retail end of the banking industry.

■ Investment analyst

As an **investment analyst** you do the research that enables fund managers to make decisions about their investment portfolios, studying the performance of companies on the markets to warn of potential dangers or to mark out the good stocks to buy. You'll research accounts, reports, announcements and statistical data for your information, poring over the internet and scouring newspapers before writing it all up in report form. Investment analysts work for stockbrokers, investment banks or investment management companies.

■ Investment banker

There are two different roles available in **investment banking**. In corporate finance you deal with mergers and acquisitions and equity and debt as well as providing strategic advice and raising venture capital. In operations you handle the clearance and settlement of transactions. Overall, the role of the investment banker is to advise clients on the most appropriate way to raise money to fund their activities and to execute transactions on their behalf.

■ Financial adviser

A **financial adviser** does pretty much what you might think, advising his or her clients on selecting the right financial products and services for their needs, which could include pensions, investments, insurance and mortgages. You could be self-employed or work for a financial services company. You'll work directly with clients, selecting the products that best suit their circumstances and will require in-depth knowledge of the tax system and the investment market.

■ Stockbroker/Commodity broker

Both these jobs are **brokers**, buying and selling for their clients. One deals in stocks and shares, the other in physical commodities (sugar, metals, that kind of thing). You need to be fully aware of what is going on with your market in order to be in a position to advise your client on whether to invest, hold or sell. Those clients could be individuals, companies or institutions – pension funds perhaps.

■ Trader

There are actually two distinct roles lumped under this title – traders and sales – which should not be confused although their roles are quite similar. **Traders** make prices on bonds, equities, foreign exchange or commodities, working closely with their banks as well as paying attention to research and market analysis. **Sales** deal in stocks and shares on behalf of the bank's clients, and issue market updates to investors they hope will be spurred into making transactions.

QUALIFICATIONS AND TRAINING Professional qualifications for **actuaries** are awarded by two bodies in the UK – the Institute of Actuaries and the Faculty of Actuaries (Scotland) – and in order to qualify you need to become a member which itself means finding employment with a firm of actuaries and passing the professional exams. The learning process is usually by correspondence and tutorials and takes a minimum of three years.

Entry into the world of **banking** can come at different stages. Banks employ school-leavers with GCSEs or A-levels and graduates with degrees in (usually) vaguely related areas such as business studies, law or accountancy. From then on you should have access to structured training schemes (these aren't tin-pot organisations you'll be joining after all). These schemes can lead to professional qualifications from the Institute of Financial Services in England and Wales or the Chartered Institute of Bankers in Scotland.

To join the world of **investment**, you will usually need a degree and often a professional qualification, the most widely accepted being that of chartered financial analyst, from the Association of Investment Analysis and Research, an international group which has the Society of Investment Professionals as its UK representative.

Financial advisers have to undertake training recognised by the Financial Services Authority (they can supply details of approved training and the organisations that provide them). This can take between two and three years.

SALARY The average graduate starting salary in the finance and investment industry is £21,157.

Online reading
Financial Times www.ft.com
Risk.net www.risk.net
Money Observer www.moneyobserver.com

Contacts

Association of Independent Financial Advisers
2–6 Austin Friars House
Austin Friars
London EC2N 2HD
(t) 020 7628 1287
(↗) www.aifa.net

Building Societies Association
6th Floor
York House
Kingsway
London WC2B 6UJ
(t) 020 7437 0655
(↗) www.bsa.org.uk

Chartered Institute of Bankers in Scotland
Drumsheugh House
38b Drumsheugh Gardens
Edinburgh EH3 7SW
(t) 0131 473 7777
(↗) www.ciobs.org.uk

Faculty of Actuaries (Scotland)
Maclaurin House
18 Dublin Street
Edinburgh EH1 3PP
(t) 0131 240 1300
(↗) www.actuaries.org.uk

Financial Services Authority
25 The North Colonnade
Canary Wharf
London E14 5HS
(t) 020 7066 1000
(↗) www.fsa.gov.uk

IFS School of Finance
IFS House
4–9 Burgate Lane
Canterbury
Kent CT1 2XJ
(t) 01227 818609
(↗) www.ifslearning.com

Institute of Actuaries
Staple Inn Hall
High Holborn
London WC1V 7QJ
(t) 020 7632 2100
(↗) www.actuaries.org.uk

Institute of Financial Planning
Whitefriars Centre
Lewins Mead
Bristol BS1 2NT
(t) 0117 945 2470
(↗) www.financialplanning.org.uk

London Investment Banking Association
6 Frederick's Place
London EC2R 8BT
(t) 020 7796 3606
(↗) www.liba.org.uk

Personal Finance Society
20 Aldermanbury
London EC2V 7HY
(t) 020 8530 0852
(↗) www.thepfs.org

Securities and Investment Institute
Centurion House
24 Monument Street
London EC3R 8AQ
(t) 020 7645 0600
(↗) www.securities-institute.org.uk

UK Society of Investment Professionals
90 Basinghall Street
London EC2V 5AY
(t) 020 7796 3000
(↗) www.uksip.org

■ Insurance

We use the **insurance** industry to make sure that any misfortune that befalls us can be covered, financially at least. We all pay into a common pool, from which we draw if disaster strikes, or which we leave for others if we stay lucky. Insurance companies cover individual property and lives, companies and reinsurance, and the work involves risk and damage assessment, policy drafting and settling claims.

You'll be good with paperwork and with numbers and you'll be happy to be based in an office. You'll have sound judgement and be confident about passing those judgements to others and about others, often in difficult circumstances. If you become an insurance broker then you'll need a sharp sales edge about you too.

Roles

■ Chartered loss adjuster

Chartered loss adjusters are impartial specialists who investigate insurance claims and report back to the insurance company, making recommendations as to whether or not the claim should be paid. The title "chartered" can be used once you've passed exams set by a professional body such as the Chartered Insurance Institute.

■ Insurance broker

An **insurance broker** is an expert on insurance who advises clients on the most appropriate cover then helps to arrange it. You act as the intermediary between the client and the insurance company; the work is very client-based and a large part of it is fully understanding the client's needs. You'll need to assess risks thoroughly and find the most appropriate cover, always acting with your client's interests in mind. For larger projects, such as insuring a ship or a plane, you would work with a number of firms to spread the load.

■ Insurance underwriter

Insurance underwriters tend to specialise in one area of insurance, such as life insurance, and are responsible for deciding if requests for insurance cover should be accepted and on what terms, assessing the risk of loss to both the policyholder and the insurance company, as well as the value of the business to the company. You need a through understanding of the risk business and will probably specialise in different kinds of work as you progress – large-scale stuff like aviation insurance or smaller but lucrative areas like property.

Contacts

Association of British Insurers
51 Gresham Street
London EC2V 7HQ
(t) 020 7600 3333
(↗) www.abi.org.uk

**British Insurance
Brokers' Association**
14 Bevis Marks
London EC3A 7NT
(t) 0844 770 0266
(↗) www.biba.org.uk

Chartered Insurance Institute
20 Aldermanbury
London EC2V 7HY
(t) 020 7417 4415
(↗) www.cii.co.uk

**Chartered Institute
of Loss Adjusters**
Peninsular House
36 Monument Street
London EC3R 8LJ
(t) 020 7337 9960
(↗) www.cila.co.uk

Online reading
Insurance Age www.insuranceage.com
Insurance Journal www.insurancejournal.com
Professional Broking www.broking.co.uk

QUALIFICATIONS AND TRAINING You can get into the world of insurance with three or more GCSEs, grade C or better, two of which would ordinarily be English and maths. Most companies run training schemes and/or you can study part-time for BTEC diplomas. You can also study on courses run by the Chartered Insurance Institute, taking their exams, although you need three A-levels before you start worrying about those.

SALARY The average graduate starting salary in the finance and investment industry is £21,157.

CORPORATE CULTURE

Look at the postcodes in the contacts list. Noticed a pattern yet? While not all jobs in the sector are based in the City of London, it is that sober-suited strait-laced square mile which defines the industry's ethos. You are handling big money and that money is desperately important to your clients and customers. You, therefore, have to appear professional, probably in a nice suit with shiny shoes, clean hanky, the lot. Having said that, the rewards, especially in some sectors of the investment world, can be generous, so you can expect the pressure-cooker atmosphere to ease after-hours with a pretty boisterous social scene. The trading floors can be aggressive, macho places and there have been well-publicised legal cases where that machismo has swung over into intimidation and degradation of women, but those are isolated incidents and most people in the finance industry have been introduced to the 21st century. In terms of progression, it's relatively easy to measure your success and failure – just look at the bottom line – so if you're good enough, you should progress naturally. It's an increasingly international career, so you should be prepared to travel, you poor thing, and language skills could be an advantage.

If you want flexibility in your work, the large institutions may not be right for you, but accountancy and financial advice offer excellent opportunities for self-employment and the joys of being your own boss.

ETHICAL QUESTIONS

The world of finance, which is strictly regulated by the Financial Services Authority, is understandably concerned with the bottom line, but this doesn't have to mean profit at any cost. Financial institutions are increasingly feeling the heat of public interest in their investment policies and are becoming more likely to consider the wider ethical implications of their business. What is the firm's attitude towards ethical investment? Does it have a policy not to invest in unethical sectors such as oppressive regimes, military hardware, tobacco, oil and animal testing? It might be telling to know if the firm knows the difference between "positive screening", where investments are made in companies that meet positive criteria like good employment practices, and "negative screening" where companies involved in certain activities such as animal testing are excluded from the portfolio.

What is the attitude of the firm to the misselling of financial products like endowment mortgages or personal pensions? How do the incentive schemes open to employees function? Is the emphasis on providing the best service to the consumer or maximising profit for the company? How does the company regard long-term investments?

Government

Although politicians are the most obvious, if not particularly attractive, face of government, in reality it's an almost inconceivably large animal. If you work for central government as a civil servant, for example, you will be one of around half a million people employed either by large government departments or smaller spin-off organisations. In local government, there are some 2.5 million people employed in a vast network of local authorities, county and district councils and the capital's boroughs. Often the roles overlap: central government will set out the principles of education policy, for example, and local government will implement them.

In whatever area you aim for, government is management on a grand scale, with hefty budgets and even heftier responsibilities. Your work will impact directly on people's lives and it's not like peddling a tin of beans – people can't just switch brands that easily. So people care, and it helps if you do too. You'll also need to be a team player. No matter who you are, you are but a cog in a bigger wheel. You'll need good communication skills to explain your plans to others and good organisational skills to get those other cogs moving. Working quickly and accurately, meeting deadlines, using IT packages with calm efficiency and motivating other members of your team will all be strings to your bow.

But you can forget one thing – politics. This isn't about manifestos or policies, this is about day-to-day management and much of what you do has nothing to do with the colour of the rosettes of the party in power. Part of your work will be implementing policy and it may be, on occasion, that you disagree. Keep your opinions for the weekend: you're paid to work for your government, local or central, not to try and change it.

■ Local government

At local government level alone there are hundreds of different jobs available, divided into seven broad areas of employment: social services, property, leisure, environmental, emergency, education and corporate. The roles cover everything from administration to teaching to recycling management, but many appear elsewhere in this book – a human resources officer does much the same job for a county council as for an IT firm, for example, and local government employs IT specialists, marketeers, horticulturists etc – so what we have here is a sprinkling of jobs *peculiar* to local government. Social services is a more specialised area, so you'll find this on page 191. Most councils have the following or similar positions, although employment and council structure can vary slightly from area to area and the councils may give the jobs different names to make them sexier (the phrase "I work in local government" has yet to work as a reliable underwear loosener).

Roles

- Benefits officer

Benefits officers work for district, borough, unitary and metropolitan councils, providing information and advice to local residents on all aspects of housing and council tax benefits. You will also process claims for benefits, checking that all the information given by claimants is correct and then calculating the level of benefit to be paid.

- Environmental health officer

This is a health and safety job covering housing, food production and preparation as well as some aspects of air and water pollution. **Environmental health officers** inspect housing to ensure that places where people live are safe and hygienic, check atmospheric pollution, ensure that standards of food hygiene are met in areas where food is prepared or sold, including abattoirs and factories, and check the safety of water supplies. Noise control can also be part of the job. There may also be an educational aspect to the work, going into local schools and communities to give talks and information. These officers work for unitary, district, borough and metropolitan councils but not for county councils.

- Regeneration officer

The regeneration of communities in certain areas is a government priority and has become a major activity for local government. **Regeneration officers** help local groups start and develop regeneration projects. These may be to do with areas such as business, transport or housing. You may also give advice or help groups get funding or arrange training, and might also promote tourism in the area to benefit local businesses and communities.

- Trading standards officer

As a **trading standards officer** you ensure that legislation to protect consumers is followed by traders. The role has two aspects: investigating complaints and monitoring the quality of services and goods. The exact work varies with the location, so if you're in a rural area you might spend a lot of time on animal health, ensuring proper transport of livestock to market for example. City-based officers are likely to be concerned with street traders and the problems of counterfeit goods. Officers in ports will work with customs to check imported items. Other areas of work include checking that adverts aren't misleading, that weights are correct and that products are safe.

QUALIFICATIONS AND TRAINING Entry requirements vary quite widely between roles and between boroughs. An increasing number of people in this sector are graduates, though for some roles A-levels and GCSEs may be adequate. You can often expect structured training, whether that's day release for a BTEC in public services or continuous professional development. You may also, for example, gain professional qualifications for membership of the Institute of Chartered Secretaries and Administrators. Alternatively, many authorities take part in national graduate development schemes to recruit and train graduates, over two years, to become senior managers. For more technical roles, NVQs and modern apprenticeship schemes are available.

SALARY The average graduate starting salary for officers in local government is £19,060.

Contacts

Chartered Institute of Environmental Health
Chadwick Court
15 Hatfields
London SE1 8DJ
(t) 020 7928 6006
(↗) www.cieh.org

Convention of Scottish Local Authorities
Rosebery House
9 Haymarket Terrace
Edinburgh EH12 5XZ
(t) 0131 474 9200
(↗) www.cosla.gov.uk

The Improvement and Development Agency (IDeA)
Layden House
Turnmill Street
London EC1M 5LG
(t) 0207 296 6880
(↗) www.idea.gov.uk

Institute of Chartered Secretaries and Administrators
16 Park Crescent
London W1B 1AH
(t) 020 7580 4741
(↗) www.icsa.org.uk

Institute of Revenues, Rating and Valuation
41 Doughty Street
London WC1N 2LF
(t) 020 7831 3505
(↗) www.irrv.org.uk

Local Government Employers
Local Government House
Smith Square
London SW1P 3HZ
(t) 020 7187 7373
(↗) www.lge.gov.uk

Royal Environmental Health Institute of Scotland

3 Manor Place
Edinburgh EH3 7DH

(t) 0131 225 6999

(↗) www.rehis.org

Standards Board for England

Fourth Floor
Griffin House
40 Lever Street
Manchester M1 1BB

(t) 0161 817 5300

(↗) www.standardsboard.co.uk

Trading Standards Institute

1 Sylvan Court
Sylvan Way
Southfields Business Park
Basildon SS15 6TH

(t) 0870 872 9000

(↗) www.tsi.org.uk

Online reading

SocietyGuardian society.guardian.co.uk

Local Government Association www.lganet.gov.uk

■ Central government/Civil service

Central government is also made up of hundred of jobs covering administration to policy work. There are 173 departments, and the civil service is one of the UK's biggest employers, having around half a million people on its books. With such a huge number of employees it's no wonder the civil service runs extensive graduate recruitment schemes.

Civil service departments work with the government to formulate policies, then civil service agencies deliver them. Civil servants work at every level, from advising on pensions to investigating fraud and formulating the policy that drives nursery education, so the jobs tend to be diverse. Each department runs its own recruitment, but there are also specialist departments – the government economic service, the government legal service, government social research, the government statistical service and the government operational research service – which recruit graduates with particular skills. In addition to that is the fast-track graduate scheme which has a number of options.

Scotland and Wales have slightly different forms of government but the recruitment processes and the types of jobs available are similar. The

National Assembly for Wales was established in 1998, providing a democratically elected and accountable body responsible for most important public services and with the power to make subordinate legislation to meet Welsh circumstances. It has two areas: the Welsh assembly government, concerned with economic development, health, education, social services, local government, agriculture, housing, transport, the environment and European affairs, and the Wales Office, which represents the UK government in Wales and Wales within the UK government. This includes steering legislation for Wales through the UK parliament and securing the Welsh budget. The Wales Office deals with a wide range of domestic issues, such as health, local government, social services, agriculture, environment, industry and transport.

Similarly, Scotland has the Scottish parliament and the Scottish executive. The executive operates in a similar way to the UK government with certain legislative and policy-making responsibilities. It is responsible for issues including health, education and training, local government, social work and housing, economic development and transport, law and home affairs, the environment, agriculture, fisheries and forestry, sport and the arts. The executive is answerable to the parliament and relations between the Scottish parliament and Scottish executive and the UK government are maintained by the Scotland Office.

As with local government, there are many, many jobs within governmental organisations that aren't peculiar to them – IT, human resources and so on – which means the government is just another potential employer to add to your list. The jobs listed below are those unique to government.

Roles

- Civil service administrator

Civil service administration jobs vary a lot depending on which of the many departments you're attached to. However, wherever you are, your role is likely to include formulating and implementing policy and researching, analysing and summarising economic or political information, policy and procedure. If this sounds dry it's because it's a bit of a generalisation; whatever you do is likely to be related to your skill (and possibly interests) and there's the added thrill of being proactive and actually influencing government policy.

- Civil service fast stream

The civil service supports the government by helping them develop and deliver policies, and administer public services. The fast stream is the accelerated training and development programme aimed at preparing you to reach a senior civil service level. There are five types of entry making up the general fast stream: central departments (covering all the major departments except the diplomatic service); science and engineering; the diplomatic service; the Department for International Development technical development option; and clerkships in parliament. There are also fast stream schemes for statisticians, economists, technology and business, the GCHQ and the SIS. Fast streamers start off with a series of postings, each of which last 12-18 months, and are given real responsibility from the start. They may be seconded to other government departments, business or industry, or to work abroad, and can expect to be appointed to a senior manager position within four to five years. Existing civil servants can apply to join the fast stream but will usually need two years' experience.

■ GCHQ management

This is a fast stream trainee appointment (distinct, however, from the civil service fast stream programme) which lasts three to five years and is aimed at getting you to **GCHQ management** level, where you'd be leading intelligence teams, developing policies and managing resources. The work is varied as there are different departments within GCHQ, but might involve research into new intelligence sources, briefing the director and liaising between departments. You'll generally start off learning what signals intelligence is all about as most, but not all, GCHQ management trainees start off in intelligence production. This is an intelligence analyst position, so you'd be responsible for providing information on "targets", which could be drug-smuggling, weapons proliferation, or a traditional political or military target.

■ Diplomatic service

The **diplomatic service** has a range of functions centred on promoting and protecting British interests abroad and advising and supporting government ministers in formulating foreign policy. Although you can be posted in embassies or missions abroad, there are also positions in the UK, through the Foreign and Commonwealth Office (FCO). You would normally spend two or three years working for the FCO before being sent abroad. When you start you'll typically deal with either a specific country or geographical area, or a specific multilateral issue at the FCO in London. This will involve being in touch with high commissions and embassies in your assigned countries, filtering information to interested parties and coordinating visits by ministers and VIPs. In an overseas posting (typically three or four years) you might be involved in high-level international negotiations, organising ministerial or trade visits, or gathering information on political, commercial or economic affairs.

QUALIFICATIONS AND TRAINING You will generally need at least a 2:2 degree, usually in any subject, though a particular role might be more attainable with a relevant degree and fast-track appointments might come easier with a 2:1 or better. If you want to nab a place on the European fast stream you will need an A-level in a European language. Progression from then on can be predictable and sometimes seems set in stone, but, as everywhere, if you have the talent and application, you will move ahead. Check out the details on the fast-track schemes for entry levels and the commitment they make to your progression.

SALARY The average graduate starting salary in the civil service is £17,712.

Contacts

The first port of call should be the Civil Service website

⊘ www.civil-service.gov.uk.

Websites for individual departments can be found via the jobs portal at Recruitment Gateway

⊘ www.careers.civil-service.gov.uk

Civil Service Fast Stream
Application Helpdesk
Pilgrims Well
427 London Road
Camberley
Surrey GU15 3HZ

ⓣ 01276 400333

⊘ www.faststream.gov.uk

Committee on Standards in Public Life
The Secretary
35 Great Smith Street
London SW1P 3BQ

ⓣ 020 7276 2595

⊘ www.public-standards.gov.uk

Foreign and Commonwealth Office
Recruitment Section
Human Resources Directorate
Room 2/89
Foreign and Commonwealth Office
Old Admiralty Building
Whitehall
London SW1A 2AH

⊘ www.fco.gov.uk

GCHQ
The Recruitment Office
Room A2c
GCHQ
Hubble Road
Cheltenham
Glos GL51 0EX

ⓣ 01242 709095

⊘ www.gchq.gov.uk

National Assembly for Wales
Cardiff Bay
Cardiff CF99 1NA
(t) 0845 010 5500
(↗) www.wales.gov.uk

Secret Intelligence Service
PO Box 1300
London SE1 1BD
(↗) www.sis.gov.uk

Scottish Parliament
Edinburgh EH99 1SP
(t) 0131 348 5000
(↗) www.scottish.parliament.uk

Online reading
Guardian Unlimited Politics politics.guardian.co.uk
Public Magazine www.guardian.co.uk/public
Public Finance magazine www.publicfinance.co.uk

CORPORATE CULTURE

For an employer of this size, it's impossible to generalise. All you can say is…
it varies. The civil service and the major government departments tend to
take themselves very seriously and are extremely committed; they work long
hours, but with perhaps less of the boozy self-rewarding of parts of the private sector. On the other hand, we've all had experience of both central and
local government officers who couldn't give a monkey's.

But for the vast majority it is a sober world, made so by its very importance.

The civil service champions work–life balance practices, enabling workers
to job-share, have career breaks and even just do term-time working. There
is a job-share database and the government is actively looking at how to
ensure that those who take career breaks or make work–life choices don't end
up with a slower career progression. Enlightened stuff.

ETHICAL QUESTIONS

Arguably one of the sectors where you can make the most difference to
people's lives through your work, but there are some considerations. Exactly
which department do you want to work for, the Ministry of Defence or the
Environment Agency? The local council's waste collection authority or its
road maintenance department?

What is the department's attitude towards and record with whistleblowers? Is there a commitment to transparency in the decision-making
process, and clear accountability for the results of the decisions made? Are
you prepared to enact the policies of the current government or council if

they go against your principles? How are individuals' conflicts of interest disclosed and resolved?

If it's your intention to enter politics, you will already have given careful consideration to your personal stance on a wide range of moral and ethical questions in relation to political parties and movements, and you have probably considered how the system in which politicians operate can be improved. At a party level, is policy formulated democratically? Are appointments transparent and fair? How does the party decide on its choice of candidate for an office? Is lobby culture something which should be encouraged, or does it just mean greater political influence for large, powerful organisations?

Healthcare

Healthcare is a profession where you will be open to higher than average risks of suicide, drug addiction and alcoholism, and it may be 20 years before you start to earn well, if at all. It's stressful, the hours are often long and arduous and the conditions can be less than perfect. Yet healthcare can be a uniquely rewarding profession, offering the opportunity to be resourceful and imaginative, and to have a practical and emotional impact on people's lives in a way that only doctors, nurses and other medical practitioners can.

There are huge numbers of people employed in the healthcare sector, and the range of jobs is considerable, so this section can only give a sample of the careers out there. Many entrants into this sector have been planning their career since an early age. However, there are increasing opportunities for career changers and mature applicants; there are conversion courses that will lead to a medical degree no matter what your degree background, and nursing diplomas and alternative medicine can be studied even if you don't have three science A-levels.

Common to all the medical careers is a need for dedication, both during training and working. Many health careers can make extraordinary demands in terms of hours and commitment. You will need to be patient with others (both colleagues and patients), tolerant of the fact you are seeing people at their most vulnerable and perhaps irrational, and yet you must be sufficiently mentally resilient to make logical decisions in stressful situations. You'll need to retain enormous amounts of technical knowledge, be dextrous and have good communication skills – the ability to listen as well as talk. And you need to inspire trust in those around you.

■ Alternative and complementary medicine

Alternative and complementary medicine isn't necessarily about aligning your chakras or eating bark during certain phases of the moon in a room full of scented candles. Complementary therapies are increasingly popular and are now often used alongside western medicine, sometimes provided by the NHS – there are five NHS-allied homeopathic hospitals in Britain.

The likelihood though is that you would be self-employed so along with your technical and personal skills you will also need to have good business, organisational and self-motivation skills to make sure your business keeps afloat.

Roles

- Acupuncturist

Acupuncture is an ancient form of Chinese medicine which uses needles to stimulate points in the body. These points are believed to lie along interconnected energy channels (meridians) which link all the internal organs and body systems together in an organic whole. Stimulating these points in particular ways can apparently control and regulate the entire body. Acupuncturists make thorough examinations of patients, which includes checking the pulses in the wrists and tongue, and find out about their medical history and that of their close family, their diet, digestive system, sleeping patterns and emotional state. Members of the British Acupuncture Council have completed a thorough training of at least three years in traditional acupuncture and biomedical sciences appropriate to the practice of acupuncture.

- Chiropractor

A **chiropractor** treats problems with joints, bones and muscles, and through this the effects they have on the nervous system. This doesn't involve drugs or surgery: chiropractors use their hands on the joints of the body, concentrating particularly on the spine, and make gentle, specific adjustments to improve the efficiency of the nervous system and release the body's natural healing ability. Like acupuncturists, chiropractors often take a holistic approach to treatment. There are two main systems of chiropractic – McTimoney, and the British Chiropractic Association – which have distinct philosophies and different methods.

- Homeopath

This is another holistic discipline, taking into account physical, emotional and mental symptoms. **Homeopathic medicine** uses minute doses of natural substances and works on the principle that like treats like, so an illness is treated with a medicine which could produce similar symptoms in a healthy person. Many homeopaths are trained in "traditional" medicine and have an additional homeopathic qualification.

■ Naturopath

A **naturopath** uses natural methods to allow the body to cleanse and heal itself. In the belief that the human body is essentially self-regulatory, naturopaths avoid drugs and use diet, hydrotherapy and psychology to rebalance the body's chemistry and general wellbeing.

■ Osteopath

The **osteopathic** approach is not dissimilar to chiropractic medicine, but has a broader approach: it's a system of manipulation, using the hands to correct joint and tissue abnormalities. By restoring physical and mental wellbeing, osteopathy makes it easier for a patient's body to function normally and use its own recuperative powers more effectively. While chiropractors tend to focus on balancing the backbone by manipulation and massage in particular, osteopaths take a holistic view of the whole body.

QUALIFICATIONS AND TRAINING For an **acupuncturist**, training (a three-year full-time course, with part-time options available) is monitored by the British Acupuncture Accreditation Board, which is allied to the British Acupuncture Council.

Those wanting to be **chiropractors** must be registered with the General Chiropractic Council, who keep an up-to-date list of approved courses (course lengths vary). Qualified doctors can study for a **homeopathy** postgraduate qualification at a learning centre accredited by the Faculty of Homeopathy; those starting from scratch can get a list of approved courses (of varying lengths) from the Society of Homeopaths.

The General Council and Register of **Naturopaths** recommends two undergraduate courses for naturopaths: one is run by the British College of Osteopathic Medicine, the other by the University of Westminster. **Osteopaths** take a four- or five-year course, combining much of the training a doctor would get with lots of clinic time with real patients; a degree at the British School of Osteopathy, which is aligned with the University of Luton, leads to a bachelor's degree (BOst).

SALARY The average graduate starting salary for therapists is £19,322.

Contacts

British Acupuncture Council
63 Jeddo Road
London W12 9HQ

(t) 020 8735 0400

(↗) www.acupuncture.org.uk

British Chiropractic Association
59 Castle Street
Reading
Berks RG1 7SN

(t) 0118 950 5950

(↗) www.chiropractic-uk.co.uk

British College of Osteopathic Medicine
Lief House
120–122 Finchley Road
London NW3 5HR

(t) 020 7435 6464

(↗) www.bcno.ac.uk

British School of Osteopathy
275 Borough High Street
London SE1 1JE

(t) 020 7407 0222

(↗) www.bso.ac.uk

Faculty of Homeopathy
Hahnemann House
29 Park Street West
Luton LU1 3BE

(t) 0870 444 3950

(↗) www.trusthomeopathy.org

General Chiropractic Council
44 Wicklow Street
London WC1X 9HL

(t) 020 7713 5155

(↗) www.gcc-uk.org

General Council and Register of Naturopaths
Goswell House
2 Goswell Road
Street
Somerset BA16 0JG

(t) 08707 456984

(↗) www.naturopathy.org.uk

General Osteopathic Council
176 Tower Bridge Road
London SE1 3LU

(t) 020 7357 6655

(↗) www.osteopathy.org.uk

Society of Homeopaths
11 Brookfield
Duncan Close
Moulton Park
Northampton NN3 6WL

(t) 0845 450 6611

(↗) www.homeopathy-soh.org

Online reading
New Health magazine www.new-health.biz
What Medicine? www.whatmedicine.co.uk
Surgery Door www.surgerydoor.co.uk

■ Allied health professions

These are roles that exist alongside the core healthcare jobs and are prescribed by doctors and surgeons. They might focus on correcting a problem, rehabilitation after surgery or an accident, or managing a long-term problem or condition. There are many different specialties: the following have been chosen to reflect the range, and might also include practitioners from the above list.

Roles

■ Health visitor
A **health visitor** is a registered nurse who specialises in assessing and dealing with community healthcare and promoting health in their practice area. The role can vary widely – you might be counselling the bereaved, supporting people who are trying to stop smoking or helping a patient come to terms with their illness. You'll need management skills on top of nursing expertise.

■ Hospital pharmacist
As a **pharmacist inside the NHS** you dispense medication to patients, advise medical and nursing staff on the safe and appropriate dosage and administration of drugs, and manage the hospital's pharmacy services. You also prepare certain formulations, keep stock replenished and securely stored, keep records and stay up to date with the latest research and developments. You might also undertake your own research. Pharmacists on the high street are essentially highly qualified retailers and their role is discussed in the retail section, but the training is much the same.

■ Occupational therapist
Occupational therapists work with people who have mental or physical disabilities, using different forms and levels of activity to restore, develop or maintain skills. Your aim is to enable people to live as independently as possible. This can be done in a variety of settings ranging from a person's own home or disabled living centres through to housing departments and hospitals.

■ Physiotherapist
Physiotherapy deals with human function and movement and maximising potential. It works to combat a broad range of physical problems, in particular those associated with neuromuscular, musculoskeletal, cardiovascular and respiratory systems. You might work alone or, increasingly, with other healthcare professionals in multi-professional teams.

- Podiatrist

Podiatrists used to be known as chiropodists, and deal with the diagnosis and treatment of problems and diseases of the feet and lower leg, as well as advising patients on how to avoid problems. These problems can range from warts and corns to fitting orthotics.

- Radiographer

There are two types of radiographer: therapeutic and diagnostic. **Therapeutic radiographers** work as part of a team using radiation to treat diseased tissue or tumours. Your work would involve planning appropriate treatment with oncologists and other specialists, then delivering it. **Diagnostic radiographers** use technologies such as x-rays, computed tomography (CT) scanning, magnetic resonance imaging (MRI) and ultrasound to produce images of organs and limbs etc. You then interpret these pictures in order to allow doctors to diagnose and treat diseases and injuries.

QUALIFICATIONS AND TRAINING A degree course in **occupational therapy** with a high practical element can be completed on a full (three-year) or part-time basis. A degree course in **physiotherapy** entitles degree holders to membership of the Chartered Society of Physiotherapy, which in turn allows you to practise in the NHS. **Podiatrists** must complete a degree course in podiatry or podiatric medicine and to practice you must belong to a reputable professional association. The role of **health visitor** is open to experienced nurses or midwives; approved one-year health-visitor courses give you the status of specialist practitioner. **Radiographers** must complete a degree in the subject and register with the Radiographers Board of the Health Professions Council before being allowed to work for the NHS. **Pharmacists** must complete a four-year Master of Pharmacy degree followed by a year's on-the-job training which ends up with another exam. They must also become a registered member of the Royal Pharmaceutical Society of Great Britain or the Pharmaceutical Society of Northern Ireland.

SALARY The average graduate starting salary for allied health professionals is £20,428.

Online reading

Intute Health and Life Sciences: Nursing, Midwifery and Allied Health www.intute.ac.uk/healthandlifesciences/nursing/

Allied Health Professionals Bulletin www.dh.gov.uk/en/Publication sandstatistics/Bulletins/Alliedhealthprofessionalsbulletin/index.htm

SocietyGuardian www.SocietyGuardian.co.uk

Contacts

British Association/College of Occupational Therapists

106–114 Borough High Street
London SE1 1LB

(t) 020 7357 6480

(↗) www.cot.co.uk

Chartered Society of Physiotherapy

14 Bedford Row
London WC1R 4ED

(t) 020 7306 6666

(↗) www.csp.org.uk

Guild of Healthcare Pharmacists

Amicus Centre
33-37 Moreland Street
London EC1V 8HA

(t) 020 7780 4077

(↗) www.ghp.org.uk

Health Professions Council

Park House
184 Kennington Park Road
London SE11 4BU

(t) 020 7582 0866

(↗) www.hpc-uk.org

Society of Chiropodists and Podiatrists

1 Fellmonger's Path
Tower Bridge Road
London SE1 3LY

(t) 020 7234 8620

(↗) www.feetforlife.org

Society of Radiographers

207 Providence Square
Mill Street
London SE1 2EW

(t) 020 7740 7200

(↗) www.sor.org

Unite/CPHVA

33-37 Moreland Street
London EC1V 8HA

(t) 0207 505 3000

(↗) www.amicus-cphva.org

■ Core healthcare

The following jobs are probably those that spring to mind when you think of healthcare but there are plenty more, taking in a full range of specialisms in surgery as well as branches such as oncology, radiology, gynaecology... the list goes on.

Roles

■ Dentist

Dentists specialise in diagnosing and treating diseases and problems of the mouth and teeth. This can be done in a range of settings, whether it's a family practice, hospital dentistry, community dentistry, armed forces dentistry or in industry; there are also teaching and research jobs.

■ Doctor

Once you've qualified as a doctor, you can choose to be either a GP (general practitioner) or a hospital doctor. The roles are different even though you're essentially dealing with the same work. A **GP** provides patients with primary and continuing care, diagnosing, treating and referring them to hospitals or specialist care when necessary. If you're a partner in a practice you'll also have a managerial role, being responsible for things like hiring other staff, paperwork and working with the practice budget. **Hospital doctors** also diagnose and treat but go on to specialise in a particular area such as paediatrics or oncology. They can also progress to the more senior position of consultant.

■ Nurse

There are different branches of nursing – dealing with adults, children, mental health and learning disabilities – and you need to choose which one to specialise in during your training. **Nurses** work in hospitals, in GPs' surgeries, in residential homes or with community healthcare teams. You will be dealing with a range of healthcare issues, from advising on contraception to managing chronic conditions such as arthritis or diabetes, planning and delivering care with other specialists. Building relationships with patients can be an important part of the job, particularly in children's nursing. It can be a very pressurised role, although this will depend on your exact responsibilities.

■ Midwife

Midwives give support, care and advice for women and their partners from early pregnancy until the baby is 28 days old. Midwives are independent practitioners and do not need to call on doctors unless there's a medical problem, but you may work with other healthcare professionals such as GPs, health visitors and social workers to provide a range of care. You can work in a variety of settings, in hospitals, clinics or homes.

QUALIFICATIONS AND TRAINING There are 13 **dentistry** schools and departments in the country, with around 400 places available annually, and the competition is hot. You'll be expected to have excellent A-levels: chemistry is a requirement, and biology is usually preferred as the second science A-level. A dentistry course usually involves five years of academic work – two years of pre-clinical study, often taken with other medical students, and three years of clinical work. There may also be the option of an intercalated year, in which you will be encouraged to take a science-related course before returning to dentistry. You should emerge with a thorough scientific knowledge and the necessary clinical and practical skills to care for and treat your patients and run a practice. For this you'll need skills in communication, management, teamwork, manual dexterity and information handling. Once qualified you must be on the Dentists' Register, which is run by the General Dental Council.

Typically, courses leading to the status of **doctor** involve five years of academic work, with an optional intercalated year (studying a science course for 12 months before returning to medicine). Following criticisms from the General Medical Council in the 1990s, courses now include a greater emphasis on communication skills, understanding cultural issues and patient interaction, as well as on picking up specific skills in the relevant environment. Once you graduate, you must apply to the General Medical Council for registration, to allow you to practise. After graduation, doctors enter a two-year foundation programme, designed to provide the generic core skills needed as a doctor. After the first year, you're fully registered with the GMC. Following the foundation programme doctors compete for a place on a specialist training post in either general practice, or one of the hospital specialties. Competition for these places has become intense in recent years.

There are four different **nursing** degree programmes to choose from. They all share a common first year and then you follow your chosen branch of nursing: adult (including midwifery), child health, learning disability or mental health. In England, most student nurses take a three-year diploma course, requiring GCSE or equivalent qualifications, but nursing students with A-levels or equivalent qualifications can take a degree course, also lasting three years. All these courses are run by universities, in partnership with local hospitals. Once qualified you can train in a number of specialised areas and, in many ways, training never stops as you keep abreast of new care procedures and pursue your own ambitions in the profession.

Three-year degree or diploma courses in **midwifery** lead to qualification as a registered midwife, or, for qualified nurses, there are shorter, though still usually full-time, courses available. Either way, the programme is a mixture of academic theory and practice, with plenty of time on placements. Once working, there is a strong emphasis on continuous professional development to keep up with changes in birthing practice.

SALARY The average graduate starting salary for health professionals £25,355.

Contacts

British Dental Association
64 Wimpole Street
London W1G 8YS
(t) 020 7563 4568
(↗) www.bda.org

British Medical Association
BMA House
Tavistock Square
London WC1H 9JP
(t) 020 7387 4499
(↗) www.bma.org.uk

General Dental Council
37 Wimpole Street
London W1G 8DQ
(t) 020 7887 3800
(↗) www.gdc-uk.org

General Medical Council
Regent's Place
350 Euston Road
London NW1 3JN
(t) 0845 357 8001
(↗) www.gmc-uk.org

Nursing and Midwifery Council
23 Portland Place
London W1B 1PZ
(t) 020 7637 7181
(↗) www.nmc-uk.org

Nursing and Midwifery Admissions Service
Rosehill
New Barn Lane
Cheltenham GL52 3LZ
(t) 0870 1122206
(↗) www.nmas.ac.uk

Royal College of General Practitioners
14 Princes Gate
London SW7 1PU
(t) 0845 456 4041
(↗) www.rcgp.org.uk

Royal College of Midwives
15 Mansfield Street
London W1G 9NH
(t) 020 7312 3535
(↗) www.rcm.org.uk

Royal College of Nursing
20 Cavendish Square
London W1G 0RN
(t) 020 7409 3333
(↗) www.rcn.org.uk

Online reading

Health Service Journal www.hsj.co.uk
NHS Magazine www.nhsdirect.nhs.uk/magazine
Nursing Standard www.nursing-standard.co.uk

CORPORATE CULTURE

If you work in the NHS then, like the civil service, you can benefit from the government's encouragement of work–life balance initiatives, which means that every NHS Trust must demonstrate its willingness to allow part-time or term-time working, job-sharing and career breaks. As we've said elsewhere, this is pleasantly enlightened. But some parts of the NHS do need that sort of light shining on them. There are problems of under-funding in certain areas, of overwork and stress, and you can be making life or death decisions with little supervision. There's also a higher than average risk of suicide, drink or drugs problems and depression within this sector. Public healthcare is a rewarding, increasingly well paid and deeply important profession, respected by the rest of the community, but it is also, undoubtedly, a double-edge sword and you'll think differently about it almost every day.

Working in private health may mean higher earnings and perhaps the joys of self-employment, but it lacks the backs-to-the-wall camaraderie of the hospital's accident and emergency departments.

ETHICAL QUESTIONS

Whilst there is a wealth of professional ethical guidance relating to the various caring professions, animal testing, bioethics and the ethical practices of the giant pharmaceutical firms are also key considerations in this sector. Although the end goal is good (making someone better) healthcare is arguably the sector in which ethical dilemmas are most likely to crop up nearly every day in some form or another.

Are you working for the NHS or a private medical firm? What are your attitudes towards private healthcare and private companies which function almost as part of the NHS? How are decisions made regarding which patients are given which treatment: purely on the basis of what is best for the patient, or are there other considerations such as the cost of treatment?

Is the organisation you would work for responsibly promoting medicines and drugs? If it's a distributor of pharmaceuticals or medical supplies, what is its attitude to provision in developing countries? Does it use just a few suppliers? Does it have a policy of fair trade with its suppliers? If it promotes complementary medicines does it do so responsibly, or is it a victim of fashion-based cures that are not backed up by peer-reviewed clinical trials? What is the attitude of the organisation to holistic healthcare? Is it the patient who is treated or just the disease?

Hospitality

There are a number of misconceptions about the hospitality sector. Those whose only connection with it is as customers often imagine it to be a clubbable sort of career where days are filled with conviviality and bonhomie, fuelled by alcohol and fine food. And those who have worked as waiters and waitresses during their student days see it as a sector filled with McJobs – spotty youths working long hours for shoddy pay.

Although you can find such examples at either end, the sector is huge and its managers are responsible for budgets of millions and vast numbers of staff, including real craftspeople working in the kitchen or behind the bar. The hospitality trade encompasses four main areas of employment: hotels, restaurants, pubs/bars/clubs and contract catering or food services, and accounts for 1.8 million jobs in Britain. For the committed soul it can be a path to both considerable financial rewards and a good deal of power and responsibility, or simply a way of becoming your own boss at the head of a thriving business.

Whatever role you take on, you'll need to be good with members of the public, with a fair notion of what makes them happy. You'll need organisational flair, the ability to work while everyone else is having fun without resorting to a hangdog look of resigned martyrdom, and you'll need the technical skills of your own particular trade. You have to work well under pressure, extreme pressure at times, and be good at melding the practical with the creative. As you move up the ladder, the food chain if you will, you need to be able to take on responsibility and learn the art of delegation.

■ Hotels and restaurants

The organisational structure of a restaurant, either in or outside a hotel, is as regimented and stratified as the army with strict demarcation between jobs, levels of command and functions within the kitchen. As in the army it is expected that you will enter at the bottom and work your way up through the ranks having learnt about the workings of the kitchen from first-hand experience. It is no coincidence that kitchen staff are sometimes referred to as a "brigade". But whether you're flinging food around in skillets or cleaning them, this remains a high-pressure world where hours are long and where there's a competitive scramble to get to the top roles.

Roles

- Accommodation manager

An **accommodation manager** is responsible for the cleanliness and maintenance of bedrooms and bathrooms within the hotel and works as a member of the management team on administration, budget control and staff supervision. In some hotels, the accommodation manager is known as the housekeeper, and these two roles (see below) can sometimes overlap.

- Banqueting manager

The **banqueting manager** has roles from the start to the finish of the business conference or banqueting process, from marketing and selling the facility at first through to ensuring the bills are paid at the end. In between these points there is coordinating the various departments to be ready for the conference in terms of rooms and catering, booking entertainment and possibly marquees. There is also a fair amount of front-of-house work involved.

- Chefs

A **commis chef** is the entry-level position, for which job titles and responsibilities vary with the organisation, but the role essentially involves basic cooking and preparation under the supervision of the higher-ranking chefs. At this level it is advisable to try the various areas of the kitchen before deciding on a direction for more specialised promotion to breakfast chef, which involves an early start at the hotel and means that you are effectively in charge of the guest's first meal of the day. As a breakfast chef you may be stationed outside the kitchen at a buffet, ready to cook meals to order, since hot breakfasts do not tend to keep well. This can be a highly pressurised environment at peak times of the morning.

The **chef de partie** is a more senior position. The term has been imported from the organisational structure of the French kitchen, where the chef de partie is responsible for the running of a particular section of the kitchen such as pastries, sauces, grill, vegetables or the larder. Sometimes the chef de partie will have a job title, such as pastry chef, which reflects this specialism. Traditionally the role would include responsibility for two or more commis chefs, although in the modern hotel kitchen the staff operate more on a team basis with the chef de partie taking a more hands-on role in addition to their training and supervision responsibilities.

The sous chef/senior chef de partie is the kitchen's second-in-command, the person who will take control in the absence of the head chef. This role involves monitoring the standard of the food being served and minimising wastage through attempting to forecast popular dishes and skilled menu planning.

Finally, the head chef is in ultimate command of the kitchen: developing new dishes, planning menus and having final responsibility for staff recruitment and retention. The successful head chef must combine culinary flair with a good head for business.

■ Food and beverage manager

As the title rather suggests, being a food and beverage manager means being responsible for the stocking and sale of food, drink and sundries for the kitchens and bars within the hotel, which are a major source of revenue for the establishment. You place orders for these with suppliers and make sure the right items have been delivered. At any given point, you'll be expected to know how much of a specific product the hotel has, although this is now aided by computerised systems.

■ Hotel manager/Operations manager

The main work of the hotel or operations manager is the monitoring of staff, coordinating those within the different areas of the hotel. In order for a hotel to function well the staff must be working as an effective team. As well as this you are responsible for preparing budgets and setting targets and sometimes for deciding marketing strategies for the business.

■ Housekeeper

A head housekeeper is in charge of the hotel's team of floor housekeepers and ensures that their efforts are coordinated. You would also be responsible for liaising with other departments in the hotel to ensure the smooth running of the place at the sharp end. The job of the floor housekeeper is primarily one of supervision and administration as you are in charge of a team of room attendants and must brief and check their work. This role is central to the smooth day-to-day running of the hotel, covering essential minutiae such as informing reception when rooms are ready to be re-let and if guests are late departing, through to the provision of clean towels and little shampoo sachets in every bathroom.

■ Restaurant manager

A restaurant manager takes reservations and greets guests as they arrive, and sometimes take diners' orders and advises on the dishes. Behind the scenes, the manager is also responsible for the recruitment and training of staff, briefing staff on the day's menus and planning staff rotas, as well as making sure that the restaurant's health and safety legal requirements are being met.

■ Industrial catering

Industrial catering is not dissimilar to the hotel and restaurant trade and many of the jobs are common to both, but it's done on a different scale. It can be for the works canteen or it can be for corporate events or particular venues. The difference comes with the attitude to the catering – working to provide cheap, nutritious meals for a company's employees is very different from trying to create a sense of occasion for a big company's launch bash. They have different sorts of stresses, different relations with hungry and thirsty customers and different time pressures. They also have different hours – and you may prefer working from 7am–3pm, providing breakfast and lunch, to working a split restaurant shift of 11am–3pm and 8pm–midnight.

Outside-event catering is undergoing a boom now that the licensing of such events has been reformed. This means that outwardly unlikely venues such as the Natural History Museum or Warwick Castle are now expert providers of excellent cuisine for corporate and private bashes.

Roles

■ Catering manager

The **catering manager** title covers a huge range of jobs, including managing the food and drink provision at resorts or on liners, running catering operations at hospitals, schools, colleges and companies, and operating the catering services at weddings or conferences. In common with many other managers within the sector you will be responsible for maintaining statistical and financial records, recruiting, training and supervising staff, managing budgets, planning menus and ensuring compliance with health and safety legislation.

QUALIFICATIONS AND TRAINING Increasingly, management roles are going to graduates, especially those with relevant degrees. Twenty years ago the idea of studying catering and hotel management at a British university was almost unheard of but the growing professionalism within today's industry has prompted a demand for better vocational education and there are now over 50 higher education institutions offering courses under the broad heading of catering and institutional management. These can cover anything from hotel and catering administration to restaurant operation and baking technology. Such courses are more likely to be found in former polytechnics and further education colleges than in the more traditional universities (there is a snobbery factor), despite the fact that the food industry is the fastest growing in the UK and is crying out for graduates to underpin demands for better standards.

A degree in **hospitality management** is, as you'd expect, highly vocational, and active work experience is an important part of most courses. Managing an organisation, understanding the industry and getting to grips with staff and resources are all core areas that are covered, while many courses offer add-on modules in areas such as IT, law, accounting, gastronomy and tourism. Most degrees offered are three years, though there are some four-year courses which offer an additional year's work placement. For **non-management roles**, NVQs or HNDs are useful keys to the door, but working your way up from the shopfloor is also a much-travelled route. In all cases, training is most likely to be on the job, but some larger companies do have formal training schemes, which can be in-house courses, day release training or modern apprenticeships.

The entry point for **restaurant management** roles is much the same as for hotels, although you may want to check exactly what each course entails. For kitchen roles, NVQs, HNDs and HNCs in professional cookery are helpful, but the chances are that you'll enter at the bottom of the pile and work your way up with on-the-job training and plenty of blood, sweat and tears.

SALARY The average graduate starting salary in the hospitality industry is £16,101.

Contacts

Confederation of Tourism, Hotel and Catering Management
118–120 Great Titchfield Street
London W1W 6SS

(t) 020 7612 0170

(⌗) www.cthcm.com

Institute of Hospitality
Trinity Court
34 West Street
Sutton
Surrey SM1 1SH

(t) 020 8661 4900

(⌗) www.hcima.org.uk

People 1st
2nd Floor
Armstrong House
38 Market Square
Uxbridge
Middlesex UB8 1LH

(t) 0870 060 2550

(⌗) www.people 1st.co.uk

CORPORATE CULTURE

For many people, by far the biggest problem in the hospitality industry is the hours. While others are enjoying themselves, you are grafting and some people can find that difficult. You have to like people and not begrudge them their fun. Perversely, the better you are at this and the higher you move up in an organisation, the less likely you are to be front of house and dealing with those people.

The key to this culture is motivation. Good managers and good head chefs are able to inspire their staff to take pride in what they do and that means creating a sense of occasion no matter what that occasion is – whether it's breakfast or a spectacular wedding, it's very important to the customer. Good managers therefore imbue a team spirit into their staff which transcends the strange hours and reminds them of the love of people and food which led them there in the first place.

Reputations in this trade are slowly made and quickly lost so a sense of involvement is vital to the success of both a business and an individual, and it's that sense of pride that feeds the profession.

ETHICAL QUESTIONS

The hospitality industry is notorious for unsociable hours and low pay, and the high level of staff turnover reflects this. Does the organisation have stated employment policies and pay a fair wage to its staff? Does it use agencies to find staff, and if so how does it vet how they are paid? If it uses predominantly migrant workers, who often come to the UK to improve their English, you might want to question what its attitude is to living wages. What is its attitude to adequate work breaks, passive smoking and taxis home for staff working late shifts? All are important quality-of-life considerations in a sector that can place workers in smoky environments and requires unsociable working hours.

Apply some thinking to the production of food (see the section on food production on page 79). Hotels, restaurants and pubs are in an ideal position to use local produce and let customers know where what they are eating has come from. Does the firm have a policy of using local produce?

Human resources

Let's get two things straight. One: "human resources" is just a posh word for the personnel department. Two: you don't have to be a "people person" to join an HR department. You need to be able to get on with people, but the kind of individual who says "I'm a people person" is usually a little alarming and will be no use in what is, after all, a specialised management department.

Aside from the recruitment industry, there isn't an HR sector. Like those in IT, you are likely to be producing a specialised service for people working in other industries; from the NHS to City banks, most big organisations have an HR department to deal with the hiring, firing, training, development and legal side of employing people. The efficient use of people is vital to an organisation's success and that means having the right people doing the job and giving them the right rewards, training and back-up to do their work happily and efficiently.

You will need to be genuinely interested in people and what makes them behave as they do, yet you'll also need the detachment to deal with situations in a fair and even-handed way, particularly in stressful disciplinary cases. You'll need excellent communication skills and be good as part of a broader team, both in terms of your department and in terms of the company as a whole. And you must, must, must resist the temptation to gossip. You'll know more about the other people in the company than anyone else, but it's not information to let loose after a couple of drinks of a Friday night.

Roles

There are a number of different aspects to HR which, even in some of the biggest companies, tend not to be allocated to one individual. You may be responsible for all aspects of the personnel issues for a single department or you may cover a single aspect of the work below for the whole company.

■ Employee relations and managing change
It's your job to maintain good relations between management and the "workers" – an essential part of a company's success. This entails not only keeping in with the unions, but also managing flexible working, dealing with share option schemes, involving employees in decision-making and

managing change. There's many who don't like change and when companies develop new strategies, create new ways of working and build new structures it can be unsettling for those at the coalface. Consulting on and setting up new working arrangements, making people aware of their new role and its requirements, establishing new reporting structures and, sometimes, managing redundancies are all part of this rather delicate area.

■ Operational research

Operational research has its origins in the statistical, mathematical and scientific techniques used during the second world war to solve practical problems – and now these techniques are used to improve managerial decision-making. The role of the **operational researcher** is to work out what an organisation's strategic and operational problems are, and then to implement solutions. This is achieved by using mathematical and computer models as well as other analytical methods, and by undertaking extensive research, interpreting data and consulting with employees. Operational researchers are employed in consultancies and the civil service and by financial, commercial and industrial organisations. It's a highly competitive field. You will need the ability to understand an argument from both sides, even if you'll often try to solve it from a managerial point of view. You'll be good with people but able to maintain a certain detachment, and you'll have tact, self-confidence and a complete lack of prejudice.

■ Recruitment

You will need to think up **recruitment** strategies for your institution as well as monitor their success and modify them accordingly. You will be responsible for finding people to fill the jobs, through advertising or other means, as well as deciding on the hoops you make them go through before allowing them to join – interviews, tests, psychometrics, and so on. It's such a specialised role that some companies use recruitment consultants instead. Of course, that's an option for you – it's a highly pressurised role that revolves around assisting clients to select and recruit appropriate staff to fill any job vacancies, as well as helping individuals to find jobs. You might work for a national, regional or local recruitment agency or for a specialist agency that recruits for specific roles (like accounting or childcare for example). You'll spend a lot of time doing things like cold-calling in order to sell the agency's services to potential clients so communication and marketing skills are quite important.

- Rewards and benefits

The rewards and benefits won't all be yours, sadly, but you will work to develop and implement an organisation's **rewards and benefits** scheme, which includes salaries and bonuses as well as additional employee benefits such as pensions. In some organisations the job will also include responsibility for life assurance, profit-sharing, company cars, medical insurance packages and relocation and expatriate packages.

- Training and development

Those involved in training identify staff **training and development** needs, through planning, organising and overseeing appropriate training. This will include things like assessing both training programmes and the progress of employees undertaking them, ensuring that employees receive appropriate training and conducting job evaluation surveys.

QUALIFICATIONS AND TRAINING To gain entry, you'll generally need a degree, ideally one which you can make seem relevant either to an understanding of the industry or of people (psychology, behavioural sciences and law are always good ones). Failing that, an NVQ at grade 3 or above. Some NVQs are recognised as stepping stones for getting qualifications through the Chartered Institute of Personnel and Development's professional development scheme – this is a four-parter, with a choice of modules you complete to earn graduate membership of the CIPD. It's available full or part-time or via distance or flexible learning.

SALARY The average graduate starting salary in HR is £17,925.

Contacts

Chartered Institute of Personnel and Development
151 The Broadway
London SW19 1JQ
(t) 020 8612 6200
(↗) www.cipd.co.uk

Recruitment and Employment Confederation
15 Welbeck St
London W1G 9XT
(t) 020 7009 2100
(↗) www.rec.uk.com

Online reading

Personnel Today www.personneltoday.com

People Management www.peoplemanagement.co.uk

Human Resources Magazine www.humanresourcesmagazine.com

CORPORATE CULTURE

If you're working in an HR department in a company, then the corporate atmosphere you're in will depend on who you work for. Like many other cross-industry disciplines, the culture you work in depends on the industry rather than the job. Having said that, you are supposed to be setting standards. You can't discipline a worker for being inappropriately dressed if you're in a scruffy T-shirt with your piercings showings, so personal presentation is usually very important, and suits and smart dressing are the norm.

It's an area which reflects many of the attributes it's trying to promote: accepting, meritocratic, slightly touchy-feely sometimes, but always with an eye for professional and personal development. Flexible working is often an option, so long as you keep an ear out for changes in employment law or for changes within your company.

ETHICAL QUESTIONS

An employer's values can be readily discerned in the way it treats its staff. Human resources as a discipline has developed over recent years to cater for a workforce comprised of individuals increasingly aware of their rights and determined to have a life as well as a job. Enlightened employment policies can and do affect decisions concerning which company people want to work for.

Attention to equal opportunities and diversity is obviously a key consideration, but so too are company policies such as sick-leave entitlement and flexibility to allow religious observance. Are the company's policies progressive, and do they go beyond the minimum required by law?

What is the attitude to trade unions? Are they recognised at all? If so is there a consultative framework in place to make sure the working relationship between management and union is as productive as possible?

Asking how the department handles redundancy and sackings might be revealing. Is the grievance procedure effective in resolving disputes? Are staff consulted about changes in the way the organisation is run? Is there an undertaking to ensure they feel valued? Does the company survey employees' attitudes and opinions?

What is the attitude towards health and wellbeing? Are efforts made to avoid industrial injuries like repetitive strain injury (RSI) in the first place? Is the company committed to paying for treatment to cure RSI and allowing the employee to work to their full potential?

Information and communication technology (ICT)

Just 50 years ago, there were only 263 computers in the world. As recently as 1990, the internet was known only to a few computer scientists. Now the web, computers and all other associated gadgets, toys and essential kit seem to be everywhere. No other industry has grown so rapidly or so expansively (the dotcom crash excepted, but that mainly took down the venture capitalists) and that means it needs a constant supply of fresh blood – you perhaps.

It's a sector synonymous with innovation: currently it's all about the development of wireless technology, the miniaturisation of personal computers and the increasing synthesis between computers and mobile phones. But whatever the technology, it has an increasing effect on all our lives, helping all kinds of companies deal with the rest of us more efficiently and in increasingly innovative ways. It's likely that you will be working in another industry, but performing an ICT role; less than half of you will work for an actual ICT company, and even then you're most likely to act as a supplier to firms elsewhere in the economy.

You will, of course, be keen on and up to speed with technology. You will, more likely than not, be good at maths and you'll have a logical approach to problem-solving. Many in this industry work in teams, often under project managers (who themselves are likely to have progressed from one of the roles described below), so you'll need to adapt to that and be able to communicate effectively with other members of that team and external clients (both inside and outside your company). And you'll also be good at hitting deadlines.

Roles

■ Analysts/Systems designers

Analysts, or **systems designers** (the job titles in this industry change as often as the software), are the people who see a problem in a computer system, and then sort out a way to fix it. You might go to a company which requires a radically new computer set-up and you will have to work out their needs and provide an answer – within budget (that's the tricky bit). You will require a range of technical skills depending on you area of speciality. In addition, you need skills in generic areas such as problem-solving, analysis, leadership, time management, project management and dealing with clients. You'll have a degree of imagination and a level of confidence – you are likely to be restructuring people's jobs (and lives) so you need the ability to explain and inspire as you sell your ideas.

If you are heading towards analysis or systems design, then there's a number of areas you can head for. **Business analysts** review, analyse and evaluate the overall business and information needs of an organisation in order to develop solutions to business and related technology problems. They tend to be recruited from the ranks of experienced IT professionals who know what the business is all about.

As a **database analyst** you would develop and maintain databases, ensuring optimum performance and sorting out problems. You analyse and design code for database access, modification and construction and are also responsible for the tables, data dictionaries and monitoring of standards and procedures.

Being a **network analyst** involves researching and recommending policies and strategies for an organisation's network infrastructure. You design, install, analyse and implement computer systems and networks, ensuring that the network is effective and that it meets the changing requirements of the organisation.

Systems analysts develop data and system processes, flow diagrams and charts and specifications to suit different systems and applications, and specialise in a variety of programming languages.

■ Developers/Programmers/Software engineers

Applications **programming** or **developing** can cover a wide spectrum. Sometimes this means working with fairly loose concepts, usually when exploring an entirely new system. Alternatively you could be doing step-by-step work, where you're following procedures already developed. But essentially you are following the analysts in: once they have specified what sort of system a company or institution needs, you go in and create it, writing code so that the computers can act and translating much of that code into a series of ready-to-use instructions that those who will use your system will be able to understand. You'll need to be logical, attentive to detail and able to understand how the detail fits into the big picture. You'll be a desk jockey, sitting and concentrating for long periods of time as you try and work through a problem of logic; you'll often need to be patient and dogged as you struggle for a solution.

You can, of course, specialise in the type of programming you want to do, producing bespoke systems for individual companies or perhaps building applications for sale in shops for the rest of us to install and puzzle over – writing applications for the general public involves a special understanding of just how stupid the rest of us are. Or you could opt for multimedia work, integrating graphics, text, digital audio and video into a single product, whether it be a disc or a site. As with web design, it's a particularly fast-moving field and you need to be familiar with commercially available systems to understand the ever-moving boundaries of the field you are working in.

Programmers work as part of a team, moving up the hierarchy. At the pinnacle is the job of project leader, which involves working more closely with the analysts, interpreting their ideas and then breaking them down into separate coding tasks for the team to perform.

■ Hardware engineers

Most of the jobs in ICT now involve software, but there are areas where designing and developing computers from scratch still occurs. As a **hardware engineer** you might be designing computers for specialist use, in cars for example. This job needs specialists such as electronic engineers, mathematicians and physicists and also requires an awareness of the customer, so you'll need great technical skills as well as the ability to understand that you're designing for a customer, not just in the abstract. Your product needs to be safe, affordable and efficient.

You will possess an original mind. You'll need the imagination to create something new from scratch and you'll need the analytical ability to make sure that your new computer matches the needs of those buying it. Chances are that your clients will be of the "I don't know what I want but I'll know it when I see it" variety, so you'll need patience and diplomacy too.

■ Trainers

Trainers are the ones who tell people all they need to know to get though their day jobs on a computer. You provide instruction about computer hardware and software to individuals or groups and facilitate meetings, workshops or conferences. You might be freelance or work as part of a large company. Alternatively a trainer can get involved in technical writing – a growing part of the industry that fills the gap caused by unintelligible user manuals provided by manufacturers. You could work for those manufacturers, for consultancies or in house, especially for companies which buy bespoke programs or systems. Again, you could be employed by the company or work as a freelancer.

- User support

Support roles require skills in presentation, client consulting and interaction, group facilitation, problem-solving and time management. The client might be the young thing on the second floor of your building who always crashes their computer, or it might be some hopeless type on the end of a phone who should never have been allowed to buy a computer in the first place. The job may involve hand-holding ("click on that, now what do you see...?"), training when new systems are put in place and dealing with the many major and minor crises that erupt in companies daily (and being able to tell the difference). The role encompasses supporting desktop hardware, network administration, software applications and upgrades, databases and other end-user and desktop products. Support might be offered via telephone, internet or face to face.

- Webmasters/Web designers

This is really a part of the software engineer's or developer's job. **Webmasters** design, plan and, often, build websites for their clients or for themselves. What you put in there depends on the client's needs, so you could have all the fun of multimedia, all the security aspects of financial transaction systems – or just a picture of a grinning chief executive and a couple of email addresses. Whatever, once the site is done, the webmaster (a title with worrying echoes of Dungeons and Dragons geekery, so try and avoid it if you can) will upload it to a server and will also be responsible for its upkeep; you might also be responsible for registering it on search engines, making links to related sites and using whatever methods are required to market it within the internet world.

QUALIFICATIONS AND TRAINING For roles as **systems analysts and designers** you will generally need a degree, most often in computer sciences, although the composition of those courses can vary considerably and affect the areas you are likely to specialise in. Alternatively, you might have a foundation degree or an NVQ in related subjects. Once working, much of the training is on the job, although there are specific training courses tailored to individual products or the companies that supply them – whether that be Microsoft, Cisco, whoever. The professional bodies of the industry also run training sessions.

Many **programmers** join at graduate level, but not all have computer science degrees. You will, though, have to demonstrate that you have logical and mathematical skills. Again, training is often on the job; continuous professional development schemes are backed by the British Computer Society, though too few employers support this.

Hardware engineers will also need a degree, possibly in electronic engineering, physics or maths. Training is largely centred on experience, not least because this isn't a growing industry, as most UK hardware firms have moved towards the more lucrative and fast-moving software end.

To be a successful **support staffer** or **trainer**, you'll need to know programs better than the people you are talking to, but that's not necessarily going to come from a degree course. So while you will be expected to have numerical and logical skills (and may be tested on them at an interview), you may also need NVQ or vocational training. CPD is also very important, but whether your employer agrees is a different matter. Experience too, is its own training.

While a **webmaster** will probably need a couple of good, possibly related, A-levels (perhaps in computer sciences, perhaps in design), you will also need to show particular technical skills – proven knowledge of HTML and Java, as well as Dreamweaver and Flash are likely to be the minimum. Web design courses are available for all levels of expertise but most web folk develop their skills on the job. It's the kind of role where playing with a new toy (for which read application) can be seen as a good thing – you're developing skills and possible new ways to present your site. And let's face it, most people sitting in the office haven't got a clue what you're doing anyway.

SALARY The average graduate starting salary in ICT is £21,285.

Contacts

British Computer Society
First Floor
Block D
North Star House
North Star Avenue
Swindon SN2 1FA
(t) 01793 417417
(↗) www.bcs.org.uk

British Interactive Media Association
Briarlea House
Southend Road
South Green
Billericay CM11 2PR
(t) 01277 658107
(↗) www.bima.co.uk

e-skills UK
1 Castle Lane
London SW1E 6DR
(t) 020 7963 8920
(↗) www.e-skills.com

Help Desk Institute
21 High Street
Green Street Green
Orpington
Kent BR6 6BG
(t) 01689 889100
(↗) www.hdi-europe.com

Institute of IT Training
Westwood House
Westwood Business Park
Coventry CV4 8HS
(t) 0845 006 8858
(↗) www.iitt.org.uk

Institute for the Management of Information Systems
5 Kingfisher House
New Mill Road
Orpington
Kent BR5 3QG
(t) 0700 00 23456
(↗) www.imis.org.uk

Institute of Scientific and Technical Communicators

PO Box 522
Peterborough PE2 5WX

(t) 01733 390141

(↗) www.istc.org.uk

Institution of Analysts and Programmers

Charles House
36 Culmington Road
London W13 9NH

(t) 020 8567 2118

(↗) www.iap.org.uk

Institution of Engineering and Technology

Michael Faraday House
Stevenage
Herts SG1 2AY

(t) 01438 313 311

National Computing Centre

Oxford House
Oxford Road
Manchester M1 7ED

(t) 0161 228 6333

(↗) www.ncc.co.uk

Society of Information Technology Management

F19 Moulton Business Park
Red House Road
Northampton NN3 6AQ

(t) 01604 674800

(↗) www.socitm.gov.uk

Online reading

Guardian Technology technology.guardian.co.uk

.net www.netmag.co.uk

Web Designer www.webdesignermag.co.uk

PC Pro www.pcpro.co.uk

IT Training www.bcs.org/server.php

Computeractive www.computeractive.co.uk

UK Web Design Association www.ukwda.org

CORPORATE CULTURE

Perhaps because the sector is still in its infancy, ICT workers are often characterised as pony-tailed twentysomethings zipping round open-plan offices on microscooters and dressing mostly in skate-wear. It's not quite like that, of course – not everyone in the industry wears a Red Dwarf T-shirt – not least because this isn't a single industry in the way that, say, law is. In ICT you're more likely to be working for a firm which isn't dedicated to computers or software. So in terms of the culture that operates, that is often dependent on the industry in which you're the ICT dude. While you won't be expected to turn up in a pin-stripe, and will often be one of the less formal compartments of the company, you'll be taking your sartorial lead, and many others, from the environment you're in.

The beauty of the work you do is that if you don't like the corporate culture where you are, you can, with a little fine-tuning of your skills (and CV), simply move elsewhere. Should you want flexible working, part-time employment or job-share, there is probably a company out there willing to offer it to you. The drawback is that the same mobile workforce is also pretty competitive, and there's a long-hours culture, especially as projects draw to a conclusion. That same mobility could also lead you abroad. The UK has a very good reputation in this field and those with the right experience can make themselves a lucrative switch to sunnier climes (so keep that Red Dwarf T-shirt handy). And once you have your own good reputation, you can make yourself freelance. Many firms prefer to take on ICT staff only for individual projects, so you are only there till the project is done. As with all freelance roles, there's less security, but the immediate cash rewards are often higher.

Perversely for a sector so young, the IT industry is stubbornly male. There's little evidence to suggest that any systematic discrimination exists – IT employers simply concede that they find it difficult to attract women into the sector, though the related area of IT sales at least manages closer to its fair share.

ETHICAL QUESTIONS

The production of most electrical and computer components is a highly polluting and energy- and resource-intensive process. Attention to how and where hardware is sourced, used and disposed of are crucial.

Another consideration might be to think through what your personal attitudes are to a firm making you use software that monitors or "spies" on employees (monitoring email, web access, keyboard use etc) – increasingly popular in the workplace. Would the firm consider the relevance and potential benefits of such a system before designing, implementing or maintaining it? How is it decided who owns the information generated?

What is the approach to the question of who should ensure that stored information is correct and complete? This is a crucial issue when considering systems which store personal information, particularly concerning money or even criminal records.

Information architecture is a term which describes how an information system is set up to help people complete tasks efficiently. What consideration does a firm give to the possibility of educating users by linking in information they may not know exists? How does the company approach labelling? Is it acceptable to simply use the shortest and most predictable labels, or is more thought given to what impact these labels might have on the people or groups being labelled?

How far does the company go to ensure that its products are as accessible as possible, for example to people with visual or hearing impairment?

Law

The law isn't all about sweeping about in a wig and a gown, making dramatic speeches to packed courtrooms then snuffling into the finest claret at your gentleman's club *à la* Rumpole. It may be like this on rare occasions, but mostly it's a lot more mundane, even at a high and public level.

Of course most law roles are highly vocational, so you're quite likely to have been planning this since your A-levels and have a reasonable idea of what to expect. Law is a diverse sector but always involves upholding the law of the land and dealing with those who contravene it. For many people, entering the legal profession means making a choice between being a barrister and a solicitor, but there are other areas you can go into with a law qualification, not least advisory and consultancy roles, local government or the academic life. So bear in mind that your choice is not bound by the job descriptions in this section alone. That said, as a lawyer (a catch-all term that covers barristers and solicitors), there's an enormous amount of scope in the type of work you undertake, whether community-based, human rights, family, corporate, publishing… the list is long. The size of practice will also make a difference to the type of work you do and the atmosphere in which you work – important considerations. So, really, although the law may remain the same, the ways in which you choose to practise can vary significantly.

For most jobs in the legal sector you will need to be – how can we put this delicately – clever. The intellectual ability to form a coherent argument, to spot flaws in the arguments of others, to cope with enormous amounts of information and to do so under the stress of long hours, tight deadlines and important issues, needs to be something your head can cope with. You'll also need to be able to communicate well and be confident in yourself and inspire confidence in others. The higher echelons of the profession do not make for an easy climb.

Roles

■ Barrister/Advocate

These roles are specialist legal advisers and courtroom advocates, whose job it is to present cases in court under instruction from a solicitor. **Barristers** are individual legal practitioners who work in chambers (groups of offices) that are headed by an experienced barrister and have a clerk to control the flow of work. You might specialise in a particular area, such as family law or criminal law. Whatever you do, the job will include preparing cases – which entails having meetings with the client, researching and preparing legal arguments and interpreting the law – presenting arguments in court, drafting legal documents and giving legal advice. Barristers have the right to appear in higher courts on contentious matters. Scotland's legal system is distinct from that of England and Wales, so the comparable role is called an **advocate** and has some small differences in training.

■ Barrister's clerk/Advocate's clerk

Although this isn't strictly a graduate role, as the majority of **barristers' clerks** enter the profession straight after A-levels, it is an excellent way in, albeit one that needs committed hard work and skill. Basically the role involves running the business and administration side of a barrister's chambers. It is a big job that will see you allocating work to the most appropriate barrister, dealing with solicitors while getting new work for the chambers, planning case details through to the court appearance stage and working closely with barristers to ensure that the case runs according to plan. Clerks joining at a junior level will normally be trained by their chambers, which might include attending courses run through the Institute of Barristers' Clerks, sometimes leading to a BTEC national certificate covering organisation, finance, management, law, marketing and chambers administration.

■ Law costs draftsman

Legal costs are a complex affair. Whether they are the costs charged by a solicitor, or the costs charged to a losing party in a case in litigation, they are often contentious. Many solicitors therefore employ **law costs draftsmen** to work out (and justify) the money being charged. It can also be a freelance job. Either way you will need to pay rigorous attention to detail, and have a thick skin. Legal bills are never popular.

■ Legal executive

Legal executives (who don't feature in Scottish law circles) work for a solicitor doing back-up roles, often focusing on a particular area of the law –

conveyancing perhaps, or company law. You'll concentrate on preparing documents or interviewing clients, the sort of detailed work that allows a solicitor to get on with the bigger picture. By becoming a fellow of the Institute of Legal Executives you can qualify as a solicitor within two years.

■ Licensed conveyancer

Conveyancing is the legal transfer of ownership of property or land from one to another. It can be a complex and tiresome business so, while anyone can now legally do it, most prefer to leave it to the pros. **Licensed conveyancers**, again only seen in England and Wales, are such pros. You might work on your own, or for solicitors, companies with large property interests or local government.

■ Solicitor

Solicitors offer legal services and representation to their clients who could be householders arguing over their neighbour's fences, companies buying large property empires, or individuals facing criminal charges. Quite a few solicitors also offer other services to complement their legal services, such as advice on property selling or financial matters. Solicitors are able to represent their clients in magistrates and county courts; with additional qualifications they can also appear in crown or high courts, but are more likely to brief barristers for that line of work. If you're a commercial solicitor, working for a business or corporate client, you might specialise in a particular area of law, such as tax or employment. Non-commercial solicitors might also specialise, but will typically deal with things like wills and probate, litigation and matrimonial law. Most solicitors work in private practices, whether they be large City firms made up of a multitude of specialists or the rural old family retainers who usually deal in wills and conveyancing.

QUALIFICATIONS AND TRAINING To be a **barrister**, you will generally need a law degree (second class or better), or a non-law degree followed by a pass in either the one-year common professional examination or the postgraduate diploma in law; to practise in Scotland you'll need a diploma in legal practice from a Scottish university. You then need to join one of the four Inns of Court and attend an approved one-year, full-time vocational course (the list of approved institutions comes from the Bar Council), after which you'll do a one-year pupillage under the guidance of a barrister (usually involving research, coffee-making and sitting in the back of a court). After pupillage, you must find a seat in an existing set of chambers, and from then on it's over to you.

Most **solicitors** are graduates too, although fellows of the Institute of Legal Executives do not necessarily need a degree. If your degree isn't in law, then you have to take the common professional examination or a postgraduate qualification in law.

Then there's the one-year vocational course, followed by a two-year training contract with an authorised firm, with an additional 20-day, usually modular, professional skills course thrown in. In Scotland, a solicitor must either take a law degree at one of nine accredited universities or do the exams run by the Law Society of Scotland, followed by a 26-week postgraduate course, then a two-year training period with a Scottish firm. Law isn't a profession you enter on a whim.

To become a **barrister's clerk**, you will need at least 4 GCSEs at A, B or C grade in "academic" subjects. Training is on the job, but you can, via the good offices of the Institute of Barristers' Clerks, go for a two-year BTEC. That and five years' service will equip you for membership of the Institute.

Law costs draftsmen, **legal executives** and **licensed conveyancers** can get in with GCSEs and A-levels and go on to specific training with the Association of Law Costs Draftsmen, the Institute of Legal Executives and the Council of Licensed Conveyancers respectively.

SALARY The average graduate starting salary in the law professions is £18,859.

Contacts

**Association of
Law Costs Draftsmen**

Church Cottage
Church Lane
Stuston
Diss
Norfolk IP21 4AG

(t) 01379 741404

(↗) www.alcd.org.uk

Association of Women Barristers

187 Fleet Street
London EC4A 2AT

(↗) www.womenbarristers.co.uk

Association of Women Solicitors

(↗) www.womensolicitors.org.uk

Bar Council

289–293 High Holborn
London WC1V 7HZ

(t) 020 7242 0082

(↗) www.barcouncil.org.uk

Black Solicitors' Network

c/o The Law Society
113 Chancery Lane
London WC2A 1PL

(t) 020 7316 5773

(↗) www.blacksolicitorsnetwork.
co.uk

**Council for Licensed
Conveyancers**

16 Glebe Road
Chelmsford
Essex CM1 1QG

(t) 01245 349599

(↗) www.theclc.gov.uk

Faculty of Advocates
Advocates Library
Parliament House
Edinburgh EH1 1RF

(t) 0131 226 5071

(↗) www.advocates.org.uk

Institute of Barristers' Clerks
289–293 High Holborn
London WC1 7HZ

(t) 020 7831 7144

(↗) www.barristersclerks.com

Institute of Legal Executives
Kempston Manor
Kempston
Beds MK42 7AB

(t) 01234 841000

(↗) www.ilex.org.uk

Law Society
113 Chancery Lane
London WC2A 1PL

(t) 020 7242 1222

(↗) www.lawsociety.org.uk

Law Society of Scotland
26 Drumsheugh Gardens
Edinburgh EH3 7YR

(t) 0131 226 7411

(↗) www.lawscot.org.uk

Society of Asian Lawyers
4-5 Gray's Inn Square
Gray's Inn
London WC1R 5AH

(↗) societyofasianlawyers.com

Society of Black Lawyers
11 Cranmer Road
Kennington Park
London SW9 6EJ

(t) 020 7735 6592

Online reading

The Bar Council's pupillage website www.pupillages.com

Bar Standards Board www.barstandardsboard.org.uk

Bar vocational courses www.bvconline.co.uk

The Lawyer www.thelawyer.com

European Lawyer www.europeanlawyer.co.uk

Consilio: the daily online law magazine www.spr-consilio.com

Law Careers Advice Network www.lcan.org.uk

CORPORATE CULTURE

This is a very formal sector, particularly for barristers, so smart office-wear is pretty much the norm. You'll be meeting with clients, who need to be reassured of your professionalism, particularly as there is often money, reputation or even years of a client's life at stake. People who work in the legal profession, particularly barristers and solicitors, are often self-confident and quick-witted; barristers in particular have a sense of drama, of the sort that comes with the territory when you're wearing wigs and robes on a daily basis. Much of a lawyer's work is done in public, so you'll need to enjoy the verbal battles and have the physical stamina to do so for long days. This isn't a frivolous job and it attracts people who have a sense of gravitas so even on the nights when everyone in the office or chambers lets their hair down, you're not likely to be arrested. And if you are, you'll know someone who can help...

Once they've completed all their training, talented barristers and solicitors can get promoted to important cases, although experience is fairly key and it's unlikely that you'd leap straight into anything staggeringly responsible without a few years of solid practice behind you. Lawyers tend to be self-employed so progression depends on results and reputation.

While 50% of entrants to the bar are women, there is a high rate of dropout after 10 years or so – barristers are self-employed so maternity rights and part-time working aren't always tenable. The Bar Council is looking into issues of equality such as these and some chambers may have more flexible approaches. Part-time work is more viable for solicitors.

The fact is though, that the law profession in the UK is often viewed as a largely white, middle-class profession. One factor in such a mono-culture may well be the cost of entry. Legal education is expensive – the bar vocational course can be upwards of £8,000 – and few students are sponsored. The method of entry to the profession can also be exclusive. Firms want great GCSEs, A-levels and a 2:1 or above, traditional qualifications that mean they recruit from traditional backgrounds. If that isn't you, then take heart that the situation is improving, but there may be extra barriers ahead.

ETHICAL QUESTIONS

Lawyers are not infrequently accused of a lack of ethics, which is perhaps unavoidable in a profession whose primary business is to argue one side of a case. Solicitors are regulated by the Law Society and barristers by the Bar Council and in Scotland the Faculty of Advocates. Amongst other things these bodies set ethical standards and rules governing qualification and fitness to practice. Judges are appointed either by the Ministry of Justice or the Scottish parliament.

Does the firm give free advice to anyone? What areas of law does it practise? Does it help firms defend themselves against unethical practices or does it help to fight rights abuses? Is the firm active in campaigning for reform to any areas of law? Is it involved solely in prosecution or defence? Does it undertake work for the Crown Prosecution Service, or individuals granted legal aid? Have the firm's fees ever been challenged or has it been compelled to reduce the amount of fees charged for a case? Do the chambers use expert witnesses and if they became aware of opposing views from different experts what action would they take?

Management consultancy

Management consultancy is a slightly nebulous profession: although it takes in a lot of graduates and second-jobbers, there's some confusion about what the job actually entails. All you have to remember is that management is the art of getting the best results out of other people and consultancy is about advising people about areas of expertise.

Essentially, management consultants are the independent gunslingers brought in to firms that may be failing, may not be developing as they should or may be embarking on a whole new direction. The management consultant should be able to come in and give the big picture, sharing knowledge, skills and techniques in order to improve the performance of individuals, groups and the whole organisation. You've got to be able to sum up a situation quickly, analyse issues and formulate answers. You'll need to be able to listen, to organise and to implement solutions. And you've got to be confident. You are, after all, the clever clogs with all the answers – and don't underestimate the hostility you could receive from employees of your target firm as you sweep in, telling them how to do their jobs. That's not your intention, but it could be the reaction you get.

Roles

As a new graduate or a new entrant to the world of **consultancy**, you're likely to play a background role at first. This will entail researching and crunching data and talking to clients as a fact-finder, as well as analysing what you find. You will be assisting the senior consultants (the best of whom will be inclusive to all members of their team) to understand the nature of the problem and the range of potential solutions, and will help them reach conclusions and then present them to a (hopefully) delighted client.

If you're working for a consultancy firm, then it's likely that you'll be required to specialise in order to develop the expertise you're going to need. So you may focus on information technology, corporate finance, human resources or e-commerce. Or you may opt for particular kinds of organisations such as local government, the charity sector or one area of manufacturing. It's really up to you to find your niche.

It's likely that your early years in the job will be spent doing the slightly drudge-like work as a junior in the office, writing and researching reports and analyses. You'll move on to closer work with the client and presenting proposals, before being given more senior roles, leading teams and running projects.

QUALIFICATIONS AND TRAINING Many consultants don't join the profession straight from university, but direct entry from graduation is both possible and increasingly common, as is entry straight after postgraduate qualification, without any of the blue-chip management experience often thought necessary. They do, though, have to be good qualifications, with business and numerate subjects highly valued. If you want to join the ranks of the specialist, then a degree in a relevant subject is more than handy – electronic engineering perhaps or computing. Whatever else is written on your degree certificate, though, it will have to say 2:1 at least if you are to make any headway. And of all the postgraduate qualifications likely to impress, you're most likely to succeed with an MBA, as you might expect. It's not a role you'll slip into straight after graduation, although Chelsea Clinton managed to do just that in 2003. Even if your dad isn't a former president, some firms will fatten you up with on-the-job training, possibly with the certified management consultant certificate, promoted by the Institute of Management Consultancy, which requires at least three years' experience in the job. Basically, you have to know your stuff and you have to be able to prove it.

SALARY The average graduate starting salary for management consultants is £25,047.

Contacts

Institute of Business Consulting
3rd Floor
17–18 Hayward's Place
London EC1R 0EQ
(t) 020 7566 5220
(↗) www.ibconsulting.org.uk

Institute of Management Services
Brooke House
24 Dam Street
Lichfield
Staffordshire WS13 6AB
(t) 01543 266909
(↗) www.ims-productivity.com

Management Consultancies Association
60 Trafalgar Square
London WC2N 5DS
(t) 020 7321 3990
(↗) www.mca.org.uk

CORPORATE CULTURE

This is a very formal sector and there's a lot of money involved, so smart office-wear is the norm. You'll be meeting with clients, who need to be reassured of your professionalism, particularly as there is a lot at stake. You'll need to be able to work alongside, and as part of, a team, getting on well with people at all levels and rising above their suspicions that you're going to cost them their job. Especially if it's true.

You will often have to work long hours as you try and understand and solve problems that might have been ingrained for years and you may end up dealing with some pretty traumatic work situations. You may also end up working abroad for long stretches if your clients are international. Wherever you are, it can be very stressful and mentally demanding and can soak up your time both in and out of work hours, with rapid deadlines and long hours of travel eating into your fun-time. It's not a job for the uncommitted. But the rewards can be great, with good pay and a large range of big-company-style benefits such as pensions, gym membership, healthcare schemes, bonuses and share options.

Within your own company, though, you will usually find a meritocracy – if you're good you'll go places quickly. If you're really ambitious and join a consultancy straight from university, it's possible to become a partner by your mid-thirties, if you've got the talent. As with many competitive environments, though, career breaks (to have a baby for example) would have to be short. It's a fast-changing world and you need to keep up.

In fact, it's a rather cut-throat business too, so if you don't progress, you won't be expected to hang around either. Assuming you're pretty bright, you will move on from your first consultancy job to project management, probably in a specialist area, and then on to more senior management roles, and up to partnership level, when your place in the car park is secure.

Culturally, it may not always seem the most diverse of professions, but that's likely to be because people have been selected from the same pool rather than anything more sinister – much of the industry is based in London and the south-east, where the HQs of the big clients tend to be. But if you have the skills, there's no reason to expect that barriers will be put in your way. They are logical managers you're dealing with.

ETHICAL QUESTIONS

Management consulting is all about getting the best out of a firm's workers and resources, but where belts are tightened and efficiencies improved, there will also be the temptation to push costly ethical practices to one side. In the search for better profits are a company and its consultants always acting as ethically as possible, not just going for the short-term, cheapest solutions? What is the management consultancy's attitude to this dilemma or does it just see pleasing the client and increasing their profitability as its sole aim? There is concern within the industry itself that the public sees management consultancy as lacking a strong ethical commitment.

Is there a commitment to think about the effects of solving a particular problem in the long term? Does the consultancy have processes to allow cross-examination of the ethics of a course of action? What does the consultancy understand by the term "stakeholders"? How does it respond if it perceives a lack of transparency in the situation it has been hired to resolve, and are there any circumstances in which it might consider informing stakeholders of a situation which affects their interests? Would it put pressure on a client to keep stakeholders informed?

Manufacturing

Manufacturing is a broad umbrella under which a great many occupations shelter. Not all these jobs have the most glamorous of reputations, though this has not always been the case. By the middle of the 19th century Britain had become the world's leading industrial power and no other nation could boast either the range or productivity of British factories. But by the beginning of the 20th century the United States had overtaken Britain's levels of production and Germany was on an equal footing. Britain's manufacturing industry continued to decline throughout the last century. At the end of the second world war, it accounted for almost 40% of the British economy. That percentage has now halved. At the end of the 1970s around 7 million were employed in manufacturing. Now that figure is just 3.6 million, compared with more than 20 million employed by the service industry.

Despite its decline, the manufacturing industry offers a vast variety of roles, depending on which product is being manufactured. There are numerous skilled and semi-skilled jobs in factories, but we concentrate on management tasks in this section. Whichever part of the manufacturing industry you end up in, you will need organisational skills, numeracy, business acumen and the ability to lead and get on with people at all levels of the business. You'll need to be good at analysis and problem solving and the higher up you go, the thicker your skin will become – the more people you're in charge of, the more people will disagree with what you do.

Roles

■ Plant manager

This is often a first general management role for graduates in manufacturing, and is sometimes known as a factory or operations manager. The **plant manager** has full operational control over what happens at the facility, including engineering, output, personnel and often logistics, sales and marketing as well.

■ Production manager

The **production manager** is responsible for the planning, coordination and control of processes in order to ensure the product is made efficiently and at a satisfactory price, quality and quantity. The work is largely logistical –

working out a production schedule, the resources needed, how much it will cost and how long it will take. Production managers are also involved with product design and purchasing.

■ Production planner

The **production planner** draws up a schedule of work, which is agreed with the production manager, containing details of the materials and machines to be used, cost of materials, mechanical and human resources, the time required to do the job, and the quality standards to be met. Planners are responsible for making sure the schedule is followed during production. You will receive regular information on progress and deal quickly with any problems, such as a shortage of staff or materials and machinery breakdowns. In a similar role, the **production supervisor** reports to the production manager or plant manager and is responsible for achieving immediate and short-term objectives laid down by the production manager, for example in output, quality, waste, yield, safety and overtime costs.

■ Quality assurance officer

The **quality assurance officer** monitors and advises on the operating procedures being used within a production plant. The role involves collecting a great deal of statistics so you need to be able to assimilate and analyse the data.

QUALIFICATIONS AND TRAINING For management roles, you will often need a degree, generally in a related subject like engineering. Most big manufacturing companies have comprehensive graduate training programmes and extensive opportunities for gaining work experience during holidays.

Manufacturers are less likely to consider applicants with non-relevant qualifications. Therefore **degrees** in subjects such as engineering, electronics, business, management or the physical sciences will improve your chances of a successful application. Manufacturing is also an area in which postgraduate qualifications, including PhDs, are looked on favourably by employers. You could, for example, take a postgraduate business course, perhaps leading to a BTEC diploma in management studies, which can be done part time or full time. A bigger commitment is the **master of business administration (MBA)** course offered by business schools throughout Europe and the US. These are usually one- or two-year full-time courses and can be expensive; your company may be prepared to make that investment in you if you can't afford it.

Non-degree holders can also progress into the higher management roles by virtue of shop-floor experience. Those looking for supervisor roles can benefit from HND/HNC and BTEC qualifications that cover basic management preoccupations and techniques, or from certificates from the Institute of Operations Management or the Chartered Management Institute, both of which offer training.

SALARY The average graduate starting salary for management roles in manufacturing is £21,003.

CORPORATE CULTURE

Production workers usually work 37 to 40 hours a week, Monday to Friday, although some may work shifts. However, managers will be expected to work outside these hours when it is necessary to attend meetings or when emergencies arise.

There is a perception that manufacturing is a male-dominated sector – there are no reasons why a woman should not take these roles, but very few seem to. Although at a later stage in your career you may be able to take work as an independent consultant or expert on a project-to-project basis, this is unlikely at first and to begin with there will be few opportunities for flexible working.

Contacts

British Standards Institution
389 Chiswick High Road
London W4 4AL
(t) 020 8996 9001
(↗) www.bsi-global.com

Chartered Management Institute
Management House
Cottingham Road
Corby
Northants NN17 1TT
(t) 01536 204222
(↗) www.managers.org.uk

Chartered Quality Institute
12 Grosvenor Crescent
London SW1X 7EE
(t) 020 7245 6722
(↗) www.thecqi.org

Institute of Leadership and Management
1 Giltspur Street
London EC1A 9DD
(t) 020 7294 2470
(↗) www.i-l-m.com

Institute of Operations Management
University of Warwick Science Park
Sir William Lyons Road
Coventry CV4 7EZ
(t) 024 7669 2266
(↗) www.iomnet.org.uk

Online reading
The Manufacturer www.themanufacturer.com
Manufacturing and Logistics IT magazine www.logisticsit.com
Manufacturing Engineer available via www.theiet.org

What you wear at work will depend on both the organisation and the role which you fulfil within it. Overalls are common in many positions as the Japanese practice of "kaizen" manufacturing techniques, prevalent in many plants now, encourages senior managers to wear the same attire as their assembly-line workers.

Thanks to skills shortages in this sector, career advancement can be rapid, although most graduate schemes will insist that you spend at least the first two years getting to grips with the basics of a variety of roles. Opportunities for climbing the ladder will be greater in higher-growth industries, such as the manufacture of pharmaceuticals and, to a lesser extent, cars and aircraft.

Whilst the manufacturing industry is vast in terms of the roles that need to be filled within it, there is often call for a candidate to be an expert specialised in one particular field. As manufacturers are increasingly willing to move production facilities to regions and countries where labour and supply costs are cheaper, there is a fair probability that at some point in your career you will be asked to relocate within the UK or work abroad. Many sectors, notably the oil and minerals exploration industries, are almost entirely based overseas.

ETHICAL QUESTIONS

All of this raises serious ethical questions. Whether it is the environmental damage they cause, the suffering they cause (military hardware), or the animal testing they rely on, it will be a rare company that could claim to be progressive and truly ethical in its practices in any of these fields. However, some claim that the only way to change some of the sector's unethical practices is from within. Could your job enact positive change – by working on greater fuel efficiency or greener fuel for cars, for example?

The military–industrial complex is often accused of being too open to a "revolving door" mechanism whereby ex-servicemen and women work for the companies from which they procured goods and services for the armed forces. Are you comfortable with this or do you consider such cosy relationships in such a powerful industry to be ethically questionable, and what is the attitude of the company in this area? Many manufacturers receive whopping subsidies from governments, a practice considered unethical in other areas of business, which helps reiterate and reinforce the closeness of the relationship. Is the company open and honest about its relationship with governments?

In the chemical industry safety standards for the protection of the workforce, consumers and public must be paramount (in 1984 20,000 people lost their lives in Bhopal, India, following a leak at a chemical factory). How seriously does the firm take its responsibility in this area?

The petrochemical industry has many interests in countries where corruption in public life is a big problem. What steps does the company take to avoid dealing with corrupt officials, or to blow the whistle on them?

Ethical concerns in the biotech industry are a very hot topic. What is the company's approach to creating embryos solely for the purpose of using their stem cells? Do they consider the principle of cloning of human beings to be acceptable?

Media and journalism

The rise in popularity of media studies as a degree subject suggests the media sector will have little difficulty in attracting recruits for the foreseeable future, yet the reality of working in the media is generally less exciting and glamorous than the stereotypes may have you believe. Most jobs within the media involve a great deal of hard work and often, at first, for a very small amount of money.

Of course there is a great deal of satisfaction to be gained from producing a TV programme or seeing your byline in a newspaper, but achieving this kind of success is notoriously difficult in a business which is highly competitive – whether we're talking newspapers, magazines, books, TV, radio or new media.

Whichever role you end up in, you will need a flair for communication, of course, and the confidence to put it into action. You'll require self-confidence and persistence and you'll often have to work long and antisocial hours. You will be able to set aside your prejudices about issues to ensure that your reporting is sound and objective and you'll be able to generate an interest in a huge variety of subjects. But most important of all, you'll be able to meet deadlines.

■ Print journalism

A journalist is the person who writes and produces material for print (newspapers and magazines), radio, TV or, increasingly, online. Once on the ladder there's a number of routes you can take – general news, specialist subjects, features or documentary – depending on your experience and expertise.

Roles

■ Editor

Newspaper and magazine **editors** are responsible for the style and content of their titles. However, other roles carry the title "editor" too, including the commissioning editors for a particular section such as features or sport. Art or picture editors are responsible for the magazine or newspaper's visual content, including photographs and illustrations.

- Editorial assistant

As the job title suggests, an **editorial assistant** supports more senior editorial staff in the administration of the commissioning, planning and production of books, journals or magazines. This is the recognised starting point for a career in editorial work. The work includes progressing publications from receipt of text from authors through to the handover to production staff; you will also act as a personal assistant to commissioning editors in work like issuing contracts and dealing with royalties.

- Journalist

The three main areas of print **journalism** are news writing, feature writing and subediting. The magazine journalist typically creates news and feature articles targeted at the magazine's readership, which is usually defined by a shared interest or social class. A newspaper journalist's roles, on the other hand, range from reporter and staff writer through to feature writer and subeditor. The work can be divided into two areas: intake and output. Intake is essentially the inception, writing and submission of the report, feature or column; the output phase, conducted by the subeditors and editors, involves ensuring that the copy is ready for publication.

- Production editor

A **production editor** oversees the production process, from the layout of copy on computer screen and choice of images to the point at which the pages are sent to be printed. The whole process is usually done on a pre-prepared layout created in specialist programs.

- Publisher

A **publisher** is a senior manager within a magazine or book publishing house and is sometimes known as a publishing manager or publishing director. The publisher oversees managers of other departments including sales and marketing, finance, rights, publicity and production, as well as editorial staff.

- Subeditor

As a **subeditor** you process all copy written for a newspaper or magazine, making sure that it adheres to house style, meets the required word count and remains within the law. You must also check that it communicates its meaning clearly and reads well, which often involves a certain amount of rewriting and summarising.

QUALIFICATIONS AND TRAINING The majority of journalists are graduates, but in many cases the degree course itself doesn't matter, although many take media studies, hoping for a more direct road into newspapers and broadcasting. If that's the route you take, then the more vocational of the courses on offer might be your bag.

For **journalism**, look for aspects of the course that study news production, elements of bias and propaganda, or the role of the press. It's as well to remember too that there are many good postgraduate journalism courses which may be an option if you want to take a different degree. There are more than 30 courses accredited by the National Council for the Training of Journalists. Beyond that, it's usually a question of experience, working your way up through local newspapers or trade magazines, gaining the sort of portfolio that suits what you want to be doing, honing your news-gathering skills and/or polishing your writing style. It's the quality of your work that will get you further, just as much as your networking skills. Work experience can be an extra way in. Impress during a stint on a magazine or newspaper and at the very least you'll have a god reference to call upon, or you could just be in the right place at the right time.

If you're heading for a job as a **subeditor**, there are innumerable subbing courses that can freshen up your skills, but make sure you go to a college with a good reputation. There are plenty of claims in the small ads of papers promising that you'll make a fortune from spotting "speling errers", but go for the ones run by colleges which also have good general journalism courses. Once you're in work, most publications will know it is to their advantage that your subbing skills are up to scratch and should be happy to send you on a refresher course.

For **production editor** roles, much the same applies, but you'll be brushing up on the layout programs that magazines are produced on. National newspapers are likely to have their own bespoke adaptations of such systems, but you can't be expected to come ready versed in that, and they'll be happy to train you on the job.

SALARY The average graduate starting salary for all media roles is £16,791.

Contacts

National Council for the Training of Journalists

The New Granary
Station Road
Newport
Saffron Walden
Essex CB11 3PL

(t) 01799 544014

(↗) www.nctj.com

National Union of Journalists

308 Gray's Inn Road
London WC1X 8DP

(t) 020 7278 7916

(↗) www.nujtraining.org.uk

Society for Editors and Proofreaders

Riverbank House
1 Putney Bridge Approach
London SW6 3JD

(t) 020 7736 3278

(↗) www.sfep.org.uk

Online reading
MediaGuardian www.MediaGuardian.co.uk
Press Gazette www.pressgazette.co.uk
Mediaweek www.brandrepublic.com/MediaWeek

■ Broadcast journalism

Broadcast journalism, which includes online roles, does contain a number of journalists who have made the leap from newspapers but increasingly the tendency is for specialists. While all entrants to the broadcast world tend to want to work for national broadcasters, there are many equally fulfilling roles in local media.

Roles

■ Announcer/Presenter

An **announcer** works at the frontline of radio and television production, introducing and hosting programmes. You might be a newsreader working with a carefully timed script, a continuity announcer providing links between different programmes, or a DJ combining music and chat in your show. Announcers have to spend time preparing their broadcasts and researching background information. You also need a good knowledge of current affairs. **Presenters** spend time planning, rehearsing and perhaps writing for the shows they take part in.

■ Broadcast assistant

Broadcast assistant is a support role with work that ranges from straight-forward administrative duties including programme logs and letter writing to arranging contracts and payment for contributors. You may also contribute research.

■ Broadcast journalist

This is a front-end, before-camera/microphone job that always looks a little more glamorous than it is. **Broadcast journalists** are responsible for the research, writing and editing of material for broadcast in a variety of factual, news and current affairs programmes on television and radio and, increasingly, the internet. The work can include generating and researching stories, interviewing people, attending press conferences, gathering appropriate images and sounds, writing up, editing and packaging stories and reports and presenting them in radio or TV studios or on location.

■ Producer

A **producer** initiates ideas for programmes and "sells" these to commissioning editors. It is then the responsibility of the producer to manage the staff working on the project through to its completion. You could be involved in any number of areas as a producer – raising money, hiring a director and crew, arranging tie-in deals, sorting out visas, damping down tantrums... What's more, with changes in the industry and increasingly tight budgets, many independent producers, especially in radio, are now often required to act as their own researchers.

■ Production assistant/Production manager

As a **production assistant** you'll be involved in every stage of the production of a programme from pre-production to post-production, providing support in an administrative role to the director and producer. A production manager works within a framework set out by the director or producer and ensures the practical work has been done so that the filming environment is ready for production. That might mean booking the set, arranging the catering and pre-warning the police that a fake robbery is about to take place.

■ Programme researcher

Researchers collect, verify and prepare information for film, TV and radio productions. Material required for programmes and films is extremely diverse and detailed research ensures that all the information to be used is as accurate as possible. Researchers liaise with producers and directors to generate ideas and draft pitches, and they may also be involved in writing scripts and briefing scriptwriters.

■ Sound technician/Sound operator

A **sound technician** has a specialist role involving working with live and recorded sound. This can include recording and balancing speech for a radio play, monitoring the sound quality, levels and tone for live broadcasts such as concerts, recording film soundtracks, or playing in music or sound effects during a live programme. In film and TV sound operators' responsibilities vary according to the type and size of production. Duties include setting up microphones and other equipment and ensuring that cables are out of sight of the cameras.

QUALIFICATIONS AND TRAINING The tendency is for **broadcast journalists** to be graduates of specialist media courses or to have pursued postgraduate courses in the same field, concentrating on radio journalism or TV work perhaps. The Broadcast Journalism Training Council accredits courses that cover all aspects of broadcast journalism. For training once you are working, the BBC and ITN both have excellent, but fiercely contested, graduate training courses.

For **online journalists**, there is still a window of opportunity for the enthusiastic amateur to make the leap. Matt Drudge of the Drudge Report is enjoying his moment in the sunshine because his own site (www.drudgereport.com) caught the attention. Most of you won't make that sort of splash but if you want to make it in internet journalism (and it's an area which will only grow in significance), then you should at least have your own weblog. You might not get notorious on the internet, but it will demonstrate enthusiasm for, and technical ability with, the medium.

A **researcher** or **producer** is more likely to have a general degree and will probably start off in an assistant's role as a way of gaining experience before moving up the pecking order. A combination of hard work, enthusiasm and luck can bring success in this highly competitive area. A sound technician will need a vocational qualification (AVCE, GNVQ, you know the sort of thing) as a sound engineer.

SALARY The average graduate starting salary for all media roles is £16,791.

Contacts

Association of Online Publishers
Queens House
28 Kingsway
London WC2B 6JR
(t) 020 7404 4166
(↗) www.ukaop.org.uk

Broadcast Journalism Training Council
18 Miller's Close
Rippingale
near Bourne
Lincs PE10 0TH
(t) 01778 440025
(↗) www.bjtc.org.uk

Radio Academy
5 Market Place
London W1W 8AE
(t) 020 7255 2010
(↗) www.radioacademy.org

Radiocentre
77 Shaftesbury Avenue
London W1D 5DU
(t) 020 7306 2603
(↗) www.radiocentre.org

Skillset: the Sector Skills Council for the Audiovisual Industries
Prospect House
80–110 New Oxford Street
London WC1A 1HB
(t) 020 7520 5757
(↗) www.skillset.org

Online reading

MediaGuardian www.MediaGuardian.co.uk

Mediaweek www.brandrepublic.com/MediaWeek

New Media Age www.nma.co.uk

Broadcastnow www.broadcastnow.co.uk

■ Books

Publishing houses usually divide themselves into three – editorial, production and sales and marketing. The last is dealt with in the earlier section on marketing, since marketing is, in principle, much the same no matter what you're selling. Production roles (which include subbing and proofreading) are not dissimilar to those in magazines and newspapers, though the product is very different and so are the timescales. There is considerable overlap in the skills required though, so we'll leave you to refer back to the print journalism part of this section.

Roles

■ Author

An **author** is a writer working in one or a variety of disciplines, from novels to poetry and plays to non-fiction. The author researches, plans, drafts and revises their work before submitting it to a publisher, either unsolicited or through an agent. Specialisms may include academic writing, writing for children, educational writing, technical authorship or translating.

■ Editor

An **editor** selects the authors and books to be printed and then takes responsibility for the style and content of those books. Much of the editor's time is spent reading and evaluating manuscripts, meeting agents and authors, and attending book fairs. After commissioning, the editor monitors the book's progress and prepares regular reports for other departments such as sales, marketing and design. This is rather an advanced role – the entry position is usually editorial assistant, a junior post to learn the job, which is where most graduates enter the world of publishing.

■ Indexer

An **indexer**, yep, prepares an index for a book, helping readers locate information quickly and easily, by guiding them to the right pages. The job involves studying books carefully, usually at the proof stage, to decide what to include in the index. Indexers use a range of reference tools to help them decide how to organise the entries, including encyclopedias, thesauruses, dictionaries and the internet, and then arrange them alphabetically, cross-referencing each item.

QUALIFICATIONS AND TRAINING If you're entering the world of books, you'll be expected to have a degree, usually in a literate subject, since words will be your currency. If you're heading for technical or scientific publishing, then a degree in the relevant subject would be nice. While postgraduate vocational training in publishing is handy, work experience is more valuable, so there's nothing for it but to dive in.

SALARY The average graduate starting salary for all media roles is £16,791.

Contacts

Institute of Paper, Printing and Publishing
83 Guildford Street
Chertsey
Surrey KT16 9AS
ⓣ 0870 330 8625
↗ www.ip3.org.uk

Publishers Association
29b Montague Street
London WC1B 5BW
ⓣ 020 7691 9191
↗ www.publishers.org.uk

Publishing Skills Group
South House
The Street
Clapham
Worthing
West Sussex BN13 3UU
ⓣ 01903 871686
↗ www.workinpublishing.org.uk

Society of Indexers
Woodbourn Business Centre
10 Jessell Street
Sheffield S9 3HY
ⓣ 0114 244 9561
↗ www.indexers.org.uk

Online reading

The Bookseller www.thebookseller.com
Guardian Unlimited Books books.guardian.co.uk
Publishing News www.publishingnews.co.uk

CORPORATE CULTURE

Working in the media tends to involve long and irregular hours, whether you're chasing stories on a newspaper or working flat out to complete a television programme in time for broadcast. It is possible to work in media jobs where the hours are more regular but these tend to be at the less time-sensitive end of the spectrum, which takes out the adrenalin kick for some, but may suit the more laid-back amongst you.

The informal atmosphere of many media organisations can contribute to an atmosphere which is fairly matey but can also be catty and back-stabbing. Most media organisations operate a wear-what-you-like policy, although journalists attending press conferences and interviews – and certainly those appearing front of camera – require a smarter wardrobe than most.

While the media sector enjoys a good record of gender equality, there are still relatively few producers, editors and journalists from ethnic minorities. There are, however, moves within the sector to address this imbalance and many media organisations are involved in diversity recruitment drives.

Much media work is done on a freelance basis. As a result there is a great deal of job insecurity within the sector. Making a living from freelancing in the media requires either nerves of steel and great conviction or else a hefty private income as back-up. The freelance nature of many of the jobs does mean there are opportunities for flexible working and for home-working, particularly if you're a writer or author. Radio and TV offer far fewer roles that can be undertaken from home.

Many people land jobs within the media without a degree or HND. Similarly, graduates entering the media can find that the subject matter of their degree is largely immaterial although it's more likely that you'll bump into media workers with arts, humanities or social science backgrounds. Despite appearances, competition for jobs is extremely fierce. In most sectors it is quite likely that you will need to do a certain amount of unpaid work experience before you are considered for a salaried position. The lack of tangible, vocational qualifications for many of the positions in the media can make trying to get a job both baffling and frustrating.

The demand for jobs means media organisations can also get away with paying lower than average salaries. The informal nature of the business means opportunities for promotion and progression are difficult to predict. There is a vague structure for career progression within most parts of the sector, but some areas, such as journalism, can be cracked within hours of graduating by some and never reached by others even if they have taken every recommended step along the traditional path.

ETHICAL QUESTIONS

As the media industry continues to expand and become more powerful, so too does the moral debate surrounding it. In the wider context of broadcasting and the print media, the industry is frequently accused of having a less than ethical approach, for example in stereotyping nations or genders. Is it an acceptable defence to claim that prejudice reflects that of the target consumer, or do you think it is the moral responsibility of the media to promote greater understanding and tolerance? Fair and balanced reporting is surely the aim of all journalists, but journalists are often not trusted by a wider public suspicious of their motives. Would your job help repair this reputation? The industry is regulated by Ofcom and the Press Complaints Commission, which publishes an editors' code of conduct.

Many media firms are owned by larger companies. Are they undermining editorial freedom in any way? Are they making you push certain products over others, or plug other media companies? Do they support union recognition? Do they respect privacy where appropriate, or do they encourage dubious practices like doorstepping those who are grieving?

The media as a whole also has a poor reputation for employing people from a diverse range of backgrounds; what is this firm's record? What is it doing to improve it? The media also traditionally pays poorly and requires long, often unsocial hours. What allowances does the firm make for this? Are there any childcare allowances or taxis home for night workers?

Not for profit

This sector has a variety of names – voluntary and community sector, third sector and charity sector – though these can mean slightly different things depending on how wide your definition is. In the broadest sense it can mean anything from charities registered with the Charities Commission to small voluntary groups and NHS trusts. The organisation Working for a Charity, which offers training and career advice for those trying to work in this sector, uses the slightly narrower definition of "general charities". This term covers national charities such as Shelter and the NSPCC as well as smaller community groups. For an organisation to meet their definition of "general charity" it needs to be independent of government and business, be non profit-distributing, provide a wider public benefit that goes beyond any membership, or be a non-sacramental religious body or place of worship.

Whichever way you slice it, charities now play a large part in British society, covering activities such as advice, advocacy and fundraising for a bewildering and expanding range of issues. This sector is growing apace as an employer and provider of services and is increasingly having to become more businesslike in its operation as competition for people's sympathy and support becomes ever more intense. Currently there are about 169,000 general charities within the UK, and these employ around 611,000 paid workers (236,000 part time). Beyond this it is estimated that there are something like 925,000 unpaid trustees who take responsibility for the governance of individual charities. The latest citizenship survey found that in April to September 2007, 73% of adults in England and Wales had volunteered at least once in the last 12 months.

To work in the sector, you need resilience, stamina and commitment and a philosophical loyalty to the cause or charity you are working for. Until you hit senior management, the pay is not especially impressive, so your staying power may be tested, but should be buoyed by your commitment to what are, in capital letters, Good Works.

Roles

- Advice worker

This is a general title that can relate to any number of fields, be it housing, jobs, legal or social problems. **Advice workers** are employed by a range of organisations such as charities, citizens advice bureaux etc. Your job is to give impartial and confidential advice, guidance and information on whichever topic your organisation is involved in. The work can be quite varied: you might interview clients and assess their needs, write reports, mediate on behalf of a client or give them legal support for court appearances and tribunals. There are also other aspects of the job which can include interpreting legislation, doing research, compiling statistics and maintaining information systems and databases. You'll also probably spend quite a bit of time making and maintaining contact with other organisations that might be relevant either to a particular client's case or to the organisation's priorities as a whole.

Charity administrator

This can be an absolutely key position in the voluntary sector. A **charity administrator** can fulfil a number of different roles depending on the size of the organisation – financial, secretarial and human resources to name but a few. This can be a linchpin job, liaising between the organisation, the public and the media. You'll probably know more about the organisation than anyone else as, to varying degrees, you'll deal with the correspondence, aspects of recruitment, accounts, minutes and agendas for meetings, mailshots and publicity... Basically even if you're not directly involved in something it'll probably pass by or through you at some point.

Fundraiser

A **fundraiser** does exactly what you think. You'll be employed (directly or indirectly) by a charity or other body such as a school, church, hospital or political party to raise money from personal and/or corporate donations to meet an annual target. It's usually a paid post rather than voluntary and the activities can be quite wide-ranging, from organising campaigns and door-to-door collections to approaching businesses for sponsorship and coming up with novel fundraising ideas. You might also have responsibility for recruiting and coordinating volunteers, although this can also be a separate role.

Volunteer work organiser

Not a volunteer yourself, as a **volunteer work organiser** you sort out recruitment and scheduling and coordination of those who are. This also includes developing volunteering opportunities, finding the best jobs for each volunteer's skills, overseeing work and providing support and training where necessary. In addition you might be involved in creating publicity aimed at promoting volunteering, and might also have other duties relating to the general running of the charity, as many smaller organisations won't have the resources to fund this as a full-time position.

QUALIFICATIONS AND TRAINING There's no set road into the voluntary sector. Most are graduates, but the discipline is less important than demonstrable commitment. Having said that, some degrees, such as law and politics for example, are more useful than others. Postgraduate management qualifications are handy skills to bring, but recruiters will be more impressed by work experience, examples of voluntary work you have done in the past and a clear grasp of the issues the charity is dealing with and the political culture you're working in. There is a feeling that the sector is becoming more professional in a commercial sense, with graduate training schemes popping up occasionally, but training is more likely to come with experience than formal courses. In jobs where you are using technical or vocational skills, such as in education perhaps, you would be expected to be as qualified as someone working in that sector.

SALARY The average graduate starting salary for charity roles is £15,481.

Contacts

Charity Commission for England and Wales
PO Box 1227
Liverpool L69 3UG
(t) 0845 300 0218
(↗) www.charity-commission.gov.uk

Institute of Fundraising
Park Place
12 Lawn Lane
London SW8 1UD
(t) 020 7840 1000
(↗) www.institute-of-fundraising
.org.uk

National Council for Voluntary Organisations
Regent's Wharf
8 All Saints Street
London N1 9RL
(t) 020 7713 6161
(↗) www.ncvo-vol.org.uk

Working for a Charity
NCVO
Regent's Wharf
8 All Saints Street
London N1 9RL
(t) 020 7520 2512
(↗) www.wfac.org.uk

Online reading

SocietyGuardian SocietyGuardian.co.uk

Third Sector www.thirdsector.co.uk

VolResource: information for voluntary and community organisations www.volresource.org.uk

Workforce hub www.workforcehub.org.uk

CORPORATE CULTURE

Not-for-profit work is very much based on merit. If you've built up a bit of experience and proved yourself talented then you'll go places. The sector is just getting used to being commercialised so there is a greater keenness to reward those doing well to stop them heading towards the private sector in search of a good deal. If you're good and committed you'll find opportunities, even if this involves moving around within the sector.

Funding limitations can act as a brake on flexible working or job-shares (such flexibility usually costs firms), but the notion of work–life balance is gaining currency, which is slightly out of kilter with the sector's reliance on volunteers for a good deal of its work.

The presence of volunteers means it remains an informal sector to work in and unless you have a formal role that involves meeting clients or potential sponsors, then casual office wear is going to be the most appropriate.

Aid work can bring opportunities to travel with the job, to disaster areas for example, but competition for those roles can be intense so if you want to raise your chances of a job in the sector, go for the less glamorous jobs and you'll find the paths a whole lot clearer.

ETHICAL QUESTIONS

The organisation may be not for profit but what is the nature of the advice it is giving? Is it pushing an agenda that you don't agree with, for example religious, medical or political? Do you think the organisation's finances are being managed as well as they could be? These organisations need sufficient income to cover liabilities and grow assets, and not for profit can still mean that directors are paid large amounts.

Ask what the aim of the organisation is, do they have a mission statement or similar? What is their attitude towards groups which take an alternative viewpoint to their own?

Does the firm publish accounts or keep them secret? Is information on directors' remuneration available, or figures showing what proportion of income or donations are spent on its core activities? A visit might well be useful: do the offices look disproportionately lavish, or the cars in the car park overly luxurious? Is fundraising paid for on a commission basis? What is the attitude towards risk, does the firm believe in the cause it is raising funds for enough to take a risk?

Property

Property, from land through construction to sale, lease and maintenance is about more than just sketching an ideal living space or slapping a few bricks together; it's an intensely social sector. Whichever aspect you work in, understanding people's needs will be central. Money features heavily in all areas, from facilities management to town planning; budgeting and the efficient use of resources are major considerations, whether you're working in the public or private domain. All of these jobs in one way or another involve valuation, budgeting and costing. It can be a gigantic task: facilities managers working for organisations such as the NHS will find themselves responsible for the work, working environment and care of literally thousands of people, from providing clean sheets and meals to operating the telephone system and buying and maintaining valuable specialist equipment. To give it a financial dimension, 25% of the NHS budget each year is spent on estate and facilities management. And that's nothing compared to planning a whole town or regenerating part of one, where community groups, legislation, budgetary demands (with enormous amounts of cash at stake) as well as the demands of industry, leisure, housing and even preservation must play a part in any of your designs. If just reading this is giving you a stress headache then it's not the sector for you. These jobs all seem to entail a certain amount of aggravation, particularly those with a social aspect, such as housing, or those where a large amount of investment is involved, so don't necessarily expect a quiet life.

This is also a competitive sector, so personality will count as much as aptitude in certain roles, particularly those dealing with people on a regular basis such as housing officers and estate agents. Relevant experience is also highly valued in every area, so if you're considering this sector it's worth trying to get work experience; if you're thinking of a career change from a related profession it will stand you in good stead to have a relevant background, set of skills and knowledge base. Bear in mind that several roles, such as architecture and surveying, require long training periods; not only is competition fierce for jobs once you're qualified, you're going to have a bit of a battle for training places as well.

Roles

■ Architect

An **architect** uses creative and technical skills to plan and design buildings. Not only this but you also plan and manage the building process, choose the building materials and sort out planning permission, construction costs and so on. You might also be involved in restoration and conservation. Architecture is an interesting mixture of the creative and the hard-headed, because unless you're Frank Lloyd Wright you're going to have to pay close attention to the wishes of your clients – you'll very rarely be given a free hand to simply create a building, and many of your commissions can be mundane. Some architects even specialise in particular areas of buildings, for example designing public bathrooms... Finding innovative solutions to design problems, compromising and fitting form and function together are the most challenging aspects of an architect's job.

■ Architectural technologist

The **architectural technologist** works alongside architects and other construction professionals and is a specialist in the sound technological performance of buildings. Skills will probably include managing and using computer-aided design, preparing and undertaking feasibility studies, and surveying and coming up with design solutions. Essentially you ensure that architectural designs fulfil performance, production, regulatory and procurement criteria and specify materials and assembly techniques. You might also coordinate and monitor construction and development, making sure it stays faithful to the specifications agreed with the client and meets the agreed standards, deadlines, cost and quality.

■ Building surveyor

Surveyors carry out structural surveys of properties, reporting on their condition and valuation. They give advice on all aspects of property and construction, work on site during the construction of new buildings and advise on repairs, maintenance, improvements and alterations to be made to existing buildings. As such, building surveyors are employed by a wide range of public and private bodies. Other surveying roles deal particularly with the concerns, legislation and practicalities of working with different types of land and usage; they include urban general practice surveyor, rural practice surveyor and planning and development surveyor.

■ Estate agent

As an **estate agent** you are responsible for the sale, letting, management and valuation of properties, whether they're shops, houses, flats, farms, factories or offices. You'll liaise with clients and organisations concerned with property such as mortgage providers and solicitors.

■ Estate manager/Land agent

An **estate manager** works for large organisations and estate owners, taking care of all the land-based business. You are concerned with the use and development of the land, ensuring it's used efficiently and profitably, and will advise on issues such as forestry, agricultural use, building and accounts. A single estate might include a range of different usages such as recreational land, private dwellings, tenanted land, woodland, farms and shooting facilities. Because of this need to manage and oversee all these different aspects you might be employed either by the estate owners themselves or through a firm of chartered surveyors with a management contract for the estate.

■ Housing manager/officer

As a **housing officer** you can work for a variety of property providers, including housing associations and local authorities, and your role will depend on your employer's priorities. For example, working in the rented accommodation sector you'd be involved in managing and maintaining properties, sorting out rent arrears and repairs, processing applications for housing and allocating property. You might be working with social and welfare agencies, which will entail understanding the way the benefits system works, and you might work for a specific group such as elderly, disabled or homeless people. You may also find that your role involves a lot of advisory work (see the Not for profit section on page 168 for more on that line of work).

■ Town planner

The role of a **town planner** is all about deciding on and managing land use, balancing the need for housing, leisure and agricultural space as well as for industrial development and transport networks. Planners play a substantial role in urban regeneration schemes. Research and design are key elements as all the needs or potential needs of a community must be considered, as must legislation and practicalities such as cost.

QUALIFICATIONS AND TRAINING Architects must take a five-year course which is punctuated with a year of professional experience after the third year, and another at the end, bringing the total to seven years. The courses are increasingly broad and include architectural history, building control, law and a whole range of related subjects. But to become an architect you must be registered with the Architects Registration Board, which approves some, but not all, courses, so check that the one you are considering isn't a ringer. "Architectural studies" could be a giveaway that it's not the real thing. The Royal Institute of British Architects offers a series of exam courses for mature entrants with several years' experience of working in an architectural practice. Once in work, the industry requires continuous professional development (CPD) training.

Architectural technologists must have a degree in architectural technology or the built environment or a level 4 NVQ approved by the Chartered Institute of Architectural Technologists. To be able to work, you need to complete the professional and occupational performance record, run by BIAT, which normally takes around two years and is polished off with an assessment interview.

An accredited course is also needed for **surveying**, this time approved by the Royal Institution of Chartered Surveyors. Once past that hurdle (for a degree or a diploma), you must embark on three years of practical on-the-job training under the auspices of the assessment of professional competence, before facing a final interview.

A **housing manager** must attain the Chartered Institute of Housing's professional qualification. If you have at least one A-level and four GCSEs (C and above), then you can start the HNC in housing studies on day release, followed by two years' part-time study for the institute's professional qualification. If you don't have the A-level, you can pre-qualify with a BTEC national certificate in housing studies and then start the HNC.

The qualifications system for **town and country planning** increasingly reflects the specialisms developing in the planning industry, with courses concentrating specifically on urban design, environmental impact and transport issues. Most courses, though, offer at least one year of training in the general skills of town and country planning, from ensuring better quality of living in inner cities, to maintaining services in rural areas. From then on, courses might focus on urban planning, town and regional planning, city and regional planning or civic design. Others will be more closely allied with property management and real estate. After two years in practice, many will sit further exams for professional qualifications such as membership of the Royal Town Planning Institute or the Chartered Institute of Housing.

An **estate agent** doesn't actually need professional qualifications to practise, but both the National Association of Estate Agents and the RICS offer professional qualifications, NVQs and the equivalent in sales, management and letting and these entitle you to membership of the associations. They're not essential, but are increasingly useful. An **estate manager** doesn't legally need a degree or a diploma either, but qualification as a surveyor is increasingly handy.

SALARY The average graduate starting salary in property is £19,839.

Online reading
The Architect's Journal www.ajplus.co.uk
Construction Plus www.constructionplus.co.uk
Building magazine www.building.co.uk
Inside Housing www.insidehousing.co.uk

Contacts

Architects Registration Board
8 Weymouth Street
London W1W 5BU

(t) 020 7580 5861

(↗) www.arb.org.uk

Association of Building Engineers
Lutyens House
Billing Brook Road
Weston Favell
Northampton NN3 8NW

(t) 0845 126 1058

(↗) www.abe.org.uk

British Association of Landscape Industries
Landscape House
Stoneleigh Park
National Agricultural Centre
Warwickshire CV8 2LG

(t) 0870 770 4971

(↗) www.bali.co.uk

Chartered Institute of Architectural Technologists
397 City Road
London EC1V 1NH

(t) 020 7278 2206

(↗) www.ciat.org.uk

Chartered Institute of Housing
Octavia House
Westwood Way
Coventry CV4 8JP

(t) 024 7685 1700

(↗) www.cih.org

CITB ConstructionSkills
Bircham Newton
Kings Lynn
Norfolk PE31 6RH

(t) 01485 577577

(↗) www.citb.org.uk

Landscape Design Trust
Bank Chambers
1 London Road
Redhill
Surrey RH1 1LY

(t) 01737 779257

(↗) www.landscape.co.uk

Landscape Institute
33 Great Portland Street
London W1W 8QG

(t) 020 7299 4500

(↗) www.landscapeinstitute.org

National Association of Estate Agents
Arbon House
21 Jury Street
Warwick CV34 4EH

(t) 01926 496800

(↗) www.naea.co.uk

National Housing Federation
Lion Court
25 Procter Street
London WC1V 6NY

(t) 020 7067 1010

(↗) www.housing.org.uk

Royal Institute of British Architects
66 Portland Place
London W1B 1AD

(t) 020 7580 5533

(↗) www.riba.org

Royal Institution of Chartered Surveyors
RICS Contact Centre
Surveyor Court
Westwood Way
Coventry CV4 8JE

(t) 0870 333 1600

(↗) www.rics.org

Royal Town Planning Institute
41 Botolph Lane
London EC3R 8DL
(t) 020 7929 9494
(↗) www.rtpi.org.uk

Town and Country Planning Association
17 Carlton House Terrace
London SW1Y 5AS
(t) 020 7930 8903
(↗) www.tcpa.org.uk

CORPORATE CULTURE

The corporate culture depends entirely on which part of the industry you are in. The underlying philosophy of an estate agent can be wholly different to that of a housing officer and neither job really compares to that of an architect. So the breadth is too wide for glib conclusions. Safe to say that you'll be dealing with people's lives in a very direct way, in the environment in which they live, and whether your job involves building it, managing it or selling it, it's not something to be taken lightly.

ETHICAL QUESTIONS

A firm's attitude to sustainable materials and construction techniques should be key, as should its attitude to energy saving both during construction and in the design of how a building functions once built. The safety of materials and structures is also of paramount concern both during and after construction.

What approach would be taken if a client wanted to build in a place of outstanding natural beauty, particularly when the structure would affect visitors' experience of the area? How are disputes between architect and client resolved?

How does the company approach the responsibilities of a landlord to a tenant, and vice versa? In surveying, how does a firm balance its responsibility to the client and to the public? Given that the work of surveyors usually leads to the development of land, how much consideration is given to the environmental impact and sustainability of the development? Are the costs of environmental protection considered an essential part of evaluating a project? Does the firm use environmental experts to help them with these issues?

Retail

Retail covers buying and selling everything you can think of in as many different ways. E-tailing (online shopping) is the new buzzword: IT graduates are no longer employed just to sort out store hardware and head-office software and systems, but are increasingly being used to develop ever more hi-tech (though still user-friendly) ways of promoting, selling and providing products to the customer without them ever leaving their homes. Internet shopping is now worth around £21.4 billion a year. Consumer research is also a growing area, as retailers seek to find better and more personalised ways to target consumers.

If you want a career in retail you'll probably have to spend some time on the shopfloor, even if your ambitions are focused on a head-office role such as merchandising. Most employers consider it essential to have a good understanding of how retailing in general, and the business you're joining in particular, works. Of course, you might be recruited directly into a head-office post, but you may well find that your employer will still insist on some shopfloor experience as part of your training.

In the more traditional retail outlets (let's call them "shops"), which still account for the vast majority of the retail trade, you'll need to have an outgoing personality, excellent communication skills and the ability to get on with everyone from warehouse staff to the head honcho. A quick mind and the ability to problem-solve in a sometimes chaotic situation (think January sales) also helps, and you'll need mental and physical stamina for those eight-till-late shopping days. Most of all, you'll have a good eye for business.

Roles

- Customer services manager

In the most basic sense the role of the **customer services manager** entails making sure a store satisfies its customers' needs and keeps them happy. It actually has a variety of settings, from head office to the sharp end on the shopfloor. This means that the precise roles will vary depending on your exact remit. You could be handling face-to-face customer enquiries or developing a customer services policy to cover the entire organisation. You'll be happy dealing with people and good at understanding their needs; communication skills are key.

■ Retail pharmacist

Retail pharmacists work in independent pharmacies, pharmacy chains or supermarket pharmacies, giving healthcare advice and dispensing prescription and non-prescription medicines. Processing prescriptions and dispensing medicines are the jobs people mostly associate pharmacists with but there are other aspects to the role, including managing people, controlling medicines and stock, liaising with medical representatives and keeping statistical and financial records.

■ Retail buyer

As a **retail buyer** you find, select and buy in merchandise that matches your store's ethos and customer base. You need to make sure that it's within the price range of the customer demographic, is bought in sufficient quantity to supply demand, and meets the quality standards of the shop.

This is a key job and can be quite stressful. A store's profitability can rely heavily on good buying policies – if you misjudge your target consumer you're going to have an awful lot of unsold lurex flares on your hands. It's a responsible job and you'll find you have quite a lot of independence, which can add to the pressure. Typically you'll be working at least a season in advance, so all your Christmas buying, for example, will be done while people are swanning around in flip-flops. The job includes visiting manufacturers and suppliers and going to trade fairs to decide on and negotiate for new ranges of merchandise. In addition you'll write reports, analyse sales figures, make sales forecasts, get customer feedback and react to customer demand.

■ Retail manager

The role of the **retail manager** varies according to whether you're working for a chain store, department store, supermarket or small independent shop. If you're employed by a really big store you might just be responsible for one particular department, or you might be in charge of a whole shop. Either way you'll be overseeing the day-to-day running of your particular patch.

You'll be trying to improve performance and sales, and are likely to be set daily or weekly targets by your head office. To meet targets you'll be expected to find the best ways of selling stock quickly and profitably. Managing and motivating staff play a big part in this, so again you'll have to be good with people. Generally speaking you'll be responsible for things like overseeing stock levels and making decisions concerning control and management of supply and storage, as well as making sure that stock you order is delivered at the most convenient time and can be accommodated in the shop. You'll also have to analyse sales figures and make forecasts relating to stock ordering, organise promotions and displays, and even monitor the competition. It's a multi-faceted role and can be stressful.

- Retail merchandiser

As a **retail merchandiser** you look after the nitty-gritty of product supply, ensuring that the right amounts are bought and that they appear in the shops at the right time and in the correct quantities. It is also your job to determine how many lines should be bought and in what quantities and you will decide how much money should be spent. You'll work with the buyers to monitor performance, forecast trends and plan stock levels. You also control the prices of the stock, setting initial prices and deciding on promotions and markdowns. The job involves a lot of analysis and numerical work, keeping an eye on performance rates, managing stock distribution, forecasting and budgeting.

QUALIFICATIONS AND TRAINING Graduate schemes will give you training in most of these roles, notably buying and merchandising, but increasingly business and marketing degrees have become valuable assets. Anyone wanting to become a **retail buyer** or **merchandiser** should have a degree, and a degree in marketing, business studies or economics will be especially useful. However, experience is the most important thing and any connection to the business, even time spent as a Saturday shop assistant, will show commitment to and understanding of the business. People-pleasing and people-managing skills are particularly useful for the roles of **retail manager** and **customer services manager**. These are jobs where it really does pay to have served your time in other positions as this will give you an enormous insight into behaviour on both sides of the till, which is invaluable in all areas of retail management.

The one job that really does need serious qualifications is that of a **retail pharmacist**, where, frankly, you need to know your stuff. As with hospital pharmacists, you need to take a four-year pharmacy degree, do an examined pre-registration year of experience and become a registered member of the Royal Pharmaceutical Society of Great Britain or the Pharmaceutical Society of Northern Ireland. Of course as you're dealing with the general public and are a frontline medical service your communication skills also need to be up to the mark, so retail experience will again stand you in good stead.

SALARY The average graduate starting salary in retail is £15,616.

Online reading
The Grocer www.thegrocer.co.uk
Retail Week www.retail-week.com
Graduate to Retail www.graduatetoretail.org

Contacts

British Retail Consortium
2nd Floor
21 Dartmouth Street
London SW1H 9BP

(t) 020 7854 8900

(↗) www.brc.org.uk

British Shops and Stores Association
Middleton House
2 Main Road
Middleton Cheney
Banbury OX17 2TN

(t) 01295 712277

(↗) www.british-shops.co.uk

Chartered Institute of Purchasing and Supply
Easton House
Easton on the Hill
Stamford
Lincs PE9 3NZ

(t) 01780 756777

(↗) www.cips.org

Institute of Customer Service
2 Castle Court
St Peter's Street
Colchester CO1 1EW

(t) 01206 571716

(↗) www.instituteof
customerservice.com

Pharmaceutical Society of Northern Ireland
73 University Street
Belfast BT7 1HL

(t) 028 9032 6927

(↗) www.psni.org.uk

Royal Pharmaceutical Society of Great Britain
1 Lambeth High Street
London SE1 7JN

(t) 020 7735 9141

(↗) www.rpsgb.org.uk

CORPORATE CULTURE

This is a sector in which it is possible to work your way up to a head-office or management role from the shopfloor; it's an industry that relies upon a close and constantly renewed connection between the shopfloor and management decisions, so the experience is useful. It is also a sector that's all about customers, business and the face of the company, so the vibe is businesslike, with a lot of office work and meeting clients involved, so you'll usually need to look smart. Retail depends a lot on loyalty, from customers and from employees, so the way you're expected to dress will say a lot about the people you're working for. Some might demand suits, others smart casual. There may be an exception to this if the store's ethos is wildly at odds with businesslike attire, but usually being presentable is the way forward – after all there's a lot of money at stake and suppliers will need to take you seriously. If you're working on the shopfloor as a customer services representative or manager there may be a uniform. If not, looking smart is important – you're representing the face of the company and trying to reassure customers. If it's a clothing store you may be required to wear a certain amount of the shop's merchandise; this will normally be subsidised.

The competitiveness of the sector, both in getting jobs and in business strategy, means that constant research is key. From the moment you get your first interview to the minute you're carried from the director's chair you should be keeping abreast of the latest retail gossip. Trade journals such as the Grocer, Retail Week and Marketing Week are essential tools. If you're talented you're likely to be promoted well within an organisation once you've had your training. This may be contingent on your experiencing different aspects of the organisation and often being a store manager will be the first step on the ladder to becoming a buyer. However, there's no set trajectory – organisations do have hierarchies and certain companies like their employees to have been with them for a certain amount of time before promotion. But in a sector that's all about maximising sales and profits, organisations work hard to ensure that anyone with the potential to do this is made to feel valued.

There are, of course, perks to be had from working in retail, and for some these go beyond a 10% discount. Buyers will usually find that overseas travel is a regular part of the job. There are trade fairs and suppliers to visit, so the work will take you all over. Merchandisers may also get to travel, particularly if they're working closely with a buying team. In other roles you're unlikely to travel as part of your regular job unless you work for a multinational, in which case there may be visits to other stores to observe different strategies, as well as possible training programmes.

It's not a typical 9–5 sector. Your job doesn't end when the shop closes, so if you don't want to work shifts, overtime or funny hours this is not the one for you. Buyers and merchandisers are most likely to be getting out and about, despite also spending a fair amount of time in the office. All the other roles have rotas to adhere to and will have to be in the shop for the specified hours, so there's not a lot of scope for breaking free.

ETHICAL QUESTIONS

There has been much criticism in recent years about how the supermarkets have a cast-iron grip over their suppliers, often to the extent that they effectively control whether their suppliers survive in business or not. Therefore asking about the quality of the relationship with suppliers should be a key issue. Standards of pay and union recognition are other considerations. Attitudes to waste reduction and pollution (packaging, carrier bags, road haulage etc) are also important.

Does the firm have codes of conduct relating both to its own business and its suppliers covering human issues like poverty wages, child labour and poor working conditions? If so, are the codes published, and have they been checked and validated by independent experts? Ask whether lines of fairly traded goods are carried, and whether the company is a member of any fair trade organisations. What is done with foodstuffs that pass their "best before" date? Are they just thrown away or does the shop support local organisations that pass food on to people in need? How do prices compare with those for identical products sold in other countries, in Europe or America for example? How does the company react to reports from bodies like Corporate Watch which claims that when a large supermarket opens it results in the closure of every village shop within seven miles?

For all retailers, consider the nature of their business and the products they sell. Does the timber on sale come from a sustainable source accredited by a reputable body like the Forest Stewardship Council? Does the company make efforts to address safety issues like the use of potentially hazardous chemicals in its products? Has it made any commitments to improve in any areas?

In internet retail, does a firm use aggressive techniques like pop-ups or misleading banners, or even data-mining techniques to target potential customers? How does it treat information gleaned from customers? Is it sold to third parties, or used for any purpose other than that for which it was originally intended?

Science

Obviously there is a certain amount of running around in white coats, sporting thick black-rimmed specs and wild hair, shouting, "That's it! What a fool I've been! If I reverse the polarity, why…". This, however, is not all you have to look forward to if you decide you'd like to work in science. For a start, you'll pretty much have your choice of area: industry, education, medicine, police work, pharmaceuticals, environment… the list goes on. Of course this will depend on your qualifications and specialities, but there is a wide range of jobs available, all of them desperate for new young scientific talent. Science is big business. Every day, over £9 million is spent on pharmaceutical research and development by the UK pharmaceutical industry. The whole sector is a big employer, with over 150,000 professional scientists working in the UK.

It's not all drug development either. You could work for the Ministry of Defence or for medical science. Medical science has an enormous array of scientific posts, from audiological scientist to medical physicist, only a few of which are described below because of the sheer number. And of course bomb-making isn't the only thing the Ministry of Defence has scientists for. For example the Met Office is one of their branches, employing meteorologists for weather prediction, modelling and research into issues such as global warming.

So there's enormous scope to fulfil your own personal preoccupations and interests if you choose to become a professional scientist. From producing makeup to mining for oil, scientists play an increasingly large part in the scheme of things.

Roles

■ Analytical chemist

An **analytical chemist** analyses the chemical makeup of substances, which could be for forensic, chemical, process development or drug-testing purposes, to name but a few. Whether you are analysing new drugs or checking food products you'll be working on new methods of analysis and interpreting data, and you may be part of the team that puts together the supporting documents for licensing applications for pharmaceuticals.

- Biomedical scientist

A **biomedical scientist** is still sometimes referred to by the old title of medical laboratory scientific officer, but the role remains the same. Biomedical scientists work in a clinical setting, carrying out tests on human samples (blood, tissue, saliva, urine, faeces etc) to help identify illness and assess treatment. You'll normally specialise in one particular area such as medical microbiology, clinical chemistry, transfusion science, haematology, histopathology, cytology, immunology or virology.

- Forensic scientist

The job of a **forensic scientist** mainly involves examining objects at crime scenes that might have trace materials on them, so you could be examining everything from bone shards to handwriting. If the case concerning the crime gets to court, your impartial findings might well make up part of the evidence for the prosecution or defence. The sort of work you do will depend on the area of forensics you work in: chemistry, biology, or drugs and toxicology.

In general these three areas deal with different sorts of crime. Chemistry tends to be associated with crimes against property, such as burglary and arson. Biology is linked to crimes against people such as assault, rape and murder. Drugs and toxicology looks at a range of issues including poisoning, alcohol levels (in drink-driving offences for example) and the presence of controlled substances. So work can be quite different depending on which area you're employed in, though in all jobs you'll need to analyse and interpret data, keep records and be prepared for cross-examination.

- Medical physicist

Medical physicists use analytical and applied science techniques alongside the knowledge and skills of other medical staff to diagnose and treat illness. This role can cover anything from managing radiotherapy to researching, developing and evaluating new analytical techniques or ensuring that treatment is accurate and safe and giving advice on radiation protection. The work uses high-tech implants and/or computer-aided techniques including radiotherapy, x-ray imaging, ultrasound, tomography, radiology, nuclear magnetic resonance imaging (MRI) and lasers.

- Process developer

A job in **process development** entails working to get the best performance possible from industrial manufacturing systems. This might involve investigating and putting into practice ways to improve product quality and quantity and reducing the costs of running the process. You might also develop new processes, make sure processing is safe, test to ensure reliability of the process and see a new process all the way through from research stage to prototype, pilot and full-scale use.

■ Product developer

Product developers work alongside research scientists pretty much across the whole of manufacturing industry, developing ideas and new research into new products or improved versions of products already manufactured. Obviously this involves investigating areas for development, making prototypes, liaising with other scientists, researchers and technicians, and analysing data.

■ Research scientist

As a **research scientist** you would specialise in one area, such as life science, maths, medicine or physical sciences, setting up experiments and fieldwork on your chosen point of investigation and publishing the results. Depending on whether you work in an academic setting or in industry this might be research for its own sake or with a particular product or process in mind.

■ Toxicologist

Work in this field is about identifying and studying the harmful effects of chemicals, biological materials and radiation on living systems and the environment and working out how these effects can be minimised or avoided altogether. As a **toxicologist** you might be assessing the effect of industrial chemicals on the environment and human health around a factory, looking at potential effects of a new drug, investigating food safety... any number of things. It will normally involve setting up field experiments and observations, isolating harmful substances, working with statistics, doing research and giving advice on handling different substances.

QUALIFICATIONS AND TRAINING These jobs are all essentially graduate posts, and a science degree is the minimum for most, despite the amount of training that you will often be given on the job. However, the exact relation of the degree subject to your chosen field will vary. A **forensic scientist** will need a life or physical science degree as a minimum requirement, and subjects such as analytical and forensic chemistry and molecular biology are particularly useful. A postgraduate qualification is even better. This is definitely a role that will involve further training to build on your earlier academic experience. It is also fiercely competitive, so anything in the region of an upper second or first in your degree will give you an advantage.

A **toxicologist**, on the other hand, needs a more precisely defined degree subject, namely a biological degree with a good chemistry grounding. Large companies with contract research facilities are likely to be the main hirers in this field, and they'll be looking to cherry-pick the best graduates, so training schemes are possible avenues not only for employment but also for skills development, provided you've got the paper to prove you're worthy.

Analytical chemists need a good degree in chemistry or another science that has involved the study of analytical science. Research positions will need postgraduate qualifications and the graduate recruitment programmes for big manufacturers tend to be highly competitive, so it's always worth going that extra mile with your qualifications.

A **research scientist** usually needs at least an MSc, possibly a PhD, plus post-doctoral research (particularly true of academic jobs), whereas a **biomedical scientist** needs to apply for state registration, so the best degree to get is a biomedical science degree approved by the Health Professions Council. You'll then need to do a minimum of a year's on-the-job training to qualify for state registration. If you've got a non-approved degree that's still in a relevant subject you might qualify for state registration after doing a postgraduate diploma followed by at least two years of on-the-job training. If you're entering as a graduate with no experience you'll need to go through a period of graduate traineeship, which usually lasts one to two years, although it can be longer.

Medical physicists, of whom the NHS is a major employer, also require impressive credentials, including a good degree in a physical science or an engineering subject. You then need to be state registered and go through different grades of training, which for the initial grade, A, takes at least two years.

After all that, **product development** seems like light relief, "only" requiring you to have at least a good science or engineering degree. Again, some of the best training is through the competitive graduate recruitment schemes, so any experience, internships, placements, enthusiasm and extra qualifications you can scrape together will be an advantage.

SALARY The average graduate starting salary in the science sector is £18,889.

Contacts

Association of the British Pharmaceutical Industry
12 Whitehall
London SW1A 2DY
(t) 0870 890 4333
(↗) www.abpi.org.uk

Biotechnology and Biological Sciences Research Council
Polaris House
North Star Avenue
Swindon SN2 1UH
(t) 01793 413200
(↗) www.bbsrc.ac.uk

British Association for the Advancement of Science
Wellcome Wolfson Building
165 Queen's Gate
London SW7 5HE
(t) 0870 770 7101
(↗) www.the-ba.net

British Nuclear Medicine Society
Regent House
291 Kirkdale
London SE26 4QD
(t) 020 8676 7864
(↗) www.bnms.org.uk

British Toxicology Society

PO Box 249
Macclesfield SK11 6FT

(t) 01625 267881

(↗) www.thebts.org

Defence Science and Technology Laboratory

Porton Down
Salisbury
Wilts SP4 0JQ

(t) 01980 613121

(↗) www.dstl.gov.uk

Forensic Science Service

Trident Court
2920 Solihull Parkway
Birmingham Business Park
Birmingham B37 7YN

(t) 0121 329 5200

(↗) www.forensic.gov.uk

Forensic Science Society

Clarke House
18a Mount Parade
Harrogate HG1 1BX

(t) 01423 506068

(↗) www.forensic-science-society.org.uk

Health Professions Council

Park House
184 Kennington Park Road
London SE11 4BU

(t) 020 7582 0866

(↗) www.hpc-uk.org

Health Protection Agency

7th Floor
Holborn Gate
330 High Holborn
London WC1V 7PP

(t) 020 7759 2700

(↗) www.hpa.org.uk

Human Fertilisation and Embryology Authority

21 Bloomsbury Street
London WC1B 3HF

(t) 020 7291 8200

(↗) www.hfea.gov.uk

Institute of Biology

9 Red Lion Court
London EC4A 3EF

(t) 020 7936 5900

(↗) www.iob.org

Institute of Biomedical Science

12 Coldbath Square
London EC1R 5HL

(t) 020 7713 0214

(↗) www.ibms.org

Institute of Clinical Research

Thames House
Mere Park
Dedmere Road
Marlow
Buckinghamshire SL7 1PB

(t) 01628 899755

(↗) www.instituteof
clinicalresearch.org

Institute of Physics

76 Portland Place
London W1B 1NT

(t) 020 7470 4800

(↗) www.iop.org

Institute of Science in Society

PO Box 51885
London NW2 9DH

(t) 020 8452 2729

(↗) www.i-sis.org.uk

Medical Research Council

20 Park Crescent
London W1B 4AL

(t) 020 7636 5422

(↗) www.mrc.ac.uk

Royal Society
6–9 Carlton House Terrace
London SW1Y 5AG
(t) 020 7451 2500
(↗) www.royalsoc.ac.uk

Royal Society of Chemistry
Burlington House
Piccadilly
London W1J 0BA
(t) 020 7437 8656
(↗) www.rsc.org

Online reading
Guardian Unlimited Science www.guardian.co.uk/science
Nature www.nature.com
New Scientist www.newscientist.com

CORPORATE CULTURE

Science employers are increasingly looking for all-rounders. Just as in IT, it's no longer enough to be a talented boffin – if you've spent years alone in your bedroom you're unlikely to be anyone's dream candidate. Teamwork and communication skills are definitely on the list of things you need to cultivate, but no matter how casual the company appears to be, attention to detail is king.

Your work will usually keep you in your particular lab or department, so you'd better be sure that the ethos matches yours, whether it's simply allowing you to wear Simpsons braces under your lab coat or sharing your intense political beliefs. There may be opportunities to escape and collect samples or do research abroad, but all roads will eventually lead to the lab. There are always conferences, however, for those in research or fast-developing manufacturing roles, so you might see a bit of travel if you've done your lab hours first. Scientific skills are also transferable, so there may be opportunities for working abroad.

Experience is extremely important in this sector, so it can take a while to work your way into senior positions. Biomedical scientists, for example, tend to need professional qualifications such as a fellowship of the Institute of Biomedical Science in order to get anywhere really senior, and to gain fellowship you need to have a higher degree or have written a thesis. That said, it's also a sector in which talent is important, so if you have the qualifications there's no reason why you can't get promotion fairly quickly after completing your trainee period (although this might last up to two years).

ETHICAL QUESTIONS

The ethics of scientific research centre on obtaining repeatable results within a system of peer review: your work is evaluated by your fellow scientists. Within each area of research there will be ethical issues to consider related to the subject matter under examination, the reason for undertaking the research in the first place, and the anticipated outcome. Science does not function in a vacuum: it can never be completely separated from the culture within which it operates and the values of that culture. Animal testing and the use of toxic chemicals are key areas of concern here, as is the more philosophical and ethical application of some scientific advances, such as genetics.

Always ask who is funding the research and why? Is it for a positive end goal? How does the company or institution secure funding? How are resources allocated within the company, by looking for the greatest potential profit or greatest potential good? Does the institution or company have a code of conduct covering its approaches to chemical use and animal testing? Has the code been reviewed by an independent expert? Is it accessible to funding bodies and members of the public? What would they do if research showed the opposite outcome to the one expected, would they bury the study or publish the results?

Social care

Linked with healthcare and local government, social care sits towards the sharp end of both, dealing as it does with those who are most vulnerable or in danger in our society: children and families at risk or in need, people with learning difficulties and people with physical disabilities or mental health problems. Social work is one of the most rewarding of employment sectors precisely because it is an area in which you have a chance to make a real difference; not just to individuals but to society as a whole. It is an essential sector which desperately needs all the bright young recruits it can get, but the comparatively poor remuneration, emotional stress and heavy workload make social work an unattractive option compared to many commercial sectors. To redress that situation, the sector is now making more efforts to compete with the commercial sector by offering better training and promotion prospects for the talented and committed.

You will need to be open-minded and ready to challenge your own preconceptions and prejudices as well as the prejudices of others. You'll need sometimes infinite reservoirs of patience and emotional resilience and have the ability to leave the job behind at the end of each day. And you'll need a sense of perspective, to put your analytical skills into practice in a rational way in sometimes stressful situations.

Roles

■ Day-care officer

Day-care officers work in day-care centres for the elderly (which can be open five to seven days a week), helping people with things like going to the toilet, bathing, washing clothes and eating as well as organising social activities like games or movement classes and working out individual programmes for clients. There's a lot of paperwork involved, as the progress of individuals is monitored and assessed.

■ Race equality worker

As a **race equality worker** you focus on promoting racial equality and reducing discrimination within workplaces, organisations, communities and the education system. Your tasks will include compiling statistics, offering advice, acting as an advocate for members of minority groups and liaising with other groups.

■ Social worker

Social workers operate as part of a team assessing the needs of various vulnerable groups in the community and finding appropriate solutions. The work can be varied, and social workers usually specialise in a particular field such as children and families, which includes **child care/protection** and **fostering and adoption**; helping people with physical disabilities to live independently; care of the elderly; or supporting people with mental health problems as a **mental-health outreach worker**.

Child care/protection is a specialised role within social work, and one that can involve physical and emotional risks. You'll be working with children who are damaged in some way, having gone through some form of abuse, be it physical, emotional, sexual or connected to substance misuse. Some will have learning difficulties, physical disabilities or mental health problems. Your work will involve visiting children and their families or escorting children when they spend time with parents or family. You'll also have to write reports, records and letters, liaise with other professionals and plan and review procedures and progress; you may also have to attend juvenile court hearings.

Fostering and adoption social work can be two separate roles, but ultimately it's all about finding out whether families or couples are suitable for placing children with, either on a short- to long-term basis as a foster family or permanently through adoption. You'll also provide ongoing support for families who take on children.

A **mental-health outreach worker** specialises in supporting people with long-term mental health problems. Your work is aimed at helping them adapt to ordinary life within the community by developing coping skills so that they can avoid being institutionalised in a hospital or hostel. You'll visit clients daily and help them with everyday tasks such as collecting benefits or making meals. You'll also do things like monitor their progress and any medication they are taking.

■ Substance misuse worker

The role of **substance misuse worker** is a youth work position that involves working in a team to provide specialist services to children, young adults and their families who have substance misuse problems. You'll liaise with a range of different social work areas, giving advice, identifying those at risk, developing and delivering constructive intervention through group and individual work, providing support, maintaining records and doing a host of other tasks. It's a big job and can be very involving.

■ Youth-offending team officer

This is a very challenging job working with young people mostly between the ages of 10–18. The role of the **youth-offending service officer** is to help prevent young people from committing crimes and to encourage offenders and their parents or guardians to examine possible causes and behaviour so that repeat offences can be avoided. Daily duties might include involving your charges in constructive activities or finding them a job or training opportunity. You'll also write reports on the young person's background for the courts and supervise community sentences.

QUALIFICATIONS AND TRAINING This is a tough sector, and although some of the roles don't need paper qualifications at entry point, a combination of technical knowledge and experience, not to mention soft skills, are essential prerequisites. **Day-care officers**, for example, don't need any specific qualifications, but communication skills are of paramount importance. Local authorities are the biggest recruiters and any further training will usually be given on the job. Likewise, **race equality workers** don't need specific qualifications, as personal qualities and experience are considered key, but a degree in law, psychology, business, management, education, social work, community work, public administration, sociology or social sciences can be helpful. Your key here is going to be interest and commitment, as well as any experience you've gleaned previously. Any training on policy and management will usually be given or sponsored by the body for whom you're working.

Social workers, **child care/protection workers** and **fostering and adoption social workers** need all the personal skills, commitment and experience mentioned above, but you also need official qualifications alongside. You'll need a degree in social work approved by the General Social Care Council; this replaces the old diploma in social work, the DipSW, and is a three-year programme. Social workers are now required to reregister every three years, and in order to do so, must have completed either 90 hours or 15 days of post registration training and learning (PRTL) within the three-year registration period. **Youth-offending service officers** will generally need a degree in social work but some employers accept nationally recognised youth work or teaching qualifications. Again, training will be given and encouraged but precisely what that is will depend on your employer and your client group. You will be expected to complete the service's professional certificate in effective practice.

Although it doesn't necessarily require a social work degree, to become a **mental-health outreach worker** you'll find that it's essential to have at least one year's experience of working with people with mental health problems, and you'll probably need to have further training. NVQs in social care or relevant subjects are good, and you can either get them before entry or work towards them on the job. NVQs and serious previous experience are also the way forward for **substance misuse workers**; you'll need to have an NVQ level 3 in social care, or equivalent. You'll also need two years' experience of working with young people, liaising with staff from different agencies and substance misuse-related work.

SALARY The average graduate starting salary for social service professionals is £21,563.

Contacts

Advice UK
12th Floor
New London Bridge House
25 London Bridge Street
London SE1 9SG

(t) 020 7407 4070

(↗) www.adviceuk.org.uk

British Association for Counselling and Psychotherapy
BACP House
15 St John's Business Park
Lutterworth
Leicestershire LE17 4HB

(t) 0870 443 5252

(↗) www.bacp.co.uk

British Association of Social Workers
16 Kent Street
Birmingham B5 6RD

(t) 0121 622 3911

(↗) www.basw.co.uk

Care Council for Wales
South Gate House
Wood Street
Cardiff CF10 1EW

(t) 029 2022 6257

(↗) www.ccwales.org.uk

Citizens Advice
Myddleton House
115–123 Pentonville Road
London N1 9LZ

(t) 020 7833 2181

(↗) www.citizensadvice.org.uk

Commission for Racial Equality
St Dunstan's House
201–211 Borough High Street
London SE1 1GZ

(t) 020 7939 0000

(↗) www.cre.gov.uk

Commission for Social Care Inspection
33 Greycoat Street
London SW1P 2QF

(t) 020 7979 2000

(↗) www.csci.org.uk

Communities Scotland
Thistle House
91 Haymarket Terrace
Edinburgh EH12 5HE

(t) 0131 313 0044

(↗) www.communities
scotland.gov.uk

General Social Care Council
Goldings House
2 Hay's Lane
London SE1 2HB

(t) 020 7397 5100

(↗) www.gscc.org.uk

National Youth Agency
Eastgate House
19–23 Humberstone Road
Leicester LE5 3GJ

(t) 0116 242 7350

(↗) www.nya.org.uk

Northern Ireland Social Care Council

7th Floor
Millennium House
19–25 Great Victoria Street
Belfast BT2 7AQ

(t) 028 9041 7600
(↗) www.niscc.info

Scottish Social Services Council

Compass House
11 Riverside Drive
Dundee DD1 4NY

(t) 01382 207101
(↗) www.sssc.uk.com

Online reading
SocietyGuardian www.societyguardian.co.uk
Community Care www.communitycare.co.uk
Care and Health www.careandhealth.com

CORPORATE CULTURE

This is a tough sector and very community based. As such there can be a culture of overwork, so there are questions that you need to ask before accepting a job, both of yourself and of your employer. One of the most important is to do with your professional development. It's important that you find out what frameworks are in place for your necessary continued professional development. Do staff at the organisation you're applying for actually get to take advantage of training offered? This is all part of how the organisation treats its workers – is there enough support, training and supervision for you there?

Because social services tends to be community based and concerned with specific issues occurring in a particular area, working abroad is not common. That said, youth work also sometimes involves cross-community and international work, in Britain or abroad, which brings together young people from different cultures and countries on joint projects.

Even if you're not working abroad, speaking another language may well be an advantage or even, as for race relations workers, extremely important for reaching your client group. Some of the most vulnerable people in our society are further isolated by not being able to communicate in English, so language skills are in demand.

Just because it tends to be a community concern, that doesn't mean there are no opportunities for progression or skills advancement within the social care sector. Promotion structures are improving, for example in youth work, where local authority youth services, Connexions partnerships and other related services all offer opportunities to move into management or more specialised posts, and there is now a range of management training programmes in place. Apart from that, promotion is based on experience, talent and perseverance.

The benefits of working in the social care sector lie in the variety of the work and the contact with others in the community. It's not strictly a desk-bound sector and most roles entail getting out and about to work with people in groups or one on one; if you're a youth worker you might work outdoors as part of a project, and in any of the roles you might travel within the local area to visit clients.

ETHICAL QUESTIONS

Like teaching, this is a sector in which all your work will predominantly be for the good. The only proviso is that you determine an organisation's attitude to freedom of speech, namely whistleblowers. Also consider, as with not-for-profit organisations, what agendas any counselling service may have (anti versus pro abortion, for example) and what your own attitude is to that issue. The British Association of Social Workers is the professional association for social workers in the UK. It gives guidance on ethical issues and has a duty to ensure as far as possible that members discharge their ethical obligations and are afforded the professional rights necessary in these professions.

Ask what the procedures are for raising grievances about another staff member's conduct. Does the firm have a formal commitment to investigate matters brought to its attention? Would the organisation agree that those in positions of authority have an ethical duty to explain their actions? Regarding the organisation's agenda, is it openly and honestly stated? Does it communicate its viewpoint to users of the service it provides at the first opportunity? Does it publish a statement defining its stance on the ethical issues it encounters in its work?

Sport and leisure

The sport and leisure sector covers sport and recreation, health and fitness and betting and gambling, and is a serious moneyspinner in the UK. Although this section deals mainly with fitness and facilities management, it's worth noting that the sector does extend beyond those activities that can only be done whilst wearing a tracksuit. For jobs in sports health see physiotherapy in the section on healthcare on page 118.

The sport and leisure sector is a boom area for both public and private organisations. Sport generates around 2% of the UK's GDP and consumer spending runs into tens of billions of pounds. Although some of this spending is on sports gear worn for fashion rather than action, Britain is certainly becoming more health and body conscious, leading to an increased use of sports and fitness facilities. Meanwhile the rising statistics for heart disease, diabetes and other lifestyle- and fitness-related illnesses has led to the government not only increasing provision for sports facilities but even sponsoring its incorporation into the NHS. If you've had a heart attack or bypass surgery, for example, you'll be referred to special classes at your local health centre aimed at getting you back on your feet and into a better lifestyle to stop you needing more invasive and expensive treatment. In addition, roles such as sports development officer have become increasingly important since recent research identified sport as having an important role to play in crime reduction and social inclusion. All local authority leisure departments now have a sports development plan. Sport England also employs people in jobs as diverse as doping control and event organisation.

To join the industry, you'll need organisational skills, you'll be efficient, and well motivated and you'll be an adept problem-solver. Good with people, you'll have excellent communication skills and you'll be able to be part of, and then lead, a team. And it will help if you know your sport and are reasonably physically fit.

Roles

■ Fitness instructor

A **fitness instructor** supervises a range of activities from stress management to the trendiest spinning class. It's common for instructors to specialise in only one or two types of activity, which might mean that you travel to different facilities in order to make up a full-time job. Depending on the sort of sessions you're taking (groups or one to one) and the type of training you're giving, you might be assessing a client's fitness and needs, devising programmes for individuals to follow, checking equipment safety, supervising the gym area as a whole or giving dietary advice; your aim is to ensure that people are getting what they want out of their fitness sessions in a safe way. You will be expected to register with the Register of Exercise Professionals.

■ Leisure attendant

As a **leisure attendant** you might work in a council-run facility or in a general health club. Duties will vary depending on what you're qualified to do; for example, you can only work as a swimming pool attendant if you have appropriate lifesaving qualifications. You may be on a rota to cover general duties such as reception, or you may be responsible purely for the activity areas of the centre, preparing areas for different activities, supervising areas and explaining facility use and monitoring safety. Cleaning changing rooms and toilets can also be part of this job. This role can be a springboard for careers in coaching specific sports or in management.

■ Leisure manager

The job of **leisure manager** can involve overseeing and promoting a range of activities including sports, drama and cultural events. You might have responsibility over leisure and sports centres, community centres, public halls, libraries, theatres, arts centres and tourist attractions to name but a few. This means that the work can vary a great deal, but is likely to include administration tasks that arise as the result of council decisions. You'll be responsible for organising new types of activities, maintaining existing service, constantly evaluating facilities and policies, working with budgets and overseeing building work.

■ Leisure services development officer

A **leisure services development officer** manages the leisure services provided by the council. You'll probably have a particular area to cover, such as parks and countryside, museums and galleries, or libraries and information services. Basically you'll be working to design and develop ways of making the service your department offers more effective and efficient, not to mention more popular with the public. The job involves quite a lot of consultation and discussion in order to decide on priorities, development plans and courses of action; there's also marketing and promotion to consider. You'll be constantly assessing the services offered and might be responsible for dealing with complaints.

■ Sports development officer

Sports development officer is a local authority job that generally entails working in a team to provide, promote, develop and manage sport and leisure activities for all sections of the community. The way the role is structured varies between authorities, but you will probably be planning and promoting activities and events for particular target groups, managing budgets, and carrying out research and forming appropriate plans of action. You will be working to get young people interested in sport, perhaps establishing priority sports and structures so that they can try different things and make as much progress as possible. It's a varied role that goes beyond this description, and you'll need good interpersonal skills for communicating and liaising with other bodies and target groups

■ Sports facility manager

As a **sports facility manager** your job is to make sure that services run well and offer what the customer wants, so this involves developing and structuring new services and promoting them to the public. You'll spend a lot of time troubleshooting and liaising with your staff as well as dealing with paperwork such as accident reports, invoices and the like, working with budgets and planning marketing strategies.

■ Theme park manager

A **theme park manager** organises the safe and efficient running of the theme park, and oversees the marketing, development and day-to-day operations. Typically you'll be in charge of the budget and will oversee all the paperwork for health and safety, building applications and so on. You'll also project manage developments within the park, monitor performance and customer satisfaction and recruit staff.

QUALIFICATIONS AND TRAINING Just being good at PE won't cut it in this highly competitive industry. Experience and enthusiasm backed up by qualifications are what employers are looking for, and moving up through the ranks as you gain these is common. For example, **leisure attendants** don't usually need specific qualifications (although if you're a lifeguard you'll need training, as will anyone overseeing a gym, but this will often be given on the job), but this is an entry-level position for many managers as it can often be the first step on a training scheme. **Leisure managers** therefore don't necessarily need a degree, but useful degree and HND/GNVQ subjects include leisure management, leisure studies, sports science, recreation management, recreation planning and leisure marketing. Experience is important and things like health and safety qualifications might be an advantage, though these might be gained as you work your way up to a management role. If you're aiming to be a **sports facility manager** it will strengthen your case if you study for the professional qualifications of ISPAL (The Institute for Sport, Parks and Leisure) or the Institute of Sport and Recreation Management.

Fitness instructors need serious qualifications as health and safety are key words in this industry. Fitness instructors must have a fitness qualification in weight training and a fitness qualification (awarded by a body such as the RSA) in at least two of the following areas: exercise to music, circuit training, aquafit or resistance training, fitness-room inductions, fitness assessment, relaxation and stress management and de-conditioned clients. It's also definitely an advantage to have or be working towards membership of the Fitness Industry Association – the trade organisation representing operators of health and fitness clubs – and a recognised qualification in exercise counselling and fitness assessment. It's not uncommon to keep expanding your skills as you find new areas of interest, so CPD is definitely a part of a fitness instructor's career plan. You should also register with the Register of Exercise Professionals.

To be a **sports development officer** it's not essential to have a degree, but you will need first-aid and national governing body coaching qualifications. The most important skills are going to be an awareness of the area you're trying to develop plus marketing and business qualifications, some of which your employer may sponsor. To become a **leisure services development officer** you'll need a degree (the subject is usually immaterial) plus two years' experience in the area you want to specialise in. Again, anything to do with business skills or marketing is likely to be extremely useful.

Although **theme park managers** don't need any particular qualifications, health and safety training is very advantageous. A degree is not required, but useful degree and HND/GNVQ subjects include leisure management, leisure studies, sports science, recreation management, recreation planning and leisure marketing. Training is usually given by employers, particularly if you're part of one of the graduate schemes run by some of the larger parks.

SALARY The average graduate starting salary in the leisure industry is £16,101.

Contacts

Federation of Sports and Play Associations

Federation House
Stoneleigh Park
Warwickshire CV8 2RF

(t) 024 7641 4999

(↗) www.sportslife.org.uk

Fitness Industry Association

4th Floor
61 Southwark Street
London SE1 0HL

(t) 020 7202 4719

(↗) www.fia.org.uk

Institute of Sport and Recreation Management

Sir John Beckwith Centre for Sport
Loughborough University
Loughborough LE11 3TU

(t) 01509 226474

(↗) www.isrm.co.uk

ISPAL: The Institute of Sports, Parks and Leisure

The Grotto House
Lower Basildon
Reading RG8 9NE

(t) 01491 874800

(↗) www.ispal.org.uk

Register of Exercise Professionals

8–10 Crown Hill
Croydon CR0 1RZ

(t) 020 8686 6464

(↗) www.exerciseregister.org

Sport England

3rd Floor
Victoria House
Bloomsbury Square
London WC1B 4SE

(t) 0845 850 8508

(↗) www.sportengland.org

Sport Northern Ireland

House of Sport
Upper Malone Road
Belfast BT9 5LA

(t) 028 9038 1222

(↗) www.sportscouncil-ni.org.uk

Sport Scotland

Caledonia House
South Gyle
Edinburgh EH12 9DQ

(t) 0131 317 7200

(↗) www.sportscotland.org.uk

Sports Council for Wales

Sophia Gardens
Cardiff CF11 9SW

(t) 0845 045 0904

(↗) www.sports-council-wales.org.uk

CORPORATE CULTURE

From the start it's important to realise that this is a sector that's all about motivation. It's quite common to start out as a receptionist or instructor and work your way to the top of the leisure tree. Experience is of paramount importance, so you need to be willing to take opportunities wherever and whenever they come up, even if it seems a lowly starting point. Enthusiasm and a positive attitude count for an awful lot, not least because this is a very customer-oriented industry. Equally it's a very professional sector, so qualifications matter, even if it's just a case of showing a potential employer that you have the motivation and commitment to get a first-aid certificate and do some work experience at a gym. That said, specific sports science qualifications are becoming more highly prized and if you haven't already qualified it's always worth finding out if you might be eligible for support.

This is a global business, so it's possible to work abroad if you're employed by a chain of leisure providers such as casinos, holiday camps or even some of the larger gym chains. Languages would be essential, although you might get some company training for this, and you might need slightly different qualifications, as health and safety laws may vary. If you're working for a local authority facility you're unlikely to have travel as a standard part of your job.

ETHICAL QUESTIONS

The fitness of mind and body have been inextricably linked since the time of the ancient Greeks: Aristotle himself established a gymnasium alongside his school of philosophy in Athens in 335BC. In practice, modern fitness centres can ironically be quite unhealthy and energy inefficient places given the chemicals needed for swimming pools and the power needed to heat pools, spas, saunas and so on.

Does the company have a policy on the use of harmful chemicals as well as a policy on energy saving? Do they use green electricity, ie from a company committed to increasing the amount of electricity generated from renewable sources? Do they use any other method of energy saving such as solar panels to reduce their consumption of electricity?

Does the firm strive to eliminate the use of steroids by people using its facilities? Does it consider any performance-enhancing substances to be acceptable in sport? What is its attitude towards dietary supplements? Does it sell or recommend any itself, and if so what is its relationship with the manufacturer?

Transport

This is a wide-ranging sector with a mixture of highly vocational jobs, such as those in the merchant navy or in aircraft piloting, and challenging organisational roles. In essence, you can either be part of the transport system or supply chain or you can organise it. There is no one image or stereotype for this sector, although the most identifiable roles, those of air cabin crew and pilots, have long been (wrongly) associated with glamour.

Roles

- Air cabin crew

Air cabin crew are responsible for the health, safety, comfort and general welfare of passengers. Your duties include instructing passengers on safety, ensuring there are adequate supplies of food and drink, preparing and serving food and drink during the flight, reassuring nervous passengers, helping those with small children or special needs and generally keeping everyone calm and comfortable. Before the flight you'll attend briefings and check the cabin. If there are any emergencies you'll be expected to deal with them in a calm way, administering first aid where necessary and getting the situation as under control as possible. People can be very demanding, so this job is not for the quick-tempered, panicky or easily annoyed.

- Air traffic controller

It is the job of the **air traffic controller** to keep the skies safe and ensure non-disastrous takeoff and landing around airports and on major travel routes by instructing pilots on speed, height, course and distance from other aircraft. Controllers use radar surveillance to achieve this and mostly work in a control tower, remaining in position for slots of two hours. Responsibilities are split between approach work, aerodrome work, air control and ground control. Essentially, however, your work will probably include communication with pilots, giving instructions about height, weather conditions and so on, keeping planes in holding patterns at busy times and organising the movement of craft around terminal buildings and runways.

- Airline pilot

An **airline pilot** is in charge of the safety of the aircraft and its passengers and crew. This involves researching the route, aircraft and weather before each flight, working out a flight plan (the precise route and height of the flight), briefing the crew, supervising loading and fuelling, doing pre-flight and in-flight technical checks on the aircraft's systems, communicating with air traffic control and passengers, writing reports and updating log-books. There are four sectors for pilots to work in: chartered or scheduled passenger services, business aviation (things like air schools, private aircraft etc) and freight.

■ Distribution/Logistics manager

Logistics isn't just one role, it's all the processes in supply-chain management. **Distribution management** is just one aspect of this and responsibilities can vary depending on what sort of company you're working for and in what area – manufacture, retail etc. It can cover transport, warehouse management and stock control. Your job is to ensure that the systems are in place to control and monitor the movement of goods. Typically your tasks will include cost monitoring, liaison with suppliers and customers, controlling the cycle of orders, managing warehouse staff and analysing performance so that improvements can be made.

■ Freight forwarder

A **freight forwarder** deals with arranging and organising the international movement of goods on behalf of companies, individuals or importers and exporters. This is all about assessing the needs and budget of the client then sorting out the best way to get the goods wherever they're meant to be as quickly, efficiently, safely and economically as possible, taking into account the nature of the goods and any special measures or precautions that need to be observed in transit. You'll sort out the appropriate packing, insurance, compliance with different countries' regulations and liaise with any other companies involved in the chain.

■ Merchant navy officer

The term **merchant navy** covers all commercial shipping in the UK, so you could be working on ferries, cargo containerships or tankers. There are two types of officers but exact tasks depend on your rank. Deck officers are responsible for the management of the ship, which includes navigation, paperwork, dealing with communication systems and coordinating the movement of cargo. Engineering officers are in charge of maintaining and operating all equipment.

■ Transport manager

Transport managers are employed by a whole range of bodies including national and local government, passenger transport companies (road, rail, air or sea), freight transport companies (road, rail, air, sea or inland waterways), the post office, breweries, supermarkets, clothing and food manufacturers, the armed services and consultancies. The aim is to ensure that passengers and freight are provided with any services necessary and are delivered to the right place, at the correct time, after the best possible journey and at the right price. You're likely to specialise in one aspect such as planning, engineering, research and development, operations and fleet management, industrial design, health and safety or environmental issues. Whatever the area, it's a problem-solving role and can have a significant IT dimension.

QUALIFICATIONS AND TRAINING Although certain areas of this sector such as the merchant navy are long established and are quite sure of what they want from potential employees, other areas, such as logistics and freight forwarding, are relatively new and quickly expanding sectors. Formal qualifications have so far not been necessary for **distribution/logistics managers** and **freight forwarders** but employers are increasingly seeking graduates and graduate schemes and formal training are becoming more common in larger companies. Degree subjects that might prove useful include the obvious transport, distribution and logistics as well as business or management, possibly with languages, or things like geography or computing. Experience and personal qualities can often be the most persuasive attributes, however. Training on the job is standard, but both roles are extremely competitive, so any work experience you can get will be an enormous advantage.

Transport managers fare a little better in the qualifications stakes. Degrees are not required, but there are professional qualifications that can be gained through the Institute of Logistics and Transport. Training is often on the job.

Air transport for both passengers and packages is constantly expanding, and the skills mix required is huge. **Air cabin crew** have an extremely demanding job for which physical fitness is important, and there are often height restrictions. Otherwise you simply require a good standard of secondary education; degrees and HNDs aren't really necessary, although languages are very useful. Getting into this job is difficult however and very competitive. You can speculatively apply to airlines for cabin crew posts, which involve training – they usually recruit between the ages of 18 and 40.

Air traffic controllers have enormous amounts of responsibility and accordingly, although there are no formal requirements before training (numeracy is a useful quality, however), there are stringent requirements during training. Applicants to the National Air Traffic Services scheme for air traffic controller training must be between 18 and 30, although other employers might not have limits. You must pass security clearance before starting work. You must also have a good standard of fitness, good eyesight, colour vision and hearing and nice clear diction. Most people enter through the NATS student air traffic control scheme at the College of Air Traffic Control, which is very competitive.

To be an **airline pilot** you must have a minimum of five GCSEs grade A–C (seven in the case of British Airways) in English, maths and preferably a science such as physics, and at least two A-levels or Scottish highers (three in the case of British Airways), preferably in maths and physics. Degrees might be a positive disadvantage, as it is rare to be accepted into pilot training after the mid-twenties. Qualifying to be a pilot involves a serious amount of work and expense. In order to fly as an airline pilot you need to have obtained an airline transport pilot's licence, which requires a minimum of 750 hours of structured theoretical instruction and 195 hours of flying training. A further six months or 1,500 hours of flying experience is needed to get your full licence. Pilots have three potential routes into training and then into jobs. You can enrol on a course at a Civil Aviation Authority approved training school, apply to an airline that offers sponsored training at one of these schools, or enlist as a pilot in the Royal Air Force, Fleet Air Arm or Army Air Corps Association and later undertake a conversion course to allow you to enter civilian flying.

There are two training routes for the **merchant navy**. Degree courses leading to a BSc in merchant ship operations, naval architecture or marine engineering are offered at some universities. Alternatively, if you train through one of the four naval colleges from GCSE or A-level standard you can achieve entry-level qualifications. Some Royal Navy qualifications will count towards merchant navy training. Any entrant to the merchant navy must do so through a training scheme relevant to the level of their qualifications, which can be applied for speculatively. If you've already got a relevant degree such as marine engineering, mechanical engineering or electrical engineering you might get an exemption from certain parts of the training. There are fast-track schemes for graduates. You need good eyesight and physical fitness, and any relevant experience will be taken into account. Most people enter by the age of 21, but this doesn't exclude older entrants, especially if you've worked in a relevant field.

SALARY The average graduate starting salary in the transport industry is £21,414.

Contacts

British Air Line Pilots' Association
BALPA House
5 Heathrow Boulevard
278 Bath Road
West Drayton UB7 0DQ

(t) 020 8476 4000

(↗) www.balpa.org

British International Freight Association
Redfern House
Browells Lane
Feltham
Middlesex TW13 7EP

(t) 020 8844 2266

(↗) www.bifa.org

British Women Pilots' Association
Brooklands Museum
Brooklands Road
Weybridge
Surrey KT13 0QN

(↗) www.bwpa.co.uk

Chartered Institute of Logistics and Transport
11–12 Buckingham Gate
London SW1E 6LB

(t) 01536 740100

(↗) www.ciltuk.org.uk

Civil Aviation Authority
CAA House
45–59 Kingsway
London WC2B 6TE

(t) 020 7379 7311

(↗) www.caa.co.uk

Freight Transport Association
Hermes House
St John's Road
Tunbridge Wells
Kent TN4 9UZ

(t) 01892 526171

(↗) www.fta.co.uk

Merchant Navy Training Board
Carthusian Court
12 Carthusian Street
London EC1M 6EZ

(t) 020 7417 2800

(↗) www.mntb.org.uk

National Air Traffic Services
5th Floor
Brettenham House South
Lancaster Place
London WC2E 7EN

(t) 020 7309 8666

(↗) www.nats.co.uk

Rail Freight Group
17 Queen Anne's Gate
London SW1H 9BU

(t) 020 7233 3177

(↗) www.rfg.org.uk

Road Haulage Association
Roadway House
35 Monument Hill
Weybridge
Surrey KT13 8RN

(t) 01932 841515

(↗) www.rha.net

Royal Air Force
PO Box 1000
Royal Air Force College Cranwell
Sleaford
Lincs NG34 8GZ

(t) 0845 605 5555

(↗) www.raf.mod.uk

Supply Chain Research Centre
Cranfield School of Management
Cranfield
Bedfordshire MK43 0AL

(t) 01234 754180

(↗) www.cranfield.ac.uk/som/lscm

CORPORATE CULTURE

This is a rapidly expanding client- and customer-focused industry, so it's not 9–5 and for certain roles appearance is important. Air cabin crew, for example will wear a uniform, but you'll also need to make sure that you look neat and presentable at all times, even on exhausting long-haul flights. Airline pilots are also expected to wear a uniform and look smart and professional. Merchant navy officers will wear uniforms or protective or practical clothing depending on the company and exact duties.

It's an international sector and distribution managers and freight forwarders are the ones most likely to actually spend time working abroad. It's quite common for both roles and languages are definitely useful. Pilots and air cabin crew will be abroad a lot of the time, just usually not for extensive periods – languages might well be helpful, however. Air traffic controllers have almost no call to be travelling through work. Merchant navy officers will do a lot of travelling, but don't always get the chance to go ashore.

In terms of moving up through the ranks, experience equals advancement. The merchant navy has a clear promotion structure, much like the Royal Navy, and this involves progressing through different roles with the chance to gain qualifications at each stage. Advancement for pilots depends heavily on the number of flying hours you've notched up as well as your skill. Air cabin crew can gain more senior positions with time and experience.

ETHICAL QUESTIONS

Transport-related pollution makes up a large proportion of the world's greenhouse gas emissions, so you should always ask a firm what efforts it is making to reduce its emissions. There is also an ethical obligation to ensure employee, passenger and public safety, particularly in the aviation industry.

In logistics, is consideration always given to using the greenest mode of transport available, for example rail or even canals instead of road? Does the company look beyond a simple financial calculation when examining the possibility of saving fuel by using toll roads? What are its attitudes to using greener fuels like LPG or biofuels? Can greater fuel efficiency be achieved by using computer software to minimise the number of journeys required? Does the firm have a strategy to avoid making journeys with empty lorries, by sharing loads with other companies for example? Aviation fuel is tax-free in the UK. Does the company agree that imposing a tax would encourage it to take fuel economy more seriously?

Travel

People have always moved around the globe looking at foreign things and picking up souvenirs – be they nomads, pilgrims or conquerors setting off to vanquish other races and give them a new flag. Likewise, maps have been around in one form or another for some five thousand years. Just because our ancestors didn't realise for quite a lot of that time that the world was round doesn't mean that they weren't trying to figure it out and stick it down in an easy to carry form. Travel is now a massive sector and growing in popularity all the time.

The events of September 11, 2001 damaged consumer confidence and, more importantly, sparked world events that are still not resolved, making many people nervous about travelling. The situation has worsened in the wake of the wars in Iraq and Afghanistan, as in many parts of the world there is anger against America and the UK for their roles in these conflicts. Tourists are potential targets for terrorists, and the increased security over travel arrangements not only makes people even more anxious, it also delays flights and makes travelling even more arduous than before.

On the bright side, people are still travelling and becoming more adventurous than ever. The travel industry can do a lot to make people feel safe again, and can influence people to travel in a respectful way that won't compound the damage done to Britain's reputation abroad.

Roles

■ Cartographer

Cartography covers pretty much everything to do with map-making, elements of which are undertaken by chorographers, cosmographers, hydrographers, geographers and others. Different maps serve different purposes, and new technologies are increasingly used to create them. A **cartographer** can expect to be involved in design and layout, information analysis, collating data using remote sensors and operating a photogrammetric plotting instrument or a digital photogrammetric workstation to view photographs stereoscopically. It's a highly specialised and technical field with a great deal to it. It is not a huge employer and entry is competitive.

■ Translator/Interpreter

Working as a translator is all about expressing things in another language using the written word, as opposed to interpreting, which is spoken. As a

translator you might be employed by a wide range of organisations, including businesses with overseas interests who need someone skilled at writing business letters and the like, banks, import–export firms, and publishers who need translations either into another language or from another language into English. This can be a very complex field, particularly if you're doing literary translation, and your writing style is as important as are your linguistic skills. It's also very competitive.

An **interpreter** provides verbal interpretation for conferences, business purposes, courts or community matters. The two different techniques of interpreting – simultaneous and consecutive – are used in different situations, so if you have a preference or a dislike for one then you need to pick your area carefully. Simultaneous interpreting is either done broadcast-style from a booth or is whispered directly to one or two people. It's mostly used for national and international conferences, meetings and informal gatherings where the delegates speak different languages but need to communicate, learn and transact business without lengthy delays. Consecutive interpretation is used for people who are not fluent or native speakers in whichever language but need to communicate in the official language in order to have full and equal access to legal, health, education, social or other public facilities. It's an overcrowded and competitive profession so you're going to have to be both talented and determined.

■ Tour manager

A **tour manager** works for tour operators and is responsible for organising trips and accompanying tour groups, making sure that the itinerary is followed and that the facilities and programme are provided as promised. You'll be there to welcome groups and make sure everyone has arrived, give information along the route, check tickets and travel documents, ensure special needs are catered for and help with any problems that might arise. You are also responsible for investigating possible destinations and itineraries and liaising with hotels, transport companies and restaurants.

■ Tour operator

As a **tour operator** you could be working for one of the big companies or for a smaller operator, creating, arranging and operating tours and travel programmes for customers. This will involve booking and arranging contracts with hotels, airlines and other forms of transport providers. It's different from being a travel agent as you will be organising and providing travel packages, while travel agencies advise customers on tours and flights and sell and administer travel products. There are lots of different roles available within tour operating, including in marketing, IT, sales and contracts. However, typical tasks include choosing which countries and resorts to use, checking suitability and quality of resorts and their accommodation, deciding how many different types of programme to offer, preparing brochures, negotiating costs, booking hotels and airlines, issuing tickets and confirming details with customers and hotels.

■ Tourism officer

As a **tourism officer** you are responsible for developing and promoting tourism initiatives in order to bring economic benefit to a particular area or site. You're most likely to be employed by local authorities, wildlife trusts, national parks or organisations such as the National Trust or the Forestry Commission. Typically you're going to spend your time liaising with local businesses and the media, making presentations, producing promotional material and creating tourist information, carrying out market research, managing budgets, preparing reports and maintaining visitor services and attractions.

■ Travel agency manager

A **travel agency manager** oversees the day-to-day running and management of a travel retail outlet. Your role will include recruiting and managing staff, motivating them to hit targets, dealing with sales figures and perhaps selling travel products yourself.

QUALIFICATIONS AND TRAINING The only roles in this sector that require formal qualifications as standard are cartography, interpreting and translating. Graduates are preferred for **cartography**, but sometimes an HND is acceptable. Relevant qualification subjects for degrees include cartography, GIS, physical, mathematical or applied science, and urban and land studies; for HNDs subjects such as urban and land studies or physical, mathematical or applied science would be useful. **Translators** and **interpreters** need to have complete coverage of at least one language as well as a thorough knowledge of the institutions, culture, attitudes and practices in the countries where that language is spoken, normally acquired through residence there. You'll also find that a degree is essential, although for translators it doesn't necessarily have to be in languages. For translators a postgraduate qualification in translating is useful; interpreters will need a degree in languages or interpreting. For **tourism officers**, **travel agency managers** and tour operators, you'll have an advantage if your degree is in languages, travel, tourism, leisure, business studies, marketing, management or journalism. This is similar for **tour managers**, who will find that a history degree might also be useful, and languages especially so. Relevant work experience is essential for most of these jobs. For **tour operators** there is a recognised industry qualification: the Association of British Travel Agents certificate in travel (tour operators), which at different levels corresponds to NVQ/SVQ levels 2 and 3. Other qualifications are available, such as the City and Guilds Travel and Tourism awards, which are available at four levels.

There don't tend to be too many graduate entry schemes in this sector. Most entry is through direct application for advertised jobs or speculative applications – this is often a good way in for tour managers. Some of the larger companies run graduate trainee schemes for tour operators, and these tend to lead to places in IT, marketing and operations management and similar roles. Most of these roles welcome any applicant with relevant experience and interest in travel, and experience can't be stressed enough as an important prerequisite. Travel agencies might favour those under 40, but if you already have experience in retail or a relevant sector that might smooth your way. Tour managers have to have a good level of physical fitness, so candidates tend to be younger, but different tours call for different types of managers, so this need not be a total bar.

SALARY The average graduate starting salary in travel service roles is £13,946.

CORPORATE CULTURE

This is a very international and client-based sector, so the culture tends towards service and professionalism as well as businesslike networking. Possibly the best way to experience this first hand is by visiting travel trade fairs and exhibitions such as the world travel market. These can be a good way to scope out what's happening in the business, what's out there, and importantly, to network and research your chosen area. Even fairs and exhibitions that are trade only will tend to have student days, so it's well worth showing your commitment and enthusiasm by doing research in this way.

In terms of choosing your role within the sector, it's obvious that a big draw is the potential amount of travel. Even desk jobs at travel agencies generally require some sort of experience of travel so that you're well placed to advise customers, and employers will generally encourage you to broaden your experience for this purpose. Some jobs, however, involve more travel than others. Tour managing is the job for people who want lots of overseas travel: it entails constantly living out of a suitcase and being continuously on the move. Translators and interpreters might also have some foreign travel in their work and the same goes for travel agency managers. Tour operators are usually office-based, although some overseas travel might be necessary to assess the suitability of different resorts and accommodation. Overseas work is uncommon for cartographers and tourism officers.

As in so many sectors, experience is the key to promotion. Particularly in travel agencies, you'll have to work your way up from the bottom of the ladder, learning all about the business before you get a crack at management jobs. In all the other roles experience is stressed time and again as a prerequisite, so you'll probably find that although promotion is possible you'll have to serve time before you get to the well-paid senior work.

Contacts

Association of British Travel Agents
68–71 Newman Street
London W1T 3AH

(t) 020 7637 2444

(↗) www.abta.com

British Cartographic Society
BCS Administration
12 Elworthy Drive
Wellington
Somerset TA21 9AT

(↗) www.cartography.org.uk

Institute of Translation and Interpreting
Fortuna House
South Fifth Street
Milton Keynes MK9 2EU

(t) 01908 325250

(↗) www.iti.org.uk

Institute of Travel and Tourism
PO Box 217
Ware
Herts SG12 8WY

(t) 0870 770 7960

(↗) www.itt.co.uk

Ordnance Survey
Romsey Road
Southampton SO16 4GU

(t) 0845 605 0505

(↗) www.ordnancesurvey.co.uk

Tourism Concern
Stapleton House
277–281 Holloway Road
London N7 8HN

(t) 020 7133 3330

(↗) www.tourismconcern.org.uk

Tourism Management Institute
64 Green Farm End
Kineton
Warwickshire CV35 0LD

(t) 01926 641506

(↗) www.tmi.org.uk

VisitBritain
Thames Tower
Black's Road
Hammersmith
London W6 9EL

(t) 020 8846 9000

(↗) www.visitbritain.com

World Committee on Tourism Ethics
World Tourism Organization
Capitán Haya, 42
28020 Madrid
Spain

(t) +34 91 567 8172

(↗) www.world-tourism.org/code
_ethics/eng.html

Do not assume that the travel sector is only about jetting off to San Tropez, or showing well-heeled clients around fine examples of classical architecture: the reality is that desk work is important for certain roles. Cartographers tend to be mostly desk-based although some jobs involve topographic or hydrographic surveying, which will give you a bit of time away from the computer screen. Tourism officers are likely to get out and about as well, making presentations and attending events as well as assessing and maintaining attractions that fall under their remit.

ETHICAL QUESTIONS

Any tourism operator should always be aware of what impact it is having on a destination, on both the natural environment and the local people. As tourism to developing nations increases, so does the need to strengthen fair trade principles to prevent exploitation and ensure that local people and businesses, both within the tourism industry and separate from it, profit and do not see their quality of life diminish.

Does the firm strive to follow the principles of eco-tourism? What policies does it have on sustainable tourism? How much of the money spent by the tourist stays at the destination with the local hotels and workers? Does it have a policy of ensuring these workers are treated fairly and their human rights respected? Is there training to allow local people the opportunity to manage hotels? What is the policy towards corruption? Does the operator respect the cultural assets of the destination, for example sacred sites? Do the hotels used live harmoniously with local residents, for example by not using more than their fair share of water?

The ethical principles at play in cartography are related to those in art in that the discipline is concerned with representation, which in turn informs the attitudes and ideas of individuals. The best-known example is the method used to project a three-dimensional globe on to a two dimensional map. Until recently the most commonly used method was the Mercator projection, which presents a Eurocentric view of the world by inflating the north and west, and deflating the south and east. The Peters projection represents an effort to remove this bias by accurately reflecting the relative sizes of countries, and thus avoiding the unwarranted focus on Europe and North America. Is the firm open and honest in its approach to cartography, in that where distortions occur they exist for a good reason? Does it use the Peters projection as a basis for its maps? What is its attitude towards maps from different cultures which use different map-making principles such as emotion or the relationships between peoples?

Uniformed services

Everyone has their own preconceived ideas about the army, police, navy and so on, and you will too. Your job, before you join, is to find out whether the myth and the received opinion are in any way near to the reality and whether it's actually what you want. Do you really want to go to war?

The armed forces offer a variety of roles that is little short of amazing: from jobs for vets to weapons experts, dentists and engineers. It shouldn't be surprising – the armed forces is a massive community, and every time they go to a different part of the world they need to take everything with them that civilian society needs, plus all the bits that make them armed. So it makes sense that pretty much whatever you do you can find a place to do it with the army, navy or RAF. You'll just have to learn how to use a gun, fly a plane or sail a boat in addition.

Firefighting is an incredibly popular career, despite the danger, stress and antisocial hours. Brigades receive over 100 applications for each post advertised – that's pretty stiff competition. Women can be firefighters, and there is a drive to recruit more, as at the moment less than 5% are women. There are a number of different roles available within firefighting, of which getting busy with a hose is just one. Fire brigades also have control positions, which are the nerve centre of the brigade, taking emergency calls and directing crews. Firefighters may also be trained as trauma technicians: you're taught basic skills to support the victim until a fully trained paramedic can take over. All these roles involve good people-management skills, dedication and commitment to the role. The police too are enjoying an upsurge in recruitment – largely politically fuelled as the government bangs the law and order drum, but there's no reason you can't exploit it.

■ Armed forces

Roles

■ (Operational) armed forces officer

There are slight differences in titles across the forces. The army calls these officers **combat officers** and the navy **warfare officers**. Either way, the bottom line is the same – you'll be in the frontline of battle, directing and operating advanced fighting systems in the air, on land and at sea, and commanding personnel. It's a stressful and dangerous position and your primary responsibility is for the people under your command – their training, welfare, morale and promotion. Other responsibilities revolve around identifying targets and figuring out how to achieve them, developing and implementing strategies, briefing, allocating equipment and roles, keeping equipment operational and motivating those under your command.

■ Armed forces technical officer

As a **technical officer** you'll be leading a team of specialists, including engineers and technicians, whose job in battle is to keep lines of communication and equipment operational. When not actively engaged you might be the project manager for a building or development project on a base, or you might oversee equipment or weapons research and development as well as the maintenance of all types of equipment and systems. You will allocate equipment and teach others to use, maintain and repair it, and you may even have to write up technical leaflets and manuals; you'll also be in charge of problem-solving in all areas, sometimes under enormous pressure. And it goes without saying that alongside your technical responsibilities are those to do with ensuring the welfare, morale and training of the people you're in charge of.

■ Armed forces training and education officer

The **armed forces training and education officer** is responsible for the continued education of all ranks, apprentices and officers and must also be a media and communications specialist. You may be called on to fulfil an operational role, but the majority of your work is on the base, assessing learning needs, planning courses and teaching in subjects from engineering to English as a foreign language and at a range of levels. Operational duties can include liaison work with local communities and translation and interpreting.

■ Support worker/Administrator/Armed forces officer

The armed forces are like any large organisation: they need human resources personnel and all the rest of it. In fact the role of an **administrator** fits in neatly with the essence of being an officer, which is really a management role – albeit one with higher stakes than most. The army calls these officers **staff and personnel support**, the RAF calls them **administrative officers** and in the navy they are known as **supply officers**. As an officer you would command, lead and manage a support team comprised of workers such as clerks, financial workers and IT staff, and be expected to function efficiently whether in Britain on a base or abroad in adverse conditions. Your team will be delivering essential administrative services, such as supply organisation, salaries, accountancy, keeping records, dealing with budgets, liaising with other bodies, registering and carrying out notification of deaths and injuries, carrying out security duties and much more. It's sort of an extreme office job.

QUALIFICATIONS AND TRAINING On the whole the entry qualifications are the same no matter which branch of the armed forces you're going into. Any degree subject is acceptable, although science and engineering are particularly valued in certain branches. Specialist qualifications are also necessary for roles such as armed forces veterinary surgeon, chaplain, engineer and so on. The most important general qualification is that you are a UK national with five years' UK residency.

There are also age and height restrictions. You must be at least 16 and no older than 32 (up to and including your 33rd birthday) on entry, although the maximum age

Contacts

Army Recruitment

(t) 0845 730 0111

(↗) www.armyjobs.mod.uk

Britannia Royal Naval College Dartmouth

Dartmouth
Devon TQ6 0HJ

(t) 01803 677 238

(↗) www.britannia.ac.uk

Royal Air Force

PO Box 1000
Royal Air Force College Cranwell
Sleaford
Lincs NG34 8GZ

(t) 0845 605 5555

(↗) www.raf.mod.uk

Royal Navy

Officer Career Liaison Centre
St George's Court
2–12 Bloomsbury Way
London WC1A 2SH

(t) 0845 607 5555

(↗) www.royal-navy.mod.uk

for officer entry can vary according to specialisation. Your BMI must be in proportion to your height and weight, ideally a BMI of between 18-28. Finally, your eyesight and health must be good.

The armed forces run graduate and pre-graduate recruitment schemes, some of which might involve help with university tuition fees among other benefits. Obviously any training needed is given by the employer in this instance, except where the role involves civilian skills that you either need to have had on application or can gain on outside courses.

SALARY The average graduate starting salary for army officers is £22,510.

■ Emergency services

Roles

■ Firefighter

Despite the title, it's not all about fire: **firefighters** help rescue people and property from a whole range of disasters and accidents. They also provide community advice and education on fire prevention and safety, and enforce fire safety standards in public and commercial buildings. Whether you're called out to deal with a fire, flooding, chemical spillage, trapped people or animals, crashes, bomb scares or any number of other emergencies, you'll need to assess the situation, give first aid and make the environment as safe as possible for fellow crew members and the people you're trying to help. It's a stressful and sometimes dangerous job, which relies on teamwork. You'll be kept as fit and alert as possible through regular drills and training sessions and will need to ensure that all the equipment is maintained. It's an extremely competitive field.

■ Paramedic

A **paramedic** responds to emergency calls, makes provisional diagnoses, gives provisional treatment then decides the best way to transport a patient to appropriate treatment and reports their condition to hospital staff on arrival. There are other duties such as checking and maintaining vehicles and equipment, dealing with violent and aggressive people and making clear-headed decisions under pressure that make this an extremely demanding job. You won't start off as a paramedic; you have to work your way up through ambulance care assistant, working with the patient transfer service taking non-emergency patients to appointments while being trained in life-support skills. You'll then work as an ambulance technician alongside paramedics on 999 calls, administering pre-hospital treatments and taking decisions on moving patients and other issues. Paramedics are advanced technicians, with advanced life-support skills and the authority to administer injections and insert cannulas and so on without a doctor present.

■ Police officer

The job of a **police officer** is to maintain law and order, protect life and property and prevent and detect crime. You'll spend time patrolling the streets, arresting and interviewing suspects, doing paperwork (there's lots of this – statements, incident reports, court documents and so on), responding to calls from the public and informing families of accidents and deaths.

QUALIFICATIONS AND TRAINING Some of the entry requirements are more stringent than others, and all of these positions are competitive, none more so than firefighting. Training and development is usually a career-long process. To be a **firefighter** you need to be at least 18, have good eyesight and pass a strenuous fitness test. They accept all graduates and holders of diplomas, as academic qualifications are not really necessary, although having an engineering or science degree might help you higher up the ladder, when you begin to need professional qualifications in order to progress. Posts don't come up that often and when they do there tends to be an overwhelming response, so anything you can do to give yourself an edge like volunteering, gaining first-aid skills and so on will help.

Paramedics don't need a specific degree or even necessarily a degree at all as training tends to be given on and alongside the job. Obviously something like life science or medical science will be useful. You can do a degree in paramedic science but it doesn't guarantee you a job. There is an age requirement, however; you must be at least 18 to start as an ambulance care assistant and you can't start as a paramedic until you're 21. There isn't a mandatory upper age limit though, and often services recruit up to normal retirement age. Many services welcome applications up to the age of 45 for accident and emergency work, and up to 55 for non-emergency work. There are two approaches to paramedic entry: in-job training or paramedical studies at a university. The most direct route to becoming a paramedic is to work for an ambulance service as a technician and train on the job. Individual ambulance trusts manage their own recruitment which means that entry procedures can vary slightly.

For **police officers** requirements are similar to those for a paramedic, although if you want to get on to the accelerated promotion scheme (Scotland) or high potential development scheme (England and Wales) you'll need a degree. These schemes are highly competitive and open to graduates and final-year undergraduates. Candidates must display the ability to reach the rank of inspector in between five and seven years and show

Contacts

Ambulance Service Association
Capital Tower
91 Waterloo Road
London SE1 8RT

(t) 020 7928 9620

(↗) www.asa.uk.net

British Association for Women in Policing
PO Box 999
Camberley GU15 9AL

(t) 07790 505204

(↗) www.bawp.org

British Transport Police
25 Camden Road
London NW1 9LN

(t) 020 7380 1400

(↗) www.btp.police.uk

Fire Brigades Union
Bradley House
68 Coombe Road
Kingston upon Thames
Surrey KT2 7AE

(t) 020 8541 1765

(↗) www.fbu.org.uk

Fire Service College
Moreton-in-Marsh
Glos GL56 0RH

(t) 01608 650831

(↗) www.fireservicecollege.ac.uk

Gay Police Association
GPA
London WC1N 3XX

(t) 07092 700 000

(↗) www.gay.police.uk

London Fire and Emergency Planning Authority
8 Albert Embankment
London SE1 7SD

(t) 020 7587 2000

(↗) www.london-fire.gov.uk

National Black Police Association
28-30 Grosvenor Gardens
London SW1W 0TT

(t) 020 7259 1280

(↗) www.nationalbpa.com

National Policing Improvement Agency

(t) 020 8358 5555

(↗) www.npia.police.uk

Police Federation of England and Wales
15–17 Langley Road
Surbiton
Surrey KT6 6LP

(t) 020 8335 1000

(↗) www.polfed.org

Police Service of Northern Ireland
Brooklyn
65 Knock Road
Belfast BT5 6LE

(t) 028 9065 0222

(↗) www.psni.police.uk

Police Service Recruitment

(↗) www.policecouldyou.co.uk

the potential to reach the highest ranks in the service. You have to go through the same entrance process as everyone else, taking physical and mental tests. The closing date for applying in Scotland is early November and in England and Wales there is a rolling programme of induction with three or four batches of people being processed each year.

SALARY The average graduate starting salary in the 'protective industries' is £20,639.

Online reading
Police magazine www.polfed.org/magazine.asp
NHS magazine www.nhsdirect.nhs.uk/magazine
Fire magazine www.fire-magazine.com

CORPORATE CULTURE

These are highly structured professions. Even on accelerated entry schemes you'll have to spend time in different roles, for example the two-year probation period for police work. After that, however, in every area once you've got the qualifications to advance promotion can come quickly, although you tend to have to rise through each rank. As the navy say: if you're good, you'll get on. In the navy you can become a lieutenant commander by your early 30s and could become a commander at around 40. After this you could aim even higher. For firefighters opportunities for promotion are good; if you're really talented and you've passed the relevant exams you could become station officer after five years. The police run accelerated promotion schemes for those who show promise so you could become an inspector in between five and seven years

Paramedics can progress reasonably fast, but must pass exams at every stage, which will take years of training.

As all these roles are, in some way or another, emergency professions, you can't expect regular working hours. Be prepared to have to work extremely long hours or, in the armed forces, to be posted abroad at very short notice. Family life can be adversely affected, as you might imagine. In the fire, medical and police services you'll be working shifts, but don't expect always to knock off on time if you're in the middle of fighting a fire.

The uniform you wear is one way of imposing the personal discipline that comes with the territory in these services. The degree of discipline depends on which of the services you join – it's much heavier in the army than in the fire service for example, and in the armed forces it applies to almost all your waking hours.

ETHICAL QUESTIONS

Many would question how ethical it is to be actively engaged in war (however just or unjust people believe the cause to be). However, others would argue that "peacekeeping", which is a major feature of being in the armed forces today, is an ethical thing to do given that it aims to prevent warring parties from fighting, the first principle in a negotiated solution. Consideration should be given to the armed services' efforts to eradicate discrimination and bullying, and towards whistleblowers seeking to expose gaps between the stated aims of the MoD and reality. Maybe your job can make a real difference.

The police and paramedics are another matter of course, but there are considerations here too such as attitudes towards whistleblowers. What would happen if you reported an act of racism or homophobia by another staff member?

3

Go get it!

You've discovered your niche and decided on the kind of work you'd like to do. Now it's time to arm yourself with the tools that will help you get the job you want – the practical knowledge that will help you find plum opportunities, write successful CVs and applications, get short-listed, pass psychometric tests, impress interviewers and negotiate the right salary and benefits.

■ Finding the perfect job

Searching for a job isn't as simple as you might think. It's not just a question of picking up the paper every week and scouring the job ads until one takes your fancy, although you may strike it lucky that way. The chances are that you'll need a much broader perspective than that if you're to find the jobs advertised in places you hadn't thought of or that simply aren't advertised at all. The most successful job-hunters use different approaches to finding the right job.

Where to look
Starting the hunt

The first place to start looking for jobs is in the press. Newspapers' online jobs sections are also useful.

The Guardian advertises creative, media, marketing and general jobs on Mondays; education, academic and research on Tuesdays; health, public services, housing, environmental and voluntary sector on Wednesdays; computing, science, technology, engineering and finance on Thursdays; and vacancies for graduates and second jobbers in the Work supplement on Saturdays. **www.jobs.guardian.co.uk**

The Independent advertises media on Mondays; education and general vacancies on Thursdays; and general vacancies on Sundays. **jobs.independent.co.uk**

The Times advertises public sector and legal on Tuesdays; secretarial on Wednesdays; and general vacancies on Thursdays. **jobs.timesonline.co.uk**

The Financial Times advertises accountancy, finance, insurance, sales and marketing on Thursdays. **www.ft.com/jobsclassified**

The Daily Telegraph advertises general vacancies on Thursdays. **jobs.telegraph.co.uk**

More... on places to look

Other websites dedicated to job-hunting include:

Fish4Jobs www.fish4jobs.co.uk
Prospects www.prospects.ac.uk
Monster www.monster.co.uk
Workthing www.workthing.co.uk

In many cases, you might be better off looking in the appropriate trade magazines. They are too numerous to mention here, but a decent online search engine like Google (www.google.co.uk) should get you on the right track.

Reading job ads
Look for clues

When it comes to recruitment advertising, even the most intelligent and clued-up jobseekers seem happy to suspend their disbelief and take everything they read in a job ad as gospel. That's not to say that job adverts lie – they just exaggerate the truth. That's why, when you turn up for an interview at the "fast-growing, young, dynamic company", you may discover that it's a brand new operation with one client, run from a garage by a middle-aged man with a word-processor and big ambitions.

Like all other forms of advertising copy, job adverts are written by copywriters – people employed to sell you the job. Many of them don't even work for the organisation that has the vacancy: they're consultants who have been briefed on the company and the job specification. The idea is to make the job sound as good as possible without telling fibs, and there's also half an eye on a wider audience, so they won't hold back in beating their own PR drum, as the ad may be seen by shareholders, customers and competitors, as well as potential recruits.

In creative terms, selling a job is just like selling a chocolate bar – with one important difference. In product advertising, the bigger the response, the better. However, a company with a vacancy doesn't want hundreds of responses. It would rather attract only a small number of the most suitable candidates. A good recruitment ad will act as a preselector, screening out unsuitable applicants by specifying the necessary qualities and qualifications as clearly as possible.

Applying for a job that you don't really want – or can't do – is a waste of everybody's time. You need to learn how to read between the lines of job adverts, to ignore the hype and focus on the facts. Few people spend long enough looking at job adverts. Research has shown that people scan them for between one and two seconds. So slow down: applying for a job isn't a race.

When you read a job ad you should ask yourself three questions. First, who is the advertiser? Second, what is the job on offer? And third, what exactly are they looking for? Only when you've answered all these questions should you think about applying for the job.

You need to be informed about the organisation in order to make a proper application. How big is it? Have you ever heard of it? Does it have a good reputation? What are its prospects, and its ethics? Find out by looking it up on the web, in business directories or in newspapers.

Like the sound of the company? Now it's time to examine the job. Remember, a job title often has very little to do with the job. Every position in the world is now described as a "manager" or "consultant". It's just a hook. You could find yourself managing the tea trolley. What you want to know is what the tasks and responsibilities are and how much you'll get paid. Often companies skate over the duties because they don't know quite what you'll be doing. Watch out for this. And beware qualifying phrases like "dependent on abilities", "subject to qualifications", or "circa", all of which usually mean they'll pay you at the bottom of the scale. An "on target earnings" figure (for sales jobs especially) might make you think "Wow!", but it's just what their best-ever performer earned once. You'll get a measly minimum amount. It's important to take into account the entire job package, not just the salary. A car, company pension and health insurance are all valuable benefits, as are promises of training leading to professional qualifications (if they offer it, they'll pay for it).

So, the company's fantastic, the job's ideal... but do you have what it takes? The advert seems to want someone with the charm of Hugh Grant, the brains of Stephen Hawking and the integrity of Nelson Mandela. Surely no one's like that?

You're right. Job ads describe an ideal employee who probably doesn't exist. This is deliberate; it keeps the number of applications down. Don't panic. If the advert says "preferably" or "ideally", it means these requirements aren't set in concrete. It's only if it says "You must be" or "You must have" that you must ensure you have the right experience or qualities before you apply.

It's all a game. Every company wants a determined, dynamic, confident, all-round marvellous person, but you can't measure these qualities scientifically. After all, a company isn't very likely to ask for a lazy sod who can't struggle out of bed in the morning, is it?

Finally, beware of wacky or outrageous ads. Some companies will try anything to grab your attention. It often means the job isn't very attractive, or the company or profession has a high turnover of staff. A great ad doesn't mean it's a great job – it just means the company has spent a lot of money. (Bear this principle in mind when we discuss CVs, (on page 240). A wacky or outrageous application is usually submitted by a candidate desperate to hide their shortcomings. But if you wouldn't trust a wacky advert, why would they trust a wacky application?)

More... on tracking down information on employers

A decent search engine is a good place to start:

Ask Jeeves ask.com
Google www.google.co.uk
Yahoo www.yahoo.com

Or try:

Guardian Jobs jobs.guardian.co.uk/employers
Prospects www.prospects.ac.uk

The speculative approach
Looking for buried treasures

It's a well-worn truism that many jobs simply aren't advertised – they are filled by candidates already working for that company, by applicants to other jobs that genuinely were "kept on file", or perhaps by the boss's son (don't worry about that one, it's always a disaster). But if you aren't finding your dream job in the classifieds section, there are ways to hunt down vacancies that weren't advertised. This entails tracking down companies that you want to work for, that might want you and that might respond to a well-crafted CV that lands on the right person's desk.

The best jobs come to those who don't just sit at home waiting for the right ad. It might seem futile, but sending your CV in to a company on spec can be an effective job-search strategy. Employers appreciate someone showing enough initiative to submit their CV of their own accord – not least because it saves them the time and money required to advertise in the press. By sending them your CV, you are at the very least showing enthusiasm, and at the most demonstrating that you are a perfect fit for a role with them. You might even end up being the only person interviewed for the job.

As with any CV (see page 240), you need to tailor your CV for the company you're sending it to, bringing to the fore the most relevant experience you have. You'll also need to write a suitable covering letter (see page 254). Every CV you post or email has to be addressed to the right person. Phone up the company you want to work for and ask for the name of their personnel manager. If they don't have one, tell the person who answers the phone that you want to send in your CV and ask who you should send it to. If it's an unusual name, ask for the spelling (there's no quicker way to annoy someone than by getting their name wrong). Also ask what the person's title is if it's not immediately obvious. You should also ask if the person would prefer to have your CV posted or emailed to them – many employers these days prefer email.

Keep track of who you've sent CVs to. No one will be impressed by a second or third copy landing on their desk within a month. You need to make each company feel that you are the only one for them, not that they are part of a blanket mailing scheme you've embarked upon in desperation. Keep a record of what you've sent to which company and when, so that you can find the information quickly and easily when you get a phone call. It's a good idea to have a "job file" in a ring-binder for this purpose, so you can update it when you need to. Make sure you note down names and details when you are on the phone – often the person calling you will not be the same one you sent your CV to. If you don't get a response from a company within a week of submitting your CV, telephone them to ask if they received your CV, and if they have any suitable vacancies.

If you do embark on a CV campaign, it's important to stay focused and keep organised, so bear the following points in mind.

Structure your days
Job-hunting is a full-time job. Although it is tempting to exploit your free time, don't start going fishing midweek or sleeping late. Get up at your usual hour, shower, eat breakfast and go to "work". The trick is to spend time every weekday working towards finding a job.

Research first
Comprehensive research is your route to success. It shows potential employers that you do your homework and keep ahead of the pack. Multiply your opportunities by researching numerous companies within your target industry and geographic region(s). If you're only prepared to work in London, don't apply to a company where the head office you'll be stuck in is in Nottingham and if London is your idea of hell, look for companies with large operations throughout the UK.

Flick through, and try and make sense of, a target company's last two or three annual reports, promotional sales materials, trade publications and any relevant magazine articles. This should familiarise you with the overall industry, your target company's corporate culture and its key executives. Your best bet for that sort of material is the internet – also a good way to find out what other people are saying about that company.

Determine recruitment patterns
Find out if a target company is recruiting in your preferred areas. You'll need to know if the company expects to be downsizing, maintaining a stable workforce or recruiting soon. If, for example, you want to work in marketing, find out that specific department's recruiting outlook. It's not uncommon for large companies to simultaneously recruit in one department while downsizing others.

Use your professional organisation
Even if you're just starting out on a career, professional associations are a great resource for job leads, mentoring and research. Find out which association represents you and your fellow workers and join that group. Professional associations can also keep you "in the loop". Contact other professionals to tell them of your goals and to ask for guidance. You never know when one might say "Call this person and say I referred you."

Keep knocking

Follow up on a letter of introduction or, if you've got lucky, an initial interview with a timely phone call. Keep it short and to the point. Ask if your letter
was received and if any additional information is desired. If necessary, leave
your message on their voicemail.

Remain upbeat

Looking for work is laden with untold emotionally draining rejections.
Don't take rejection personally. Share feelings with supportive people. Avoid
getting too excited or too discouraged. Reward yourself with a special treat
at each step in your job search. Apply for multiple jobs simultaneously and
view interviews as opportunities to work on your interviewing skills, not as
do-or-die situations. This alleviates your stress because all your eggs aren't
in one basket.

Using recruitment consultants
Approach with caution

Bright, well-qualified job-hunters are to a recruitment consultant what a
lottery winner is to a Ferrari dealer – a precious commodity. If they find
you a job, they pick up a commission. Unfortunately, this means they do
not necessarily have your best interests at heart. Always remember that the
consultants are working for the employers. They will tell you they are giving
careers advice, but you should not always trust it: it may be advice that fits
in with their commercial objectives.

Despite this, a good recruitment consultant can be a great asset in your
search for the right job, as long as you approach them with the right attitude
and understand the rules of engagement. The first thing to remember is to
do your research before signing up with a consultant. Most recruitment
consultants specialise in one or two areas of the job market. It is also becoming more common for employers to sign up with a "preferred" consultant.
Check you are signing on with the right agency: if necessary ring up any
companies you would like to work for and find out which consultant they use.
This will probably mean signing up with several different agencies, although
three or four should be enough.

Stories abound of job-hunters who waste time and money chasing
positions for which they are patently unsuited. A recruitment consultant is
not an insurance against this happening to you. Find out how the agency
operates before you sign on the dotted line. A professional consultant should
conduct a thorough interview with all prospective candidates before sending them to meet clients. If the agency simply tells you to fill in a form and

they'll put you on the database, the chances are you are wasting your time. An interview with the consultant is important because, not only does it give you an opportunity to check out the recruiters and ensure that you like them and trust their judgement when it comes to putting you forward for jobs, it is also your chance to sell yourself to them and make sure you're top of their list of recommended candidates. Naturally, it helps if you go to that interview well prepared. Do your research before the meeting. Have some idea of the area you'd like to work in. And be clear about what you have to offer. What are your strengths and weaknesses? If you're not sure, talk to your parents, friends or past employers.

Perhaps the most common abuse practised by consultants is not briefing candidates before sending out their CV to a potential employer. Do not sign on with an agency unless it agrees to check all potential jobs with you first. This ensures your name will only be put forward for jobs that really interest you. According to the Recruitment and Employment Confederation (REC), the industry body for consultants, it is now standard practice among its members to ensure candidates agree each application, so make sure the agency is a member of the REC when you sign up.

Recruitment consultants specialise in job ads promising a "lively working environment", "excellent career prospects" and "first-rate remuneration". But, when the big moment arrives and the job offer is on the table, make sure you are clear about the terms of employment and feel it is the right job for you before you accept. If necessary take some independent advice.

Recruitment consultants can be very useful; they can get you the job that you want. But they will try and sell you the job they want to fill, so be very sure that you want that job. And finally, despite all the above warnings, try to be open and friendly when you meet them. Treating a consultant with suspicion will not pay dividends. It is a maxim of human nature that people help you more if they like you.

More... on recruitment services

Recruitment and Employment Confederation
15 Welbeck St
London W1G 9XT
(t) 020 7009 2100   (↗) www.rec.uk.com

Get help!
From those paid to care

If you had a machine in your living room that was capable of printing £20,000 or £30,000 a year in used notes, you'd take pretty good care of it, wouldn't you? If it needed mending, you'd take it to a qualified, professional repairer. If you thought it could print even more money, you'd seek the advice of an expert on how best to upgrade it.

Aren't you just such a money-making machine? Yet where do you go when your career is coughing up error codes? Whose advice do you seek when you crave promotion or a new challenge? Survey after survey reveals that, more often than not, we seek the expert opinion of... our friends and family. With all due respect to your mates and your mum, what do they know about the industry you work in, the opportunities for training and development or the chances of promotion?

There's nothing wrong with seeking advice from your mates or your family. Their opinions can be useful since they know you better than anyone and can tell you "Oh, you'd hate that job" or "You'd be great doing that." But, unfortunately, they (especially your mum) will tell you that you can do almost anything and, ego-boosting though that is, it's not much help if they don't have the inside knowledge of how employment works.

So where should you go for personal attention? When it comes to dealing with the money we earn, we can hardly keep the banks, building societies, insurance companies and independent financial advisers from beating a path to our door and advising us on how we should save and spend it. But when it comes to earning the money, to career planning, it's a very different story.

Pick up your local Yellow Pages and in between cardboard boxes, cargo handling and carnival goods, you will probably find a modest section entitled careers advice. But as you let your finger do the walking down each entry, how do you know whether the advice proffered by Aardvark Career Consultants is expert or value for money? Most of the government-sponsored careers guidance services, for example, are geared towards the long-term unemployed, not towards recent graduates. Some people knock on the door of private consultancies, where they find themselves paying up to £300 for an interesting, but ultimately irrelevant psychometric test. Others end up in the arms of recruitment consultants who offer advice with one eye on the commission they will receive for filling a vacant position.

As a starting point, it's always worth going back to your university to see what they can offer. This might feel like a retrograde step, especially if you are already in your first or second job. But those who do go back are usually pleasantly surprised. Actually, there's no need even to go back to your own university: there is a reciprocal agreement between many universities which enables graduates to receive free guidance from any university careers advice service for up to three years after they graduate. Services vary depending on resources, but most recent graduates should be able to speak to an adviser. And you can be sure that when you go to a university careers advice service, staff will adhere to a set of standards and a code of conduct.

Job clubs
Sharing the pain and the pleasure

Job-hunting can be a difficult task when you're not getting the results you want and you've nobody to support your quest. But gather a few friends together and you could make things a lot easier, particularly if you get really creative and form your very own job club.

Setting up a job club might seem like expending a lot of effort that could otherwise be applied to job-hunting. But when you've had one knockback after another a support group can be useful. Having a good network of friends and social support can help preserve the optimism and self-esteem that are so essential to the job search. Even sharing your rebuffs can be valuable. If you know that it's common to have a number of rejections, you realise it's not your problem – it's just *the* problem.

Decide how formal you want your job club to be. Is it going to involve a few of your mates chatting about their career aims or will it be a slightly larger group with a structured series of seminars? Whichever you chose, work out how often you're going to hold your meetings and where. But avoid gathering at the table nearest to the bar, as your job-hunting aims are likely to end up a little out of focus. Set out a timetable of topics that need to be covered, such as speculative letters (see page 227), interview techniques (page 262), networking (page 236) and CVs (page 240). If you're feeling entrepreneurial, find a guest speaker who will appeal to the masses, hire a lecture hall, do some marketing and charge an entrance fee for the great event.

Remember that most jobs are not advertised so you need to get used to the idea of networking if you want to maximise your chances. Be realistic about networking opportunities derived from the job club. Even though people in the job club aren't going to provide you with jobs, hopefully they can give you access to the people they know. It might be for a 15-minute telephone conversation or even a quick coffee. The most useful way to use contacts is to get insider information about a particular sector or a particular role. And usually people are quite happy to talk to you about their job because it's flattering.

When your job club's theme for the night is interviews, why not try a dry run? Don't think of it as role-play but as a practice question-and-answer session. Brainstorm for questions or work from an interview skills book. Afterwards, evaluate the appropriateness of the responses and try and come up collaboratively with better ones. Remember the aim is to hone interview technique and build confidence so feedback about someone's performance should be couched in positive terms. Once you've been to some interviews and assessment centres you can share those experiences with the group – particularly when you haven't been successful. Offer up the questions that you were asked and, if you're brave enough, all those duff answers that you gave. See if the others can come up with something better. At least you'll learn something for next time.

Job clubs are supposed to be cooperative environments that offer support and encouragement. But what happens if two of you are chasing the same job? Consider the competitive aspect on a case-by-case basis. Rather than focusing on the friend from the job club, consider them as just one of the dozens and dozens of other candidates who will be vying for the role.

Ultimately, your club will be about providing the camaraderie that's necessary when undertaking a difficult task. With some luck, a measure of humour and a lot of hard work, you're likely to have a lot of fun. And who knows, you may find that job you've been looking for.

Careers fairs
It's just another kind of speed dating

Careers fairs are ideal places to meet potential employers. Where else would you get the chance to meet dozens of recruiters in one day? When they arrive at individual universities, it is known colloquially as the "milk round". And don't overlook the smaller fairs, where some of the big employers who do venture outside the major cities will often be less inundated and may be able to give you more time. But before you don your best bib and tucker and go hunting, make sure you're prepared: many employers interview on the spot. And do locate your best bib and tucker – employers need to be able to picture you in their companies rather than on campus, so it's worth digging out the suit.

Prepare your CV
Make sure your CV is ready and that it looks good on paper, especially if you created it originally to send round in an email. And ensure your CV is appropriate for general distribution and not job-specific. Ask a careers adviser to help prepare and check your CV for you. They will advise on content and

presentation and should spot typos. The longest queue at any careers fair is for the photocopier. Arm yourself with plenty of copies of your CV before you go.

Plan your strategy

There may be up to 150 companies at the bigger fairs, so plan which ones you want to see in advance. Get to your target stand before the busy midday period. Most fairs will be advertised on the bigger jobs websites or in the newspapers; some newspapers, such as the Guardian, run their own fairs. Check out their websites or ring up the booking numbers to see which companies will be there and plan accordingly. Graduate Prospects (www.prospects.ac.uk) also carries very good listings of careers and graduate-recruitment fairs. Having decided who you want to see, think about what the employer will want to see from you, such as a portfolio or examples of work. Make sure you have enough background detail about the company and its market.

Make appointments

If you know a company will be at a fair you plan to attend, call them up to find out if you can make an appointment to see them on the day. Some may ask you to just turn up at the stand and introduce yourself but some will allow you to name your time. And when you turn up and it's chaos and you can't get the attention of your "date" because of all those milling around, just wait your chance and quietly explain you've been trying to attract his or her attention since 10.30. They'll note your forward planning and commitment.

Practice makes perfect

Don't head for your top-choice company straight away. Present yourself to a few others first as a warm-up so that when you get to the ones you care about, you're fluent and ready.

Follow up

If you strike up a good rapport with a potential employer, follow up with a carefully crafted letter explaining where you met them and that you'd like the chance to talk more about possible employment opportunities.

Cold calling
Introduce yourself

Given that so many jobs aren't advertised, you do have to dig around. The hardest way to do that can be cold calling – literally picking up the phone and ringing target companies to see if they want you. It can be difficult, and you may have to steel yourself for that first call, but it is a proven method of finding employment. You may have to call people at least five to eight times to get results. A lot of frog-kissing is required in order to procure a prince. Before you reach for the phone, bear some of this in mind:

Think before you dial
Know who you want to speak to and what you want to get out of the conversation. Do some research about the company to find the name of the best person to contact and the section or job within the firm that you have your sights on. Specific objectives help you stay in control of the call. When phoning for a particular job, be clear about the role you want.

Be nice to the PA
It is important to develop a good relationship with the PA. He or she determines who speaks to the boss and who doesn't. Where possible, attempt to obtain the PA's name early in the conversation, and then use it.

A little spin goes a long way
Dodging an experienced PA requires more than a pleasant manner. An implied familiarity with your target decision-maker or his or her colleagues can help. For example, if somebody else in the organisation gave you the name of your target, try saying "Rupert Smith in the press office recommended I give Belinda a call – is she there?" If all else fails, call early before the PA arrives – you may be surprised who picks up the phone.

The pitch
Having got hold of your decision-maker, explain who you are, where you're calling from and why. How you say it can be more important than what you say. Pace, intonation and confidence are very important. If you can get over that first hurdle then you're on your way because it's more difficult for someone to cut you off after the first minute. Energy, enthusiasm and clarity are always welcome. Get to the point and avoid repetition.

Be cooperative
If you give people alternatives to choose between it is harder for them to say no. For example, if you ask someone whether this is a convenient time to talk

or should you call later, regardless of which alternative they choose, they enter a psychological contract to talk to you that's difficult to break.

Build rapport

As with the PA, use previous contact with the organisation as a hook. It puts you in the "warm zone". You know someone they know and that means you have something in common. Try to speak at the same speed as the other person. If one person talks very fast and the other slowly then there's a perception of a mismatch. Communicate information in small chunks and give the other person a chance to respond in between. And when job-hunting, avoid asking for a job outright. Ask for advice or information about the industry. Most people tend to be flattered when people seek their advice.

Keep them talking

The longer someone stays on the phone, the stronger the psychological bond. Even if the conversation doesn't result in the job offer you were seeking, you can still extract valuable information that could make your next call a winner. Ask what qualities they are looking for in an employee and use that information to tailor your own message. And if this person can't help, perhaps they could suggest someone else who could?

Dealing with rejection

Keep a log of your calls and categorise the responses. Most people will say "No" because they're too busy or have no budget: it's nothing personal. If somebody is rude, politely bring the conversation to an end. Don't dwell on the encounter. Remember that rudeness is a reflection of the other person's failings: perhaps frustration at not being a decision-maker, severe stress or plain bad temper.

Networking

A little more conversation, a little more action

Any job-hunter can develop a network of useful career contacts without a company director in the family. Networking is easy if you know how, and job-hunters who develop their own employment contacts need never be short of careers advice and job offers. All it takes is the know-how to get in the loop.

Employer websites

The internet is an excellent networking resource, but it has to be used in the right way. Entering career-related phrases into a search engine tends to bring up generic information and recruitment agency sites. Instead, consider who you would like to be your future employer and visit their website directly. A well-maintained company website can offer more employment news than the most well-informed employee and a thorough browse of its pages can be as productive as having a personal conversation with the recruitment team. The site should provide the most up-to-date information about jobs and recruitment and may also give specific information about how to apply for jobs before any other source does so.

Recruitment agencies

One of the major aims of recruitment agencies is to build a large network of employer contacts. By joining an employment agency you are essentially networking with hundreds of businesses. There are hundreds of recruitment agencies and they can all make beneficial contacts on your behalf. Job-hunters who register with four or five recruitment agencies can immediately gain a massive range of employment contacts. Agencies are, as we said earlier, working for the employers, not for you, but they have a list of direct phone numbers, and you don't.

Work experience

Work-experience placements can be an excellent way for job-hunters to establish a network of contacts for the future – an opportunity to meet the very people that have inspired them to pursue their chosen career. There are few other situations that offer career-minded individuals the chance to meet established professionals in a working environment. However, bear in mind that some employers take on hundreds of work-experience candidates throughout the year. In competitive industries, candidates will have to work very hard to stand out and develop relationships with employees.

Paid employment

Embarking on any paid work is a valuable networking resource, putting job-hunters in contact with other employees who can provide them with valuable insights into different career options.

Social occasions

Career contacts are not always made via obvious, employment-related routes. Social occasions can also be productive places to meet new people with useful contacts and inside information. It's not the done thing to exploit these ruthlessly – by demanding a job interview while the wedding vows are being recited at the front of the church, for example – but there's nothing wrong with asking for a number and following that up with a more formal conversation later in the week.

Inside information
Turning tittle-tattle to your advantage

Most of us love to have a good gossip. There is something deeply satisfying about getting the latest low-down on so and so or such and such. Much of this tantalising tittle-tattle tends to centre on family, friends and celebrities. But when the subject turns to work, as it often does, gossip becomes more than interesting. It becomes useful. Especially to job-hunters.

Throwaway comments about what is happening in a particular office or industry can be incredibly helpful to job-hunters looking for their first break. They can suggest where the jobs are or, at the very least, where they may be. There is a trick to exploiting this sort of market intelligence – you have to know where to find it, and how to use it. Some of the most beneficial gossip you can get is actually not heard, but read. Sector-specific journals are jam-packed with useful snippets. You'll find out who is expanding, who is diversifying, who has just collected an award, who has just delivered improved sales, which company has managed to raise its share price. You get the general idea. And yes, we agree, this sort of news is not as sexy as some, but if you really are keen to get that first break put down the glossy monthly and pick up that industry mag.

To supplement your gossip gathering it makes sense to attend events where you are likely to catch people talking shop. You probably already know the more obvious places to go to: conferences, seminars and award presentations. But be aware that it can also pay to be on the lookout at informal parties and dinners. Friends of friends may just know something and they may just mention it.

It is crucial not to talk too much at these occasions. You've got two ears and one mouth: use them in that order. That way you'll be able to hear what is going on around you and not miss out on those vital bits of conversations. And when you do eavesdrop on something particularly juicy, what then? Say something like "Excuse me, I couldn't help but overhear you saying XYZ. That's something I'm interested in; would you mind telling me a little bit more?"

Once you have garnered a fine piece of insider information, apply it. How exactly? Yes, you've guessed it... by penning a captivating letter. Be direct and assertive. State, upfront, your "in" for writing. For instance, "I am delighted to hear that your company has just won a new contract." Or, "I understand you are thinking of entering the German market." Then introduce yourself and express your interest in joining the team. Provide a brief paragraph on the way your skills and qualifications would add value. Conclude with a pointer to future action. You can afford to be a bit pushy. Try something like "I will call your PA next week to see if we can arrange a time to meet."

It would be great to be able to say that just one nugget of gossip will lead you to your dream job. But you know better than that. Persist in keeping your eyes peeled and your ears to the ground. And be sure to use this research to best effect. But one word of warning: remember not to accept, at face value, everything you hear or read. By its very nature, not all gossip is reliable. Some people will be motivated to speak out because they want to promote themselves and may overstate the truth. Others will feel unhappy about where they work and may twist the facts in a negative way. So, wherever possible, verify what you've learned with another source.

■ Questions of application

Once you've found the job to apply for, the fun has only just begun. Now you've got to present yourself on paper and online as the perfect round peg for that little round hole.

CV surgery
Writing the story of your life

What may feel like the world's most tedious task – puffing yourself up and bragging about your accomplishments on paper – doesn't have to be so painful. Just remember one thing: your CV should stand out from the crowd. Employers, especially the big-name ones, receive hundreds of CVs for a single position. To get your CV to the top of the stack, you must express your qualifications for the desired job in a concise, clear and aesthetically appealing manner.

Organise your life
It's all about function versus chronology. In functional CVs, you group your skills into categories and then briefly list your past job titles at the bottom. This format is usually reserved for career changers who want to de-emphasise huge gaps of unemployment or a lack of direct experience. Recent graduates and others on a consistent career path usually opt for the chronological format. These CVs list your jobs (and duties for each) in reverse chronological order. If you're a typical graduate, it's probably best to stick with the chronological format. Most employers expect to see that format and it best highlights your education and relevant work experience.

Categorise your achievements
When organising a chronological CV, you should outline sections of your experience, education and skills to communicate what you have accomplished. Human resources representatives and employers take less than a minute to scan your CV, so showcase and organise items into several concise and relevant segments. If you've just graduated from university and have not yet been employed, place your education section first, directly below the letterhead. In addition to the basics – university name, degree and graduation date – you can include relevant coursework that applies to a desired position, academic honours or awards. If you skated through university with anything over a 2.2 feel free to put it on your CV. Other categories might

include: relevant work experience; volunteer experience; computer skills; publications; activities and honours; language skills; and travel.

Make it look good

Along with effective organisation, appearance can make or break your CV. When creating a sexy CV, keep the following points in mind:

FONTS Whether you email, fax, or post your CV to prospective employers, you should try to keep your font plain and easy to read. And select a reasonable size – anywhere between 9 and 12 point should be acceptable. Use a sans serif font like Arial or Verdana, not Times New Roman. These will come out much clearer in faxes.

FORMATTING Just because you have Microsoft Word and all its formatting capabilities, your CV doesn't have to look like a Costa Brava holiday brochure. Myriad fonts, colours, and graphic embellishments don't really help, so use minimal and purposeful formatting. Simple bullets will best separate your duties and skills; use bold and italics sparingly. Formatting should highlight your accomplishments, not draw attention away from them. Less, in this case, is definitely more.

PAPER Even if you don't snail-mail your CV to employers, you should have hard copies on hand to bring to interviews. These copies should be on tasteful CV-quality paper. White, off-white, cream and grey are the easiest to read. Just like your socks, your covering letters, mailing envelopes and CVs should all match.

Content

Now that you know how to organise your CV and what it should look like, you need to know what to put in it.

ACTION WORDS When describing your prior job experience and duties, use active language. Instead of starting your sentence with a noun, start with an active, descriptive, impressive verb. For example, if you were a customer service representative, you actually "assisted customers with product selection, trained and supervised 15 new employees and organised special promotional events". Don't think of this as an exam paper – action verbs and flowery language are required.

NUMBERS That's right, numbers. Always include numbers, percentages and amounts in your job descriptions to back up your achievements. How many people did you supervise? How much money did you raise? How many wild bears did you feed during your stint at the zoo? How much did sales increase under your direction? This approach immediately highlights the kind of impact you've made.

LENGTH Keep it to two A4 pages. No one wants to scan through three or more pages of your long-winded accomplishments and experience. If it doesn't all fit – which it won't – cut it down to the most relevant and impressive items. You should tailor your CV to match the job description, so be sure to cut and paste accordingly.

Now it should be the Beyoncé of CVs, gyrating its booty across the employer's desk, leaving the rest behind like a stack of graceless lumps. And if your skills match what an employer is looking for, you'll be snatched up for an interview. From there, it's up to you: show them you're as good as that pretty piece of paper says you are.

Interests and hobbies
You're a rounded human being, right?

Keeping their private lives secret may be a full-time job for some footballers and MPs but if you want to get your dream job, then make what you do in your private life as public as possible.

Detailing your interests and extracurricular activities is always a bit embarrassing, like writing an ad for the lonely hearts page of the local paper. But your CV will probably be read by people who will have no other insight into your personality, skills or potential than what is laid out before them. Many employers now scan CVs for more off-beat interests as evidence of creativity, personality and enthusiasm. An intriguing list of free-time pursuits can also make up for lack of work-related experience, gaps in your knowledge, or even missing qualifications.

Some employers value extracurricular activities higher than others, but many companies, particularly those in client-facing industries, are seeking as diverse a group of employees as possible. After all, the V in CV stands for "vitae" – Latin for life – and the "Interests" part of your application is the ideal opportunity for you to prove that you have a life. A wide range of interests always looks good because the employer will want to see that you can fit into different environments with ease. Why make an unsubstantiated claim like "I work well in teams" if you can demonstrate it by telling the employer you play hockey for a local club? Many job advertisements now specify a range of desired traits, so match these to your leisure interests. Offer variety and avoid lists. Specific detail is what makes it interesting to the reader, so give examples and emphasise any significant achievements related to your interests.

If you are, for example applying for a management trainee position, your interests should point out your interpersonal and leadership skills. Writing down "Captain of football team" is not as good as "While captain of my university football team I organised practices and led the team to a national final." There are a few no-nos. Steer clear of extreme sports as these suggest you are a compulsive liar. Mentioning your pets will make you sound nice but wet. List polo as your favourite pastime and employers may think you'll buy the company if the fancy takes you. Should you lie? Of course not, but there are ways of making the most of even a pathetic ragbag of interests. For example, a passion for, say, 19th-century French literature sounds much more positive than an interest in "reading".

References
What's in a name?

Your mate Phil may be a well-connected professional who thinks you're the bee's knees, but if you've never worked with him his value as a referee is nil. Don't underestimate the power of the referee.

Tucked away at the end of most job applications, the request for references can seem unimportant. Compared to exam results, details of work experience and the interview process, the words of an academic tutor or someone who you may have only spent a week working for may not seem to carry much clout. And yet employers rarely fail to contact referees – or to rely on the information they provide.

It's important to put some thought into choosing your referees; if you only saw your personal tutor once a term, they are probably not the best person to pick. Instead choose a seminar leader or lecturer that you got on well with, and whose subject you enjoyed. But speak to them before you nominate them to ensure that they are happy to be a referee and that they feel they know you well enough to write an accurate reference.

Employers are looking to find out as much about you as possible. Academic references supply a variety of information, about attitude, discipline and how you get on with other people. They can be especially useful if you didn't get the results you expected. If you got a third and were on course for a 2:1, academic referees can confirm the reasons – if there were personal problems, for example, or a specific explanation. Employers will take this kind of information into consideration, which means that a bad result doesn't necessarily damage your chances of a good job.

Assume that your references will be followed up, so don't try to fake it. And don't feel anxious about what referees will say about your potential: most employers are interested only in the facts, rather than subjective opinions about how you will do a job in the future. Employers tend to rely on interviews, tests and role-plays to give an idea of how a candidate will perform in the future. References are information on how you have been in the past. The best references are always those with the most factual information. If you have an academic referee make sure they have your CV so they can draw attention to other aspects of your experience besides your degree. It's simple: the more positive information employers have about you, the more likely they are to say yes.

Plugging the gaps
There's more to you than you know, you know

If your experience, education and interests still only take up half a page, you're probably not selling them well enough and you're allowing the value of your CV to leak away. The chances are that you have all the attributes to hand, but you just need to show them off better. Try some of these solutions:

Explain
Most employers check dates when they go through CVs. They would be suspicious of any break that is unaccounted for. But if you've taken a few dodgy detours throughout life and learning, all is not lost. Employers are looking for an explicit path through education and employment. If this is missing make sure you explain what was happening during that time. Reassure a potential employer that you were gaining knowledge, developing skills and generally making yourself super-efficient.

Reflect
Frequently people have very useful experience that employers would love to hear about. But it's omitted from their CV because they think it's not relevant to the job they're applying for. If you've taken time out to develop a business idea, been on a three-month retreat or pursued a dream of some kind, explain this in a way that is useful to employers. Think about what your aims for that period were and what you achieved. Even if some life event was forced upon you, or you made a mistake, what did you learn from it? How did it challenge you? All of this is worth putting on your CV. Many people try to gloss over a gap and make out it's not there – but you can make an asset out of it.

Skew positively
Don't be afraid of reinterpreting what you've done. There's nothing wrong with positive skewing of attributes. For example, if you've been off for a year, you've been reflecting. Take care to balance that with some practical experi-

ence too, however, otherwise you'll be seen as a dreamer. If you've been bumming around on the beaches down under, clearly you've taken the opportunity to develop initiative and teamwork skills through solo and group travel. As long as your experience shows that you can initiate and be creative and innovative, and that you're somebody who has taken control of your own life, it will improve your CV.

Demonstrate

Some kind of work experience is essential. It doesn't matter whether it's paid employment or not. And it doesn't have to be specific to your career path. You can use voluntary experience to successfully demonstrate that you are a rounded person and that you have practical competencies. It provides a very rich source of experiences that interviewers can draw on. So if you haven't got any, get some pronto and stick it in your CV.

Refresh yourself

Employers love to think that candidates have a balanced lifestyle. They like the idea that at the weekend you can relax and go rock climbing. Then you can appear on Monday morning refreshed – rather than exhausted after having taken a lot of work home with you. Mentioning your hobbies will add to your CV only if they bring out qualities that appeal to the employers, however. Anything that demonstrates social skills is helpful and the more you can indicate your interest in life the better.

Show passion

One final attribute to demonstrate is enthusiasm. Use terminology that indicates that you are alive and proactive and have energy. CV phrases should be dynamic. "I would love to..." is better than "I am prepared to...". "Enthused by challenges" is better than "Manage to cope under pressure". Above all, show passion, demonstrating that when you commit to something, you really go for it.

CV lies
Telling the whole truth

Unless you want to spend the rest of your professional life living in a complicated (and deeply unfunny) farce, don't be tempted to lie on your CV. Getting a job can be highly stressful and candidates feel pressure to enhance their achievements in order to present themselves in the most favourable light. Some are tempted to lie in the mistaken belief that everyone else is doing so. Certainly, while the fibbers are still in the minority, lying on CVs is on the increase. The common distortions include bogus or exaggerated qualifications, changing the dates of employment to hide career gaps and exaggerating the pay received in a previous job.

Every job-hunter faces the challenge of presenting their qualifications and past experience with as positive a gloss as possible. So just where does harmless exaggeration end... and outright deception begin? It's a difficult question to answer in the same way that it is hard to define what are company perks and what is simple theft. While exaggeration is widespread and generally accepted, it is unwise to resort to outright lies. This is not merely moral advice, it's also expedient. Outright lies about qualifications or invented jobs will work against you.

At best, the cost of lying to future employers is the embarrassment of being found out. At worst, it can lose you the job. Under the terms of a contract of employment, prospective employees are required to tell the truth. A CV acts as a personal history form and if a job offer is made on the basis of information contained in a CV that the employer believes to be correct, then the employer is legally entitled to withdraw the job offer if they discover the CV contains false information. So be honest. And if you feel it means you're missing out somewhere along the line – well, you've got the moral high ground and a clear conscience. That's worth something. Isn't it?

Multimedia CVs
Log on, but don't tune out

In today's multimedia age, choosing the perfect format for your CV is not always as simple as deciding between Helvetica and Palatino, selecting double or single-spaced type, and remembering to buy a stamp for the envelope. Now the technology exists for you to create a full multimedia display – an extravaganza of sound and vision to impress future employers. But will it really work? An all-singing, all-dancing CV, including photographs or a brief video in which you introduce yourself sounds great in theory. But in practice is it really just the 21st-century equivalent of that 1980s' cliche – a CV sent on brightly coloured paper to make it stand out from the crowd – and often the quickest way to speed your name into the reject pile?

Email etiquette
Now is a good time to remember the old adage about quality not quantity. What counts is delivering the relevant information that will stimulate employers to invite you to an interview. Emailing a CV is undoubtedly a faster method of sending information than the post and generally solicits a

quick response. Yet bear in mind that less technically minded employers may not have the necessary software to view documents created in the latest multimedia format and adding heavy files containing images can drastically increase the time it takes them to download your message. Be brief and succinct – employers are looking for facts, clearly communicated, in a succinct way. Photos which are heavy files and take time to download rarely persuade employers to see someone. In fact, unless you are applying for a job in an industry such as computer games or graphic design where a multi-media CV might showcase relevant skills, flashy add-ons are more likely to alienate than impress a potential employer.

One possible option is to design your own website and then direct people to look at it. But this requires the employers to take time out to find the information. However, there are ways to make the most of the internet and send your CV online quickly and helpfully.

AVOID ATTACHMENTS Don't send your CV as an attachment: paste it into the body of the email. Employers often ignore attachments because they worry about viruses and don't want to waste time with files their computer can't translate.

SUBJECT LINES If you're submitting information to a database, add a subject line, which may include the reference number of a specific job, or a description of your skills.

USE NOUNS Online information is often scanned by computers to comb the text for words that indicate job titles, technical skills and levels of education or experience. Most of these words are nouns rather than verbs.

USE BUZZWORDS They are the key to an online application. Computer screening systems often rank CVs by the number of buzzwords in them, so don't forget to include them. Use words likely to attract those in your chosen field. For example, if a job ad asks for "retail management" skills, make sure your CV includes those words.

If you do send your CV by email, you'll need to send a covering email note that briefly and courteously explains just what you are applying for. Don't mess it up at this point. Email is a fast and often informal medium, but don't let the bad habits you've got from emailing your mates spoil things at this late stage. This isn't the time to demonstrate your habitual rambling, your poor spelling or your cavalier attitude to punctuation. Treat it as you would a printed covering letter. Write it out and re-read it beforehand and cut and paste a properly written letter into the email (you may need to reformat it a little). Then print it off – it may be handy to know what you said if you are called to an interview.

Verbal CVs
No time to be tongue-tied

So let's assume that the networking, visits to careers fairs and brazen buttonholing of important people at weddings have paid off. Your CV is pin-sharp on paper. Now you need to make it sound good too.

Most recruiters make their decision on the impression they get from a candidate and on what the candidate says – not on what is written on the CV or application form. So every job-hunter should have a well-practised verbal CV that they can trot out anytime anyone asks. It happens so often that people have a very impressive written CV, but when they're asked at an interview what they do they run themselves down with a limp statement that barely does them justice.

Talking about our strengths and successes is considered immodest, even arrogant. But unless you are lucky enough to find a third party willing to sing your praises for you at interview, you will need to overcome your fear of promoting yourself. Being able to give a good verbal account of yourself will stand you in good stead in other situations too. It's something that you should use all the time when you are networking and socialising in business. It's about selling yourself. You never know if the casual inquiry at a business lunch about what you do could be from a potential employer.

Just like a written CV, the best verbal CV is a brief one. Use no more than a few sentences to sum up the type of experience you have and how you want to be perceived and positioned. Practise your verbal CV out loud on your friends and mould it into a slick declaration that can be brought into play when required. Choose your words carefully. Some words are more likely than others to make the interviewer sit up and listen. Avoid negative words like "but" – alternatives like "however" or "and" have similar meanings but can seem more positive. Steer clear too of self-deprecating statements such as "I don't really know much about this..." or "I'm not sure if I'm qualified enough for this..." This doesn't mean that your verbal CV should cover up weaknesses or attempt to portray you as some kind of superhero, but an interview is hardly the time or place to start sharing your self-doubts.

So when do you present your verbal CV? Don't dive in straight away, but don't miss the cue either. It's often a simple one, such as "Tell me about yourself" or "What can you bring to the role?". One size rarely fits all so the key to being offered a job often lies in reshaping the verbal CV to make it relevant for the employer. Sometimes it may be better to concentrate on one area of your expertise than another. A job-hunter who learns something about the company they want to work for will always put themselves at an advantage. Employers are looking for people who are genuinely interested in working for them and who will bring an advantage to the business. Too many job-hunters fail to do their homework and present themselves so badly that they don't give themselves a fair chance.

Application forms
Ticking the right boxes

You'll always need to keep your CV up to date and ready to send off at the drop of a job ad, but when you set about answering an advert does your heart sink when you read that you need to send off for an "application pack"? Well, yes, but not half as much as when the thing thumps on to your doormat. It's huge! It's cracked the floor tiles! It'll take ages! But falter now, and you've fallen at the first hurdle. Some companies use these massive applications knowing that they will filter out the lazier amongst you, so make sure you steel yourself to tackle it. Don't be the dozy one.

Remember when you were taking exams and the teachers harped on about reading the exam paper carefully and answering the questions properly? Well, it's not much different here – and you've got as long as you like (so long as you don't miss the application date). Once you go through it carefully, you'll begin to realise that it isn't that daunting and if you follow these steps, you'll sail through this bit at least.

Read the blurb
The application pack will usually consist of more than just the application form. The original advert, job description (what the job entails), person specification (what sort of individual they are looking for) and some background information on the company in question are often in there too – which is why it made so much noise on the doormat. It's all there for a reason: to help you learn more about the company and the job so that you can decide if you really would fit that role. Read all the extra bumf properly and make sure you know exactly what they are looking for. That way, you can make sure your answers are the kind that will impress.

Do your research
Read up on the company you're applying to and research the industry, sector and particular role you're after. Check the company's website and read around the careers area so that you can drop in jargon words. Do a draft. Never dive in and write straight on the application without knowing exactly what you're going to write. Even if you're nifty with the Tippex.

Answer all the questions

That's pretty obvious, but it also means don't volunteer information that isn't asked for. People tend to say things that can then be used as evidence against them. Remember, what employers are doing is checking you off against a list of educational achievements, skills and work experience that they have in mind for the job. They don't care about your morris dancing, at least not in a good way, so don't add any extra bits of information. Where a particular question is not relevant to your background or experience, write "not applicable" in the space provided; otherwise it'll look like you've either forgotten or not bothered to answer it.

Use the right keywords

There are clues in the advert, job description and person specification as to what the employer wants; you will often have those skills, but you need to persuade them that is the case. The best way to do that is to speak their language. If they ask for someone who's a dynamic team leader or works on their own initiative, give appropriate examples of when you last did those things in a work-related situation (your experience of holding the kitty on hen parties has not given you key budgeting skills) and try and use the same keywords. These will jump out at the employer when they are flicking through the stack of applicants.

Take time to consider the personal statement

Application forms are by their nature uniform documents but the personal statement is there for you to set yourself apart from the crowd and sell yourself. Address each point in the person spec faithfully, again trying ever so subtly to ally each of the skills they are looking for to your own experience. But stay focused – don't write a novel (and certainly not a work of fiction). The function of a personal statement is just to get you through the door and you're most likely to achieve that by filling the statement with further evidence that you have the skills and qualities the employer is looking for. The worst thing to do is to write a personal statement that anybody could write, so try and bring the dry factual sections of your application to life by elaborating on key relevant points. Inject a hint of personality to your personal statement, but please don't try be a wild, crazy guy. Think laterally, but try and give the impression of sanity.

Choose appropriate referees

This will nearly always be your current employer or a lecturer from university if you have little work experience. Always ask before using someone as a referee. That way, they won't be taken off guard when they're approached by the company ("Who?") and will be more inclined to give a considered and comprehensive appraisal of your work.

Treat online forms the same as hard-copy forms

In many electronic formats a program scans for keywords so it's even more important to make sure that you're mentioning words out of the advert or job spec because that's what's going to get you to the top of the heap.

Do a final check

Put loads of effort into your dummy form. Ensure that there are no spelling mistakes or grammatical errors. Keep it concise and avoid repetition. Use a range of examples to illustrate your experience. When you've written your dummy read it back and ask yourself some honest questions about it, even if you're sick of the sight of it. Ask a friend if you feel you've re-read the same stuff too often, but whoever reads it must ask, "If this landed on my desk and I was a recruiter would I want to see this person?" The answer may well be "No". But try again, don't despair. You'll get it right next time and you may have hit upon just the words to grab the employer's attention.

The dos and don'ts of application forms and CVs

Recklessness

Like they told you at school: read the instructions carefully before you start. It's easy to forget this invaluable lesson when it comes to filling in application forms. If the form says "Use black ink", don't make your prose purple. If it says "Write in block capitals", don't present a joined-up scrawl. Putting your qualifications or work experience in chronological order "with the most recent first" may seem illogical, but if it's what they ask for, it's what they want.

Bribery

Typing your CV on pink flowery paper or, worse, spraying it with perfume, will not impress. Your potential employer might have an allergy to Calvin Klein (or it could remind them of their ex or their mother). And never, ever enclose a gift. A decent employer won't accept it. An indecent one will probably harass you as soon as you start work.

Ignorance is no excuse

Every employer knows you'll be applying for several jobs. That doesn't mean they want to be reminded of it when they receive your application form or CV. Never write "Dear Sir/Madam". Never ever get their name or title wrong. Don't, for example, put "I'd love to work in publishing" when the company is actually a book distributor. Tailor each letter or application to individual jobs in individual organisations. That means doing thorough research, on the internet and in your local library. Don't be afraid to call up to check names and ask for information packs or annual reports.

Carelessness

Messy writing might be a sign of genius, but it won't help you get a job. Neither will lots of crossings out, overwriting or creative use of Tippex. As far as an employer's concerned, a sloppy application form equals a sloppy employee. Practise in rough first. If you can, type your form or letter, unless the job ad specifically requests a handwritten application (beware – they may analyse your handwriting). CVs should always be typed.

Illiteracy

Your teechers diddent learn you rite? Tuff. All employers expect prospective employees to have a basic grasp of the English language. A poorly spelled application will make them seethe with frustration, however fantastic the content. Always check for misspellings, grammatical errors and typos. Beware computer spell-checks that may Americanise some words and ignore other errors. And avoid habits you've picked up from texting your mates too often. Nothing is ever gr8. The best bet is to ask someone else to read your application before you submit it.

Fraud

Research shows the practice is rife, but lying about your qualifications is a mug's game. Many employers now demand exam certificates or make thorough background checks. If your lie is discovered some years down the track, your successful career could be over.

Impersonation

Don't lie about your hobbies and interests. Say you speak fluent Russian and you can be damn sure that your interviewer will turn out to be a former KGB agent. Worse, you might find yourself posted to the company's Moscow office. Claim you enjoy reading? Make sure you can talk about the last book you read – and make it a good one (leave the SAS stories aside for a day or so).

Exceeding the word limit

Your CV should not resemble the first draft of Crime and Punishment. Unless you're nearing retirement, a CV should never exceed two A4 pages – one if you can manage it. A letter shouldn't be more than one page. And don't try cheating by using two-point type: as a general rule, 10–12-point type is the minimum you should employ in most fonts. Invest in some good quality white paper (a torn-out sheet from a notebook won't do). Don't enclose supplementary pages in an application form unless you're asked to do so.

Submitting a mug shot

Unless you're applying to a modelling agency, sending in a photo won't aid your job application. Holiday photos and party snaps will make you appear frivolous, passport photos will make you look like a real criminal. Do you really want to be passed around the office and be judged on whether you're hot or not (it does happen)? If a company wants to see what you look like, they'll ask.

Confessing to past crimes

So you failed your biology GCSE? So you got a "U" in your general studies A-level. Keep it to yourself. However good the rest of your exam results, the failures will stick out like a sore thumb. Leave them out – this isn't the same as lying. Sacked from your first job after three months? You still worked there for three months – it's still experience (don't write that you were sacked). Avoid unexplained gaps. If you started a course, then transferred, an employer will understand.

Covering letters
Your first chance to impress

If you send off your CV or application form with a covering letter, the likelihood is that the letter will be read first. It is, therefore, your first chance to sell yourself to a prospective employer. So don't waste it.

A covering letter isn't just a piece of paper in which you wrap your CV: it's the first stage in your marketing assault on the job market. Like it or not, you're a commodity, and if you can't sell yourself, you won't be much use to an employer competing in the marketplace. As the old cliche has it, you don't get a second chance to make a first impression. The recipient of your letter will read it and form judgments about your personality and your suitability for the job. Use it as a chance to highlight your strengths and any experience that is relevant to the job. Pick out points from your CV and elaborate on them. Don't just say "Please consider me for the job as 'x'. I enclose my CV." With a letter like that, however good your CV is, it'll probably just end up in the bin, unread. Another bugbear is the standard letter: it's always obvious when you've just changed the name and job details and it doesn't inspire much confidence in your enthusiasm for the job.

If it's handwritten, make sure you whip out your best fountain pen, but ideally type it out and print it off. Get the recipient's name right and get your facts straight. Don't say you saw the advertisement in the Guardian when it was actually in a trade magazine. If you're unsure about anything, check it. And before you put pen to paper, or fingers to keyboard, you should bear in mind "the three Cs". Organisations prefer conciseness and clarity over comprehensiveness.

Use just one side of A4, with no more than four paragraphs on it. Structure your letter in three parts. The first part sets the scene and explains why you are writing. The second provides supporting evidence or information about you and is your chance to show what sets you apart from other candidates. Always accentuate the positive; for example, if you didn't get a class of degree that reflected your ability, highlight the amount of time you spent on student activities. The third part is for next steps, such as "I look forward to hearing from you." When you've finished your letter, read it carefully. Have you got your main points across? Do you sound like a good, interesting candidate? Then show it to someone else for comments, such as a careers adviser. Always keep a copy of your letter, so you don't get caught out at interview.

Speculative letters
If you're sending your CV on a speculative basis, all the above still applies. You still need to show you know what the company does and what your role

in it should be. You still need to know who you are writing to and you still need to spell it all correctly.

Don't say "I'll work for nothing." You'll only sound desperate. Don't use coloured paper. Once in a while it might work but more often than not it alienates readers. Don't say "I want to work for a big company." Be more specific and show off your knowledge of the company. If you want a job in competitive industries like the City or the media, don't ask for a job upfront. Ask to come in for a chat or to shadow someone. Then shine once you're in. Make sure you know lots about the company and its activities – and namecheck them in your letter.

Howlers to avoid

Before you send your covering letter of infinite charm and perspicuity, just check you're not committing any of these howlers:

FORGETTING TO PROOFREAD YOUR LETTER FOR ERRORS AND TONE Make sure your letter has no spelling, typing or grammatical errors. Job applicants are frequently deselected because of such mistakes.

ADDRESSING THE LETTER TO THE WRONG PERSON Call the company and find out the name and title of the person to whom you should address your letter. It shows initiative and resourcefulness, and will impress your reader that you figured out a way to address them personally. Use their name and title and don't try to guess their gender.

USING SOMEONE ELSE'S WORDS Make sure that your letter sounds like you, not like something out of a book. Your covering letter, as well as your CV, should be an accurate reflection of your personality. Employers are looking for knowledge, enthusiam and focus.

BETRAYING YOUR IGNORANCE ABOUT THE COMPANY AND THE INDUSTRY This is where your research comes in. Don't go overboard – just make it clear that you didn't pick this company out of the phonebook. You know who they are, what they do, and you have chosen them.

BEING TOO INFORMAL Promote yourself as a professional. Your letter should be as close to a business proposal as you can get – not a plea for an interview. What do you offer that is of value? What objectives can you help them achieve?

TALKING TOO MUCH ABOUT YOURSELF Downplay "I" and emphasise "you". Try to convert "I haves" into "you wants" for the employer. What can you do for the organisation that will create interest and make them want to interview you?

BEING TOO COCKY If you meet all the stated requirements for the job, spell this out in your letter – but don't lay it on too thick. Accentuate the good match between your skills and their needs.

LACKING FOCUS Structure your letter so that each part achieves a particular goal. State the purpose of your letter in your opening paragraph. Keep the letter organised. Decide on the focus of your letter and ensure that all points reinforce the topic.

DRONING ON TOO LONG Keep it simple and clean – not cluttered. Use no more than seven lines, and preferably five or fewer, per paragraph. Vary the sentence length. None of the sentences should be very long, but you don't want a staccato stream of very short sentences. One page is the maximum for letters.

SENDING PHOTOCOPIES Send original letters. Don't send copies that look mass-produced. Don't use typewriters or dot-matrix printers and never hand-write your letter.

FORGETTING TO INCLUDE A COPY OF YOUR CV Remember that the one purpose for a covering letter is to get your CV into the hands of the employer and to obtain an interview.

FORGETTING TO ASK The primary goal of your covering letter is to get an interview. Be sure and ask for one at the end of your covering letter. Be prepared to initiate the follow-up communication yourself and let your prospective employer know you will be doing this. This may be just enough to get them to hold on to your letter and give it a more thorough reading.

We've done the work for you

Work with these sample letters to get a feel for what makes a successful covering letter. But remember, they are just a guide – don't use them as a template.

Standard speculative letter. Vary it according to the nature of the company.

Dear Mr Brown,

I am writing to enquire if you have any vacancies in your company. I enclose my CV for your information.

As you can see, I have had extensive vacation work experience in office environments, the retail sector and service industries, giving me varied skills and the ability to work with many different types of people. I believe I could fit easily into your team.

I am a conscientious person who works hard and pays attention to detail. I'm flexible, quick to pick up new skills and eager to learn from others. I also have lots of ideas and enthusiasm. I'm keen to work for a company with a great reputation and high profile like (insert company name).

I have excellent references and would be delighted to discuss any possible vacancy with you at your convenience. In case you do not have any suitable openings at the moment, I would be grateful if you would keep my CV on file for any future possibilities.

Yours sincerely,

R. White

Standard, conservative style for sectors such as business, law, accountancy, retail. Don't send a letter like this for a creative position – they'll stick it straight in the bin.

Dear Mr Black,

Please find enclosed my CV in application for the post advertised in the Guardian on 30 November.

The nature of my degree course has prepared me for this position. It involved a great deal of independent research, requiring initiative, self-motivation and a wide range of skills. For one course, (insert course), an understanding of the (insert sector) industry was essential. I found this subject very stimulating.

I am a fast and accurate writer, with a keen eye for detail and I should be very grateful for the opportunity to progress to market reporting. I have not only the ability to take on the responsibility of this position immediately, but also the enthusiasm and determination to ensure that I make a success of it.

Thank you for taking the time to consider this application and I look forward to hearing from you in the near future.

Yours sincerely,

A. Brown

Letter for a creative job (in this case to be a copywriter). The aim of a creative letter is to be original and show you have imagination but understand what the job entails. Balance is essential: don't be too wacky, or it will turn off the reader. Be careful who you send this sort of letter to. As a (very) rough rule of thumb, if they wear suits to the office, this isn't going to impress them.

Dear Ms Green,

* Confused by commas?
* Puzzled by parentheses?
* Stumped by spelling?
* Perturbed by punctuation?
* Annoyed at the apostrophe? (And alliteration?)

Well, you're not alone. It seems that fewer and fewer people can write. Unfortunately, there are still a lot of people who can read. So they'll spot a gaffe a mile off. And that means it's a false economy, unless you're 100% sure of yourself, to write your own materials. (Or to let clients do it for themselves.)

To have materials properly copywritten is, when one considers the whole publishing process and the impact that the client wishes to make, a minor expense. Sloppiness loses clients, loses customers.

There is an answer. Me. Firm quotes are free. You can see some of what I do on my multilingual website at (insert web address). If you like, I can get some samples out to you within 24 hours. And, if you use me, you'll have some sort of guarantee that you can sleep soundly as those tens of thousands of copies are rolling off the presses.

Luck shouldn't come into it!

With kindest regards,

B. Blue

Online applications

The use of e-recruitment methods has revolutionised UK graduate recruitment in recent years. Online applications (Olafs for short) are now the norm, with 76.9% of employers surveyed by the Association of Graduate Recruiters (AGR) in 2007 accepting online applications only. But many online candidates are reportedly furious at how their applications are being treated. Research has shown that female graduates in particular are deselecting themselves at the application stage, denying themselves the chance of going for posts they are capable of filling because of the tortures of the online application procedure. Negative factors include the time taken to complete an application (from six to 30 hours); technical blunders such as sites crashing and erasing applicants' responses or saying that a word limit has been exceeded when clearly it has not; and concerns about confidentiality, for example rejecting an applicant on the basis of a previous personality test stored on the database. Another complaint is lack of feedback: spending hours on a job application only to receive an automated rejection five minutes later, without any reason given. However, some employers are beginning to take a more sensitive approach to online recruitment, and in the meantime you will save yourself some grief if you bear the following advice in mind.

Select the jobs you actually want
Research has shown that graduates end up applying for jobs because of the ease of accessing online forms, rather than because of their suitability for the role. Try to avoid spending time filling out applications for jobs you don't really want or for companies you know nothing about. Instead, invest more time in those you do want. Employers can spot who is genuinely interested in the job they are offering.

Virtual reality
Completing an application online can feel as though it is "unreal". Remember, an actual recruiter will see your forms. Don't be overly casual and carefree with your answers. Make sure you spend as much time preparing your answers for an online form as you would for a paper-based one. Think about what you are writing and the way you express yourself; don't just type in a response as though you are writing an email to a friend.

Familiarise yourself with the form
Once you have logged on to the form, find out what information is required from you. What questions do they ask? Do they want you to attach a CV? Also, familiarise yourself with how to navigate around the form. Some forms

allow you to dip in and out of each section, whilst in others you must move through every page to get to the one you want. Check all the links, as these are not always clear and can be misleading.

Technicalities

Remember, this is the internet. Computer crashes and dropped connections do happen. Be warned that some pages expire after a certain amount of time, even if you are in the middle of writing. For questions that require longer answers, always prepare and keep a copy of your responses. Don't just type your answers into the online form, as the information can easily be lost.

Submit your form ahead of the deadline

Aim to send in your application ahead of the deadline. If you wait until the last minute, you may have problems accessing the company's website, as 80% of candidates try to submit their application forms during the last few days. Even if you do access the website, the link to the job and your application form might have expired automatically. And you might experience technical difficulties when you try to send your form; the last day for submission isn't the day to be frantically contacting the organisation for technical help.

■ Interviews

So far, it's all gone well. You've found the job, you've got your CV into some sort of shape, written a perfect covering letter and – bingo! You've got the job interview. This can be the tricky bit. Interviews can be scary experiences and the only way to quell your fears is to follow the advice of the scout movement and "Be prepared."

Do your research
Show you care

The best place to start is by finding out as much about the company as possible. Ring the company's marketing department and ask them to send you a copy of the annual report. You don't have to be a whizz with figures to make sense of it. Use it to find useful nuggets of information that you can drop into conversation at your interview. Look up the company's website which is likely to be full of background information, history and up-to-date news. The more you know before your interview, the more confident you'll feel and appear.

You may be more knowledgeable about the company than the managing director, but when it comes to the interview itself no amount of preparation can prevent the butterflies in your stomach, the dryness in your throat and the pounding of your heart. A little adrenalin is healthy, but what you don't want is to appear like a startled rabbit caught in the headlights. So try to keep it in perspective: an interview is not a firing squad. The worst thing that can happen is that you don't get the job. Take sensible precautions: wear something comfortable, leave yourself plenty of time to get there, use the toilet before you go in and ask for a glass of water (in case your lips stick to your teeth). A few (quiet) deep-breathing exercises will make you look and feel less agitated.

Before you go in to the interview visualise success. Imagine yourself sitting there being cool, calm and collected and answering all the questions. Visualise someone coming up to you at the end and saying, "That was fantastic, you've definitely got the job." The idea is to make yourself feel more relaxed – you don't want to come across as cocky or too laid-back.

It's unlikely you'll get the first job you're interviewed for, or that you'll be offered a job after just one interview, so you're probably going to have to go through the process all over again. What's more, unless you stay in the same job for the rest of your life, you'll face many more nerve-racking interviews during the course of your career. The good news is that you will get better at it – practice doesn't make perfect, but it helps. And comfort yourself with this thought: in a few years it will be you who gets to sit on the other side of the desk.

A question of timing
Morning glory or afternoon delight?

"I'm delighted to inform you that you have been short-listed for interview. We are seeing candidates over these two days and as you are the first person I've called, you can name your time."

If you get this phone call, what do you do? The first thing is not to panic and blurt out the first time that comes into your head. The second is to calmly get out your diary. When it comes to picking the time that will offer you the chance to make the biggest impact, there are various schools of thought. Most non-experts automatically assume that it is best to be seen last, but in fact quite the opposite is true.

If you are being seen as part of a large group – the interviewer might be seeing 20 people over two days – a few principles apply. Never opt for the first 9am slot of the day, as there is a good chance the interviewer will be running late. They might be hassled after struggling to find a parking space, or similar, and consequently distracted. But it's still desirable to be fairly early in the day; the second or third slot of the day is probably the best, as the interviewer will still be fresh but is now entirely focused on what the interviewee is saying. If you are one of the first, your answers are still going to sound fresh and you can be the one to make a good impression and set the standard. Remember that interviewers will start hearing the same sorts of answers from subsequent candidates, and the more you hear something the less interesting it sounds. The slot straight after lunch is probably to be avoided because some people can feel a bit sluggish after eating, and the same applies to the late afternoon. However, there is some evidence that interviewers can become more relaxed and better disposed to a candidate in the last interview of the day as they know they are about to leave the office.

Once the selection process gets down to the last five or fewer candidates, the time of the interview should becomes less relevant as the best people will shine through no matter what time of day it is. Whatever time you agree – and this shouldn't need saying – make sure you get there on time. If you can, do a dummy run to find out how long it takes, and aim to get there half an hour early so that any minor mishaps needn't cause a disaster. If there is an almighty cock-up and you know you're going to be late, ring them as soon as possible to let them know, and to perhaps rearrange a different time slot.

What to wear
And what not

Deciding what to wear to an interview often causes more angst than it needs to. If you know you're going to start a job-hunt, decide what your interview outfit will be and stick to it. If you can't bear the agony of choice, pick out your lucky underwear too (though the luck it brings this time will hopefully be of a different kind). You should be going for jobs in the same sector and at a similar level, so wear what is appropriate. It might be a smart pinstripe for a job in the City, but something slightly less formal for a teaching post perhaps. The impression you're trying to give is that you will fit in, so check out what those in the job you want are wearing and adjust accordingly, bearing in mind that what you wear in the job is often a notch or two down from what you wear to get the job. For men, make sure your trousers don't show too much hairy leg and women should watch the skirt (not too short) and the neckline (not too plunging). And go easy on the jewellery. Your bling might not be everyone's thing.

This isn't the time to show off your individuality. The fact that you are a free spirit, not to be contained by the conventions of the wage-slave classes is of no interest to your interviewer who will be looking for people to work with, not against. Wearing your favourite trainers when everyone else is in black brogues will just show that you are not a "team fit". In other words you would stick out like a sore thumb alongside your potential colleagues. And they won't take that risk.

Whatever you choose, make sure it's clean. Check your outfit a week or so beforehand if possible to give you the chance to take it down to the dry cleaners if necessary. Make sure you too are clean and groomed (and shaven if relevant). And avoid too much perfume or aftershave, especially if it's trying to drown out a subtle undercurrent of garlic or curry.

Body language
Don't fidget your way out of a job

However well qualified, experienced and well rehearsed you are, you won't impress an interviewer if your body lets you down. You may have the eloquence of a politician and a vocabulary to rival Shakespeare's, but the story your body language tells is more important than anything that comes out of your mouth. As for those little embellishments on your CV ("I was captain of the rugby team, student union president and Nelson Mandela's penfriend, honest"), you can rehearse the details all you like, but you won't be able to disguise the facial reddening, sweating and toe curling that proclaim

"I'm a big fat liar." So how can you make sure that your physical attitude, delivery and manner don't let you down?

Most people have no idea how other people see them. They don't see their habitual expressions and they can't tell if their words are backed up by the tone of their voice and posture. When you prepare for an interview it's important not just to practise what you have to say, but how you say it. The best way to see how you appear to others is to practise in the mirror. If you can, you should videotape yourself and ask friends for feedback. If there's nobody around, practise with your cat. The more prepared you are, the more relaxed and confident you'll feel – and appear.

When it comes to the interview itself, adopt an open position. Sit up comfortably and lean slightly forwards so you look alert and attentive. Breathe slowly. And make sure your clothes aren't too tight: it won't give a good impression if you make a gesture and your shirt buttons fly off. Just remember the mnemonic ROLE, which stands for relaxed, open, leaning and eye contact. You have more control of your body language above the waist, so beware of tics lower down, such as picking your fingers or twitching your feet. They can make you look unconfident.

There is no point attempting to lie – or exaggerate – in an interview. Just be yourself. If you say what you mean and mean what you say your verbal and non-verbal communication will match. Any interviewer worth their salt is interested in who you really are.

Tough talking
Sample questions and answers

An interview is likely to start with a few pleasantries ("Find your way here OK?"), a gentle introduction ("So, talk us through your current job"), and then the climb gets a little steeper. Certain questions tend to pop up again and again and "Tell me something about yourself" is one of them: a green light to babble on about your love of wood-whittling and Renaissance poetry. Resist the urge! Focus on the three or four key things on your CV you want them to remember and talk about those.

"Where do you see yourself in five years' time?" is another classic, but it's surprising how many interviewees flounder about and mumble something like "Oh, doing this job and really enjoying it." The interviewer may be easily pleased, but they're more likely to chalk you up as a low-achiever or unimaginative. You could take the opposite tack and answer "Doing your job": bold, but risky. A better, if vague answer is "Building on my successes here and moving up within the company."

But some questions can't be dodged by mellifluous generalisations.

Fiendishly technical questions such as "What would you deduce from a down-swing in the energy current and a fluctuation of ohm levels, followed by a faint burning smell?" may either have to be bluffed through with confidence or answered with a simple admission that you don't know. Management consultancies are famed for asking horribly long-winded questions requiring weeks of preparatory work. One, for example, asks interviewees to choose between being reincarnated as a bunny rabbit or a snake. Quick! A slimy reptile or a stupid fluffyhead? Think, think!

Asking a question about the question will give you time to think. But there will always be questions that have the potential to leave you blank. It helps to keep in mind that the motivation for all questions boils down to three basic tenets: can you do the job, will you do the job and will you fit in here? Angling answers to the first by telling them about your skills and abilities, the second by demonstrating enthusiasm and the third by highlighting your track record of teamwork will help keep you focused under pressure.

But there's no need to put yourself through the mill more than necessary. Being prepared for the tough stuff will enable you to do more than sit there gawping like a guppy when the questions get really hard:

"What are your strengths and weaknesses?"

WHAT NOT TO SAY Complete honesty is not advisable (admitting you have a drink problem or a roving eye won't win you any points). Say you have no weaknesses and you'll appear arrogant and devoid of self-awareness. And reciting a long, obviously prepared list of your admirable qualities won't do you any favours either.

WHAT TO SAY The interviewer is looking for someone who is realistic about their strengths and candid about their weaknesses. You need to come up with examples to back up your claims of strengths and be able to describe the actions you take to prevent your weaknesses from manifesting themselves. So if, for example, being disorganised is your problem, explain how you've learned to make lists and prioritise.

"What achievement are you most proud of?"

WHAT NOT TO SAY Passing grade eight piano might be your proudest moment. And you're doubtless pretty chuffed that you sailed through your GCSEs without reading a single book. But the interviewer doesn't really want to know that. The general rule is: if it isn't a skill relevant to the job you're going for (or it portrays you in a bad light), leave it out.

WHAT TO SAY Think of something you achieved using skills you can transfer to the workplace. Have you ever worked under pressure to meet a deadline or organise an event? Or have you managed a budget, however tiny, either at university or during a summer job? Show off the skills you have. Save sentiment for your wedding speech.

"What do you like doing outside of work?"

WHAT NOT TO SAY The truth (watching Coronation Street, getting sozzled, playing with your Nintendo Wii). We all do it, but don't highlight it. Don't witter on about your wonderful family or partner or you may give the impression that you're not willing to work long hours when necessary.

WHAT TO SAY Research the employer to discover the sort of people they're looking for. If, for example, their website says they possess a "work hard, play hard" culture, you might say, "Quite a few of my colleagues at work are also my friends outside of work. So we like to have the occasional drink or meal out together." Mentioning that you play a team sport is also a good idea. Some interviewers believe candidates who play team sports are also more likely to be good team players.

The trick question: "Sell me the pencil/notebook I'm holding."

WHAT NOT TO SAY "That'll be 50p, please." Don't look shocked or disdainful and don't start laughing. This is a poor question which aims to see how you deal with a question you can't have prepared for and how you react under stress. It doesn't actually test anything because, unless you're going to become a pencil salesman, it's irrelevant to the job.

WHAT TO SAY It may be a rubbish question, but you have to deal with it. Try to work out what's going on in the interviewer's head by asking questions such as "Do you mean I'm a salesman for a pencil company and you're a potential customer, or do you just want me to talk about the qualities of the pencil?" There's no right or wrong answer.

"Would you ever break the rules to get a job done?"

WHAT NOT TO SAY "Rules are made to be broken." You want to prove you're flexible, not a troublemaker. "Never." Only automatons are saintly. Be careful – there's a critical difference between breaking a rule once to benefit your organisation and breaking rules repeatedly because you find them restrictive.

WHAT TO SAY Explain that you'd break a rule only if there was an opportunity or challenge to which you'd have to react quickly or the company would lose out. Finish by saying that you'd go straight to your boss and tell them about the incident.

"Have you ever been fired?"

WHAT NOT TO SAY Don't lie. Never slag off a previous employer.

WHAT TO SAY Give good reasons why it happened. There are two good ways of getting round this question. The first is to blame your underperformance on personal circumstances such as ill health and stress that they are now completely mitigated. The second is to admit you made a wrong career decision. You thought the job would involve x and y, when it actually involved a, b and c. So you lost your motivation and deserved to be fired. But you've learned your lesson: you're doing lots of research into this job and understand its demands, so you'll never lose enthusiasm for it.

The illegal question: "Do you have/want kids?"

WHAT NOT TO SAY "That's none of your effing business." Under European Union legislation interviewers may only ask questions that can be directly related to the job at hand. Questions about personal circumstances that have no impact on your ability to do your job are illegal. If an employer asks, they're probably ignorant about the law.

WHAT TO SAY It depends how much you want the job. You could say "I'm not answering that as it's discriminatory", but you're likely to blow your chances. If you really want the job it's best just to answer the question honestly and then explain why it's not a problem and won't affect your performance.

It's your go
Sample questions to ask

At some point in every interview, it will be your turn. The interviewer is likely to sit back and say "So, anything you'd like to ask us?" A feeble "Um, no, I... er... think we've covered everything" isn't likely to impress too much. So have some prepared. But before you pick and choose from the following list, be sure to consider the culture of the organisation you are hoping to join and the nature of the person doing the selecting. Be careful to adopt the right tone and to convey a positive attitude. You want to ensure this opportunity works for you, not against you.

"What are the most enjoyable and the least enjoyable aspects of the role?"
This can show that you like to know what sort of challenge you are going to face and that you like to get properly prepared for it, all in the expectation of being able to rise to it.

"You mentioned there will be a lot of presenting/researching/liaising; what do your most successful people find most satisfying about this part of the role?"

This question can serve two purposes. It can demonstrate your listening skills. Also, it can associate you with being successful in the role and finding it satisfying.

"What types of training opportunities can you offer?"

This is one of the classic questions as it can highlight that you are keen to advance your skills and add further value to a company.

"Is there a chance for promotion in the future?"

This is another classic question, and in a similar vein. It can emphasise a determination to make progress and to do so over the long term.

"Can you tell me how the role relates to the overall structure of the organisation?"

With this question you are drawing attention to a preference for teamwork. It looks as though you want to know where you would fit in and how your contribution would affect the rest of the company.

"How would you describe the work culture here?"

Here you are signalling that you want to be able to operate at your optimum and that to do so you know you require a positive environment. This, in turn, can indicate you are a good self-manager who is aware of how to get the best out of yourself.

"In what way is performance measured and reviewed?"

This question can flag up that you appreciate the importance of delivering real results. You can be seen to be someone who understands the value of commitment, reliability and returns.

"What are the most important issues that you think your organisation will face?" Or "You have recently introduced a new product/service/division/ project: how will this benefit the organisation?"

These variations both show that you are interested not just in the job but in the employer behind it. It will be apparent you have done some research, done some thinking, and are now eager to hear their analysis.

"May I tell you a little more about my particular interest in communicating with clients/developing new ideas/implementing better systems..."

Okay, so this is a cheeky and obvious way of getting permission to blow your own trumpet but then that's what this interview is all about.

"Do you have any doubts about whether I am suited to this position?"

This is a rather more brazen way of emphasising some of your strengths. It suggests you are open to constructive criticism and willing to learn from the experience of others. In addition, it gives you a real chance to address any weaknesses the interviewer may think you have. Finally, it allows you to finish on a high, restating why you think you are the right person.

Multiple interviews
Now what do they want?

Most jobs will be offered on the basis of one or two interviews. But some go to a third. Even a fourth. Rumour has it that MI6 even goes to seven. But that's supposed to be a secret. What on earth is there left to say?

If the employer is doing their job properly, each interview serves a clearly defined and distinct purpose. The key to success is to identify and plan for each one as exhaustively as possible.

Written and practical tests, interviews that test your motivation and management ability, and psychological interviews to evaluate personality are all fairly typical of the sorts of interview a job hunter can expect to face. You can prepare for some of these (the ones that test your intellectual capacity), but not for others (management skills and personality). Needless to say, when you are in a position to prepare, do so assiduously.

Even where you can't prepare, there are still certain points to bear in mind. Think beforehand about the questions that are likely to come up. A psychological interview assesses drive, determination and reliability. Interviewers will be looking for self-awareness – people who have thought about their life and what they've learned from it. The best thing you can do is to ask yourself what challenges you've met and how you've overcome them.

Finally, remember what you have said to each interviewer. It's possible that your interviewers will compare notes, and that at some stage you'll be asked to elaborate on an answer you gave in an earlier stage in the interview process, so be clear and consistent in your answers.

Interview expenses
Will they chip in?

You've been offered an interview for your dream job. It's a long way away and getting there is going to be expensive, but the company won't reimburse your travelling expenses. Is it worth the risk?

It used to be the norm for employers to pay travel costs, but a growing number are refusing to pay these expenses, and with an unplanned train ticket to London costing more than £100 in some cases, you might question whether it is worth going. So what can you do if you find yourself in the situation where you have been invited to interview but can't afford the cost?

Firstly, always establish what the employer's position on interview expenses is. If no mention is made of them, then you should ring and find out. Make sure you know whether it is a preliminary or a final interview. Often employers will only pay for final interviews. Remember, if you refuse a job you might not get your expenses reimbursed. If you know you can't afford the cost of the trip to a first interview, ask the employer if it could be done over the telephone.

Interview jokes

The chances are that trying to crack gags in an interview situation will go down like a lead balloon. But a little humour can sometimes break the ice and certain employers will actually ask you to tell them a joke. It's not an unusual scenario for PR or sales jobs, for example. One of the jokes below was told during an interview for a job with an investment bank. The standard advice that counsels against telling jokes in interviews is not a lot of use when faced with a request for one. So to make sure you're prepared here's a list of ten jokes that have resulted in job offers. The first four are the safest. The next five could receive a mixed response. The final joke is an example of one to avoid. Swearing is unanimously regarded as best avoided, but worse still is anything that hints at a negative attitude to management – not a laughing matter. Reuse at your own risk.

Safe jokes

Did you hear about the two men who were stopped by the police for being drunk and disorderly?

It turned out that the first had been drinking battery acid and the second had been swallowing fireworks. One was charged and the other was let off.

An American had been for a job interview in the English countryside and on the way back he asked a local farmer for directions. "Excuse me dude, could you possibly tell me the quickest way to London?" The farmer said, "You driving or walking, lad?" The American replied, "Driving." The farmer nodded, saying, "Yup, definitely the quickest way."

(Don't use this one for a job in the rural industries.)

I was driving along in my car, when my boss rang up and said, "You've been promoted." That made me swerve a bit. Then he rang up a second time and said, "You've been promoted again." I swerved even more. When he rang up a third time and said, "You're now managing director," I went into a ditch. A policeman came up and asked, "What happened to you?" I replied, "I careered off the road."

A ragged piece of string went into a pub and asked for a drink. "Are you over 18?" asked the barman. "No," replied the string, "I'm a frayed knot."

Risky jokes

A visitor to a monastery was being shown round by the abbot when a monk shouted out 64. All the other monks roared with laughter. Another then called out 15, again to much laughter. "What's going on?" asked the visitor. "They know each other's jokes inside out," said the abbot. "So rather than tell them each time they've numbered them. If one calls out a number they think of the joke and laugh. Have a go..." The visitor called out "45" and there was a small ripple of polite laughter. "I'm afraid," said the Abbot "that's not very funny. Try again." So the visitor called out "56" and there was uproar. "Must have been a good joke." "Yes," said the abbot wiping his eyes. "And we've never heard it before."

Why are they putting accountants at the bottom of the ocean?
They found out that, deep down, they're really not so bad.

(Maybe not a gag for a job in the financial sector.)

How many social workers does it take to change a light bulb?
None – they form a self-help group called "How to cope with life in the dark".

(Again, there's a time and a place for this one.)

What do you call a woman with one leg?
Eileen.

You can always tell a Yorkshireman, but you can't tell him much.

And one to avoid

How many managers does it take to change a light bulb?
Five. One to notice that it needs changing, one to prepare a budget, one to sign it off, one to order it from supplies and one to tell their secretary it needs replacing.

Take our quiz to discover your interview fate

When it comes to job interviews are you a textbook example of professionalism? Or do you break all the rules?

---

1 In preparing for the interview you:

a Research the company, think about what questions they'll ask and memorise appropriate answers

b Re-read your application and double-check the job description

c Fantasise about how you'll spend your first pay cheque

2 You get to the interview:

a With five seconds to spare (but only because the tube broke down)

b Fifteen minutes early (you planned for possible delays)

c With your boyfriend/girlfriend/best friend there for moral support

3 The interviewer goes to shake hands and you:

a Make eye contact and offer a firm grip

b Refuse their hand on the grounds of personal space

c Squeeze their hand so tightly their eyes almost pop out

4 To start with, the interviewer seems nervous and appears inexperienced. You:

a Ruthlessly deploy your knowledge of body language, sitting back with steepled fingertips, and wait for them to get their act together

b Ignore their insecurity as best you can

c Try to put the interviewer at ease; you smile and ask a few gentle questions

5 Asked about your past experience, you:

a Reveal you've only had two sexual partners but spent a long time with each of them, arguing that quality is better than quantity

b Explain the skills you've developed through university projects, work placements and other responsibilities

c Recite what (you hope) it says on your CV

6 Asked about your weaknesses, you:

a Roll up your shirtsleeves to reveal a rather unimpressive bicep

b Admit to a tendency to want to get everything done by yesterday

c Tell them that you struggle with anything technical

7 Asked about any personal strengths, you:

a Say you're very interesting

b Recount last Saturday's heroic drinking session

c Explain how your communication abilities help team dynamics

8 Asked about your greatest achievement to date, you reply:

a Coming second in the school egg-and-spoon race

b Winning employee of the month on a work placement scheme

c Getting through university

9 Asked why you want to join the company, you:

a Go on about how legendary the Christmas parties are said to be

b Detail the company's successes and its plans for the future

c Simply state it would be a great opportunity

10 Asked about your willingness occasionally to work overtime, you:

a Say no; overtime is overrated, and besides you've got a busy social life

b Agree instantly; you don't want to appear uncommitted

c Say yes; but only if absolutely necessary to meet a deadline

11 Asked about any hobbies, you:

a Talk about your interests and how they improve your skills

b Refer to the masonic handshake you gave them earlier

c Say you like reading books and going to the cinema

12 Asked if you have any questions, you reply:

a Where does everyone meet for after-work drinks?

b What are my career prospects with the company?

c How often are pay rises awarded?

13 To ensure you make a lasting impression you:

a Lather yourself with aftershave or drench yourself in perfume

b Finish on a positive note about your suitability for the position

c Tell them how much you really want the job

Points

1.	a 0	b 5	c 10
2.	a 5	b 0	c 10
3.	a 0	b 10	c 5
4.	a 10	b 5	c 0
5.	a 10	b 0	c 5
6.	a 10	b 0	c 5
7.	a 5	b 10	c 0
8.	a 10	b 0	c 5
9.	a 10	b 0	c 5
10.	a 10	b 0	c 5
11.	a 0	b 10	c 5
12.	a 5	b 0	c 10
13.	a 10	b 5	c 0

How you scored

0–35

Well, aren't you just a little angel. Straight to interview heaven for you. You're an image of perfection for interviewers and the target of envy for everyone else. You go into an interview armed with valuable information and convincing answers. Once in there you apply your communication skills and general persuasiveness to great effect. Keep that halo polished – though don't necessarily get it out in front of your friends because nobody likes a clever clogs.

40–65

You are in interview purgatory. Neither the best nor the worst, you are somewhere in between. You get the answer right, but often only half right. Consider improving your self-confidence. Take a fresh look at your potential. Do a skills audit so you know where your real strengths lie. And think harder about how all this relates to the type of job you're going for. You need to master the art of being your own best salesperson.

70–130

No surprises where you'd be heading for. Yep, that's right, straight into the fires of interview hell. You are every prospective employer's nightmare. Difficult, egotistical and sometimes just downright socially inept, you are considered, at best, a time-waster. If you're happy to carry on as you are for a bit longer then don't go changing. If, however, you are serious about getting a job, then you need to get to grips with the basics of selling yourself, and what is left of your soul, in an interview.

■ Interview tests

At a second or even third interview, some companies might give you a few tests to attempt. What those tests are will depend on the job in hand. For a journalist job, for example, you might be asked to write a short news story or subedit a mistake-laden couple of paragraphs. But some companies will really want to test you...

Assessment days
Prepare for action

It's usually the bigger firms that do it, particularly the ones that have much vaunted graduate training schemes, but many companies now put applicants through the peculiar joy that is the assessment day.

In fact, it's usually more than one day – most often it's two, at a special assessment centre run or hired by the company's human resources department. Once you're there, they'll put you through hoops which could include case studies, role-playing, negotiation exercises and team challenges. In addition, psychometric testing is often used to test numerical and verbal aptitude.

Perhaps the toughest graduate recruiter is the armed forces, which puts its potential recruits through a three-day assessment known as the Regular Commissions Board. As well as the physical challenges – recruits must complete an obstacle course that includes scaling a 2.4-metre (eight-foot) wall – the ordeal is mentally testing. Candidates are tested on four areas of potential: elasticity of intellect under stress, problem-solving, physical ability and personality and character. Most leave mentally and physically exhausted.

Many assessment centre tests involve strict time constraints that offer employers the added bonus of assessing potential employees' ability to cope under stress. One such test is the "in-tray exercise" in which candidates are given 60 minutes to analyse and prioritise a file of papers. This is used by the civil service assessment centre, along with policy exercises and cognitive tests, to choose the annual intake of graduates who join the civil service's fast stream. In-tray tests and teamwork exercises are also used at investment banks. However, most investment banks also subject potential recruits to rigorous one-to-one interviews which are likely to test economic understanding and up-to-date financial awareness.

So how do you cope? The growth in scientifically-based tests means there is no point trying to act a part, because you'll be caught out. So stay relaxed and enjoy yourself – most of these new procedures sound more terrifying than they actually are, and by appearing calm and organised, you'll be more impressive than the candidate who's all fluster and bluster. But to be calm, you ought to be prepared. So here are some of the more common tests you should be ready for.

Personality tests
You are who you say you are

Many employers use personality tests such as the Myers–Briggs Type Indicator (MBTI) to give them an insight into the way you interact with people as well as the way you work. The MBTI programme defines people as having one of 16 personality types. These types are arrived at through answers to four questions (or "preferences") designed to show your preferred way of approaching things. Candidates taking a particular MBTI test answer the same four questions, each of which offers a choice of two answers. A typical question might be "Would you rather work under someone who is a) always kind? b) always fair?" Each option is coded so you end up with a four-letter code that reveals your personality type.

Since there are no right or wrong answers, there's not much you can do to prepare (although there's no harm in it). Where a company might usefully use Myers–Briggs testing is to help gauge a "team fit". They might have a vacancy in a team of introverts who need livening up a bit, or they may need an intuitive type to give a better sense of the bigger picture. There's no way you can know this, unless you happen to have the results for everyone you may be working with. But it's an interesting experiment and may help you find out a little more about yourself. Treat it as such and don't let it worry you. Trying to second-guess it won't help at all.

Preferences: your ways of doing and seeing

EXTROVERTED (E) OR INTROVERTED (I) Extroverts prefer to focus on the outer world of people and things, while introverts prefer to focus on the inner world of ideas and impressions.

SENSING (S) OR INTUITIVE (N) Sensing types are prone to focus on the present and concrete information gained from their senses, while intuitive types, their polar opposites, enjoy anticipating the future and like to focus on the big picture.

THINKING (T) OR FEELING (F) Thinking types are naturally quite analytical, tend to base their decisions on logic and aim to be fair when dealing with people. Feeling types are able to empathise and base their decisions on values and people's feelings.

JUDGING (J) OR PERCEIVING (P) Judging types dislike working under time pressure, preferring a planned and organised approach to life. Perception types get energised by last-minute time pressures and enjoy a flexible and spontaneous approach to life.

Personality types

Your four-letter code defines you as one of the following 16 personality types.

1. **THE SUPERVISOR (ESTJ)** You are a natural leader. You have clear ideas on how things should be and you can get others to see your way of thinking. You are honest, direct and confident. You value facts and figures, order and efficiency.

2. **THE INSPECTOR (ISTJ)** You prefer to work alone. You are prepared to put in long hours for the things you think are important but will do very little on tasks that do not seem to offer any real value. You are reserved, organised, loyal and dependable.

3. **THE PROVIDER (ESFJ)** You are a people person. You are warm and sensitive to others. You "read" them very well. You enjoy serving them. You like a structured, routine environment. You prefer the practical to the theoretical.

4. **THE PROTECTOR (ISFJ)** You want to believe the best of people. You have a strong need for harmony and cooperation. You like to be liked. In fact, without positive feedback from others you become disheartened and insecure.

5. **THE PROMOTER (ESTP)** You are a doer. You are not interested in long explanations. Neither are you interested in the "right way" to do things. You are focused purely on results and if that means taking risks or tackling things differently, so be it.

6. **THE CRAFTER (ISTP)** You are interested in how and why things work. Detached and analytical, you excel in finding new solutions to practical problems. Although you may not respect traditions, you are loyal to your own internal value system.

7. **THE PERFORMER (ESFP)** You are the sociable one. You are fun-loving and adore being centre of attention. You live for the moment. You crave new experiences. The theoretical and impersonal bore you.

8. **THE COMPOSER (ISFP)** You are the quiet, serious, reflective sort. You may be creative, open-minded and adaptable. You seek out beauty. You avoid conflict. You are not interested in leading or controlling others.

9. **THE FIELD MARSHAL (ENTJ)** You are an organiser. You take charge. You can absorb lots of complex, contradictory information and make decisions quickly. You can easily turn difficult problems into smooth solutions.

10. **THE MASTERMIND (INTJ)** You are a strategist. You are logical and analytical with an ability to think long-term. You can turn an idea into a 10-step action plan. You expect high standards of yourself and those around you. Competency is key.

11. **THE INVENTOR (ENTP)** You get excited by the new and the challenging. You are lateral, resourceful and intellectually quick. You are outspoken and assertive. You have a low tolerance for the mundane and may neglect things that fall into this category.

12. **THE ARCHITECT (INTP)** You are a creative thinker. You come up with new ways of doing things and you suggest alternative solutions to existing problems. You are quite individual and maybe a little distant.

13. **THE TEACHER (ENFJ)** You can place the needs of others before your own. You have a real concern for how others think and feel. You can facilitate groups well and have good people-managing skills.

14. **THE COUNSELLOR (INFJ)** You are very intuitive about people. You are gentle and caring towards them. You tend to act instinctively rather than to set rules or guidelines. You are not interested in either leading or following others.

15. **THE HEALER (INFP)** You are interested in making a difference. You are happiest serving the greater good. You want to help people. You are reflective, laid-back and can enjoy your own company.

16. **THE CHAMPION (ENFP)** You are a go-getter, enthusiastic and energetic. You will turn your hand and your mind to almost anything that interests you. And you usually achieve quite positive results.

A suitable job

According to the theory, this is how the jobs then match up. You can take it all with as large a pinch of salt as you fancy. There's a lot of worth in the Myers–Briggs model, but it's not watertight and knowledge of your type should never stop you from finding a job that appeals to you. People of all types can find success in all fields. What matters most is finding the best job for you within each field and the working environment that suits you.

1 & 2 Military leader, police officer, judge, financial director, business manager, business administrator.

3 & 4 Teacher, social worker, child care worker, health practitioner, human resources executive, librarian, psychiatrist, psychologist.

5 Sales executive, marketing executive, public relations executive, entrepreneur.

6 Engineer, pilot, anything to do with computers.

7   Actor, singer, photographer, fashion designer, interior designer, anything to do with sports.

8   Artist, musician, linguist, anything to do with animals or the outdoors.

9 & 10   Judge, lawyer, professor, computer consultant, corporate director, entrepreneur.

11 & 12   Scientist, engineer, mathematician, strategic planner, systems analyst, web designer, anything to do with new media.

13, 14, & 15   Teacher, social worker, child care worker, health practitioner, librarian, psychiatrist, psychologist, personal coach.

16   Writer, journalist, politician, diplomat, entrepreneur, teacher, counsellor.

More… on Myers–Briggs

The Myers & Briggs Foundation www.myersbriggs.org
TeamTechnology www.teamtechnology.co.uk/tt/t-articl/mb-simpl.htm

---

IQ and aptitude tests
Being a clever clogs may not help

You probably think you're pretty intelligent. You may have a degree and think that says it all about you. But you could be wrong. The much-vaunted expansion in the higher education system means that plenty more people are emerging with degrees and many of them will have comparable qualifications. For many jobs a good degree just gets you to the starting line, and tests are the additional hurdles you have to clear. So some employers look to intelligence – that innate quality which is not dependent on education – as an indicator of potential to succeed. It is assessed by tests that measure verbal, spatial, numerical and abstract reasoning.

How high individual employers set the bar depends on the nature of the work. Scientific research and some legal jobs for example require exceptional reasoning ability so employers look for high IQ when recruiting. It's less significant for positions such as retail management where interpersonal skills are more important. Most IQ scales use 100 as the average score and those who go on to higher education usually score 110 or more. Around 5% of the population will score 125 and a score of 135 would place you in the top 1%.

However there are very few jobs where just being very clever is enough.

The dream employee is one who combines a high level of conventional intelligence with other attributes such as motivation, emotional intelligence and communication skills. For some roles being too intelligent can be a disadvantage; employers who are selecting with an eye to promoting effective teamwork look for a mixture of complementary skills. It's generally acknowledged, for example, that the chair of a group should not be the cleverest person as such an individual would be likely to dominate proceedings. There's also an argument that the higher up you are in an organisation the less IQ matters. Those in senior positions need an ability to deal with change, solve problems, make difficult decisions and talk the talk. Intelligence could get in the way.

Although you can't significantly improve your IQ or natural aptitudes, knowing what to expect from a test and getting a bit of practice will help you do justice to yourself. So bear in mind the following:

- Many people lose marks because they don't read the initial instructions carefully.
- Don't worry about being a bit nervous. A little extra adrenalin can help you perform better.
- Don't spend too long on any one question. If you can't do it quickly move on and come back to it at the end.
- Be honest in personality tests rather than trying to provide the answer you think is wanted. Many tests are designed to make dishonesty glaringly obvious.
- Ensure you're provided with detailed interpretation of how you did and what that means. There's much you can learn from test feedback.

Psychometric tests
Getting to know you

Many employers now use psychometric testing to assess the personalities of potential employees. There are several kinds of test but usually candidates have to answer questions on their preferences and interests which reveal their aptitudes and how they get on with colleagues. It's not unlike a Myers–Briggs test, but this time it's to see whether you would fit in at work, rather than just to find out what you're like.

Psychometric tests assess you in two main areas: ability and personality. You might take the test with pencil and paper or on a computer. You may be asked to take it in an assessment centre, test centre or online. Some employers even set a pass rate that you need to achieve to progress further. The thing is not to stress about it. If they decide that you aren't right for the job or career in hand, then great – you're better off out of it. If you think they're wrong, well, there are always other opportunities.

There are two types of specific ability tests: attainment and aptitude. Attainment tests examine the skills and knowledge you already possess and are usually pitched to test for skills you'll need in the job. Aptitude tests are more a measure of your potential, relying not on what you already know, but on what you can improvise, on what your natural abilities and aptitudes are. They often take the form of verbal and numerical reasoning tests. There are also more specialised aptitude tests which can be used if you are applying for particular careers in IT, science or engineering.

Personality questionnaires are designed to see what you are like. As with Myers–Briggs, there's no right or wrong answer and it's more a question of a cultural or team fit – will you get on with everyone else, are you the kind to enjoy the work?

If you are given a test at interview, don't be tempted to fill in the answers you think the interviewer is looking for. If you're too perfect, they'll smell a rat. If you have to misrepresent yourself, is it really the job for you? There might be problems if you get the job because there could be things you won't be able to do.

There are some very ropey psychometric tests around and you'll have little way of knowing if you are being tested with a reliable one. But a well-designed test can produce a reasonable degree of accurate information about a person's character and, by extension, how they are likely to behave at work. It's self-assessment, after all.

More... on psychometric tests

Mindtools www.mindtools.com
Peoplemaps www.peoplemaps.co.uk
Liam Healy & Associates www.psychometrics.co.uk

Group tests
When to speak up and when to stay silent

By the time you reach the final stages of the recruitment process, you have probably already demonstrated that you have the skills required to do the job. At this point employers may take a closer look at your communication skills, your ability to analyse problems and how you work in teams with people you don't know. You may be given problems to solve, strategies to think up or perhaps you'll be asked to ford a raging river with two paper cups and a lollipop stick. Whatever they throw at you, at this stage it's time to ease off the self-promotion as recruiters are looking for candidates who are conscious of others in group exercises. Don't let your negative feelings surface. Remember that this is a test and recruiters will be watching that you listen as much as you talk, that you respect others' opinions even if you don't agree with them, and that you help the group stay focused on the end result. By concentrating on helping the group to succeed, you'll set yourself apart.

To sail through group tests you will need:

TO BE A TEAM PLAYER It may be a cliche, but demonstrating that you can work successfully in a team and listen to others' points of view is vital.

CONFIDENCE You could be dealing with both clients and candidates on a daily basis and you can't do this if you're lacking in this department.

COMMUNICATION SKILLS You need to be articulate enough to express your views coherently. If you find yourself stumped for an answer, don't ramble on or give a monosyllabic response. It's better to say, "I'd like some time to think about that. Can we come back to it?"

ANALYTICAL SKILLS The ability to analyse a problem and identify solutions is crucial. In many jobs it's important to be able to understand a client brief and the client's objectives.

TO UNDERSTAND THE INDUSTRY Some knowledge of the industry in which the company operates will be more than useful.

If all this sounds a bit daunting, don't worry. No employer is expecting you to be perfect and come top in every group test. If you are strong in some areas, but weak in others, employers can focus on those weak areas in their training programmes. Group tests are very much about the individual – employers don't want cloned templates.

Be a Swot
Analysing yourself – and them

Some companies may ask you to bring a Swot analysis to one of your interviews, or they may ask you to produce one during an assessment day. Any request for an analysis during this whole process can bring a little moisture to the palms but a bit of deep breathing and preparation can make all the difference. Swot stands for strengths, weaknesses, opportunities and threats. It's much beloved by the sort of manager who reads books with titles like "Who Moved My Cheese?", but this isn't a time to be cynical, it's a time to be analytical.

Swot-ing yourself

You can use the Swot framework to present, either to yourself or to a potential employer, a summary of what you are good at and what needs improving. Essentially, it's a system of asking yourself questions under the Swot headings and understanding where the answers take you. So ask yourself the following questions, and write down the answers. Think about what you think you are good and bad at and what other people may see as your strengths and weaknesses. Don't be modest. Be realistic.

STRENGTHS
- What advantages do you have?
- What do you do well?
- What skills and qualifications do you have?
- What do other people see as your strengths?

WEAKNESSES
- What could you improve?
- What do you do badly?
- What should you avoid?

OPPORTUNITIES
- Where are the opportunities facing you?
- What are the trends in the industry you want to join that you can take advantage of?

THREATS
- What obstacles do you face?
- What are others in your industry doing?
- Are the required specifications for your job changing?
- Is changing technology threatening your position?

Employers make ask you to do a Swot analysis on yourself, but it could also come in very handy when someone asks in an interview "What are your strengths and weaknesses?" The depth and seriousness of your answer could well catch them out.

Swot-ing the company

You can also perform the same trick on the company, whether bidden or unbidden. It may be that you are asked to produce one for an interview or during assessment. But there's nothing to stop you producing one before you have an interview. If it doesn't seem right, if all the questions are of a completely different kind, then you don't have to thrust it upon them. And in some areas, it might be completely inappropriate. If you're applying for a research post in an archaeology department then this kind of analysis is likely to have them scratching their beards in bewilderment. But in some cases, whipping out your Swot is likely to impress upon your potential employers your commitment, intelligence and managerial know-how. For a company, the questions are pretty much the same as for you. Here are some sample answers for a typical small company.

STRENGTHS

- Small managerial team is flexible and responsive. Unburdened by bureaucracy.
- Predictable level of work flow enables a high degree of commitment to customer care.
- Strong reputation.

WEAKNESSES

- No presence outside of current small marketplace.
- Small number of staff means shallow skill base in some areas and vulnerable to sickness and/or turnover.
- No new products or services coming onstream.

OPPORTUNITIES

- Likely expansion of sector.
- New technologies offer possibilities for new products and services.
- Central and local government are offering grants for expansion in this sector.

THREATS

- Technological developments may be expensive or change the market beyond recognition.
- A shift in emphasis from a large competitor could swamp market position.

By presenting such an analysis, you are also starting a plan for the future of the company. This sort of strategic thinking can be very impressive if done well, but beware of trying to second-guess a company or industry you don't know well enough and beware too of causing offence. Don't slag off a company's website as a weakness if the man responsible for it is sitting in front of you. When you are introduced, bear in mind the job titles of those you'll be dealing with (ask if necessary) and improvise if you have to.

■ Decision time

Handling rejection
It happens to us all

Despite all your effort, despite your best suit, your best questions, your wit, intelligence and penetrating analysis, they don't want you. They offered the post to someone else. They've made a decision and you aren't it.

Rejection is hard to cope with. It can be extremely dispiriting, knock your confidence and make you reconsider almost everything about yourself and what you've been doing. Inevitably, your well-meaning friends will spout the same sort of cliches as when your last partner dumped you: "Better off without them", "Plenty more where that came from", and "If they can't see that you'd be perfect, then more fool them". It didn't help when you were chucked and it won't help now. So let yourself give in to the misery for a few minutes, drop-kick the rejection letter in the vague direction of the bin, and then get started all over again. Something is obviously not working.

Find out first if that something is beyond your control. Were you applying for a job that might have a gender stereotype, or racial prejudice? Was there an in-house candidate?

Was there any incompetence on behalf of the interviewer? Did anything happen before, during or after your interview which might explain your rejection?

Now consider if it is you, and not them. Crucially, get feedback. Find out why. But don't just listen to what they tell you – apply it. Start by looking at your CV. Ensure that it is a great brochure for your skills and accomplishments. Make any changes necessary and then believe in them. It is not just a piece of paper; it is you. Now replay the interview. Was there anything else you could have done to sell yourself? Were you really present? That is, were you listening, actively, to the questions, and answering them in the best possible way. Review your presentation too. What employers want these days are job-hunters who look like they'll fit in. Did your dress sense and personal grooming on the day match the work culture you were seeking to join?

Once you've considered all this, assess the sorts of jobs you are going for. Are they the right position for you, in the right area at the right level? At this point it is often worth visiting a careers service again, and finding out where your talents are and where you should be directing them.

None of this changes the cruel reality of rejection. Disappointment, disillusionment and disgust really can undermine you. But whatever has gone wrong so far, it must not affect the way you continue your job search. Every new interview must be treated with the same attention to detail as the first. Only this way will you eventually find success. Because you will.

Interpreting rejection letters
It's not what they say, it's how they say it

Sometimes, it's not just the rejection, it's the manner of it. And while you are right to take a good long look at yourself if you get knocked back, there are some responses it's just not worth getting worked into a lather about:

THEY SEND YOU AN EMAILED ATTACHMENT CALLED UNSUCCESSFUL-AT-INTERVIEW.DOC This really speaks for itself, but it's probably the result of admin staff failing to think, rather than the mickey-take it seems to be.

YOU GET A LETTER WHICH TELLS YOU THEY WILL KEEP YOUR DETAILS ON FILE This means usually diddly-squat. Employers who say this obviously don't have a strategy for dealing with unsuccessful candidates. If you were a good fit for the organisation but not for the role, you should get a tailored letter inviting you to apply for other jobs, and other relevant departments should be alerted to your suitability. When you're not a good fit, you shouldn't be told something that gives you false hope.

YOU GET A LETTER, BUT IT'S JUST A COUPLE OF LINES "I regret to inform you that after careful consideration you have not been successful on this occasion." Employers should give feedback and where that involves objective information, such as the results of aptitude tests, they are often happy to do so. However, final interviews are a lot more subjective and employers are wary of saying anything that could be seen to be discriminatory. It is always worth ringing them to ask if they could be more helpful.

THEY SAY, "WE'LL RING YOU ON FRIDAY," BUT THE PHONE CALL NEVER COMES Some people, even senior managers, just hate giving bad news and even though their intention is to ring they often can't bring themselves to do it.

YOU NEVER HEAR ANYTHING FROM THEM AGAIN Ring if you want to, but, if a company hasn't bothered to contact you, it's unlikely that you will hear anything positive.

UNHELPFUL OR DISMISSIVE FEEDBACK This is the worst kind of feedback a company can give. Saying you just weren't suitable, but not expanding on why, is terrible practice. Twenty-something line managers can often have an arrogance that isn't matched by their experience. They may only have worked in one or two companies and be extrapolating from this limited experience.

DECIDING THAT THE JOB WASN'T THERE AFTER ALL It may be that the person making the hiring decision has failed to communicate with the person who authorises the financing of the job.

YOUR RECRUITMENT AGENCY TELLS YOU THAT THE JOB'S YOURS, BUT NOTHING EVER COMES OF IT This is common when an agency is involved and is almost always due to a failure of communication between the agency and the employer.

AT INTERVIEW YOU ARE OFFERED THE JOB, BUT WHEN YOU GET HOME YOU RECEIVE A LETTER SAYING YOU HAVE BEEN REJECTED Believe it or not this does happen, and it is obviously heartbreaking. But a verbal contract is impossible to prove, and the organisation will always maintain that it was a misunderstanding. It is of course a classic cock-up between interested parties in a large organisation.

Keep on keeping on
Don't let them grind you down

You should certainly think about what you've done wrong and whether the job was always a long-shot or not right for you anyway, and consider as many cock-up theories as you like, but don't give up. Keep constructive. If the rejections seem to be piling up, then consider temping until something does come up (see page 295). The position could expand your skills set and lead to other opportunities. At the very least it will top up your bank account. If you are looking for a job full-time, be professional about it. Structure your day. Regardless of your approach remember that you are talented, you are qualified and you are still just in the very early stages of finding what is right for you.

You got the job!
Blimey! It worked!

After all that, you've got a job offer. Congratulations! Someone likes you, thinks you are intelligent and diligent. They want to work with you. How great is that?

But there's no need to snap their hand off quite yet. There's plenty of pressure to take the first job you are offered. What with parental coercion ("We're not supporting you any more", "It's time you found your own place" etc), the burden of student debts and the desire to join your peers on the career ladder, it's easy to make a first-job mistake. So before you take up any job offer (and especially if you've been offered more than one), take time to weigh up what you will be saying yes to.

Now that can be easier said than done. Some potential employers will understand the difficulties involved. They appreciate that job-hunters are looking around and that they need time to make up their minds. But others are less flexible. The moment they give you a job offer they expect you to leap up, shake their hand and take it there and then. If you don't, they may threaten to withdraw the offer and leave you with nothing.

If you find yourself in such a situation, go with your instincts. If you are being pushed into making a decision, trust your gut reaction. But this advice comes with a caveat. Remember what it is you want to do with your career. In the rush to say yes or no, and perhaps in the urgency to just get started, it is easy to lose sight of your objective.

Fortunately, you don't have to immediately accept or reject most job offers. Most large companies are prepared to wait a while for an answer. This is because large companies are often slow-moving so there is usually no need for a rapid-fire response. In this case you should simply send a letter acknowledging receipt of the job offer and informing them that you will be in touch in the near future. In the meantime you can haul in any other offers before finally making a decision.

Smaller or medium-sized companies may not be able to give you this luxury. By their very nature they can be more dynamic. Their business must keep going, with or without you. So, out of fairness to them you should make your decision within a couple of days. Sought-after candidates may be able to gain extra thinking time.

None of this alters the fact that choosing whether to take up a job offer can be difficult. You're dealing with nothing less than that all-important first break. Whatever you do, make sure you get the basics right. Find out exactly how long you've got to make your mind up. Gather as much information as possible about the job or jobs on offer. If you've got another interview approaching, ask if it can be brought forward. If you're still waiting to hear back from an interview, contact human resources to determine exactly when a decision will be made. If they sound sympathetic, explain your situation: they may just be able to let you in on something. Finally, always be courteous when rejecting a job offer. You don't want to burn your bridges. You never know when you may come across a particular person or their company in the future.

Starting salary
Where to begin?

"Can you give us some idea of your salary expectation?" is the question that strikes fear into the heart of every interviewee. Just how do you answer? Pitch it too high and you look unrealistic and overly confident; pitch it too low and you undervalue both yourself and your ability to do the job. For most of us, salary is one of the most important factors in taking a job – and yet it is often the subject that is hardest to discuss.

Research is essential when it comes to proposing a reasonable salary. When you're sourcing every job ad under the sun, note the salaries for the posts you're interested in and you'll soon get an idea of what's being paid elsewhere and what you can safely ask for. And research the company which is interviewing you – a big company will probably offer a far different salary package to a smaller one.

The most important thing to remember when discussing your salary is that it is a negotiation. The first figure you mention probably won't be the figure you agree on, and it is a figure from which you will only negotiate down. The key is to negotiate from a position of strength. In other words you have to believe that you are bringing something to the table. Even if you're a recent graduate, you still have unique skills to offer and it's important to bear that in mind. Asking for a slightly higher salary will not affect the interviewer's decision to give you the job. If an employer indicates a salary range, they will pay the top figure if they find the right person for the job. If you're not comfortable asking for the top amount, then go for just above mid-range; it's important to give the impression that you are worth a decent salary.

Perks
To truly assess a job offer, you need to look at the whole package rather than just the size of the first pay cheque. Are you being offered the following perks?

PENSION PROVISION There's a lot of concern about a pensions timebomb, and while it may all seem a long time off, you will need a pension scheme, and sooner than you think. If your employer offers a good scheme, it's a perk worth hundreds of thousands of pounds.

JOINING BONUSES An unsophisticated approach but pretty effective. Many larger employers offer a simple cash incentive for joining. The average payment is around £2,000 and is most common in the financial sector, but other industries, such as teaching or social work, offer "golden hellos" or help with student loans in some areas.

SPONSORSHIP FOR FURTHER TRAINING Some people leave university with the intention of never taking another exam again. But there are undoubtedly big long-term prizes for those prepared to put in the work and study for further professional qualifications. Your employer is effectively paying for you to become more employable.

COMPANY CAR Many blue-chip sales and marketing roles entitle you to a company car – and your job would be difficult without one. It's a perk that offers instant one-upmanship, but beware, you may be stung for a truly vast tax bill. In fact, you might be better off opting for a car allowance paid to you monthly like a salary and then buying your own car.

OPPORTUNITIES ABROAD One of the joys of working for an international blue-chip company is that you could work internationally early in your career, either as a secondment or as part of your training. Similarly, the Foreign Office (obviously), oil firms and some consultancies may put you on a plane to somewhere exotic – but be aware that your hotel room and the airport lounge may be the only sights you take in.

FREEBIES Sometimes it's the little things that make a difference. Some employers are so keen to have you work every hour God sends that they offer free in-house catering (they charge it to clients), free onsite gyms (keeps you fit – less sick leave), free neck massages and free eye tests, for example. With a pretty basic gym membership costing around £50 a month and about £20 a week on five lunches, these perks could be worth around £1,500 a year. And this potentially on top of private medical insurance: Bupa membership for a healthy non-smoking 23-year-old is somewhere between £420 and £600 a year but really depends on the individual. Most retail companies will offer staff discount cards. Some will have clothing allowances.

MENTORING It's a jungle out there – and sometimes you'll want someone to watch over you. Ask the human resources department whether the firm operates a "buddy" scheme pairing you with, say, someone who joined the company a year before you. Their role would be to offer you friendly advice on dress codes, placement choices and office etiquette, for example. Mentoring programmes, through which you get to discuss your progress or concerns with someone who isn't a direct line manager, are also extremely helpful and can help you to make key decisions at important stages in your early career.

UNPAID LEAVE By law you're entitled to four weeks' paid holiday a year and some employers will offer you more. However, human resources depart-ments are becoming increasingly open to staff sabbaticals, allowing members of the firm to take unpaid leave to travel or pursue a pet project for a few months before returning to the fold. As a recent government survey demonstrated, many of us appreciate the opportunity for flexible working more than a pay rise and offering this opportunity can help companies retain talent.

RELOCATION PACKAGES If your skills and talents are much in demand, some of the biggest employers from around the country will be tripping over themselves to snap you up. They may also throw in a relocation bonus to help make the transition into working life smoother. Some of the biggest recruiters offer new-starts a (taxable) incentive to relocate. Relocation packages are particularly prevalent in sectors where there is a skills shortage, but the biggest employers tend to extend the offer to all new recruits. Employers hope that it will cover your deposit, first month's rent, some new clothes and shoes, and maybe even your travel expenses for a few weeks.

■ Other ways in

Sifting through the ads, banging out CVs and pestering the "right" people aren't the only ways into your dream job. There are alternative routes that you might want to bear in mind.

The small-business route
Starting small

The jobs pages of the mass media tend to be dominated by big companies, and the recruitment market as a whole is geared towards those corporations that have the resources to swamp milk rounds, give pep talks and place eye-catching adverts in newspapers and on the internet.

Working for a small company is something many job-hunters never consider. The kudos and financial rewards associated with being part of a vast corporation are often an irresistible force. Job-hunters usually cite a whole raft of reasons, including the training, the opportunity for foreign travel, the structured career path and the camaraderie between colleagues of a similar age and background.

And yet... Working for a small company will give you broader, more senior experience much more quickly. You're far more likely to become central to a small firm's success or failure early in your career, and that experience can pay off further down the line. And there's no reason why you shouldn't receive decent training, albeit often of a less structured nature. Whereas a large company will have a glamorous programme that may involve travel, a small firm might make you do an evening a week, which is just as useful. Small businesses tend not to make a great play of what they offer.

This informal approach benefits employees in other ways too. Going into a major company may scare some who find it too aggressive and commercial. The small firm gives you the full panoply of business but is less stressful. As most small companies are out of London there is also the factor of cheaper and less tiring commuting to consider. If you do this first you have a better chance of surviving in a bigger company later. Consider, too, the fact that small firms are often at the cutting edge of change within an industry. They are the ones who come up with seminal ideas and products that are later taken on board and copied by household names.

If you decide that small firms are the way forward, you need to check in local papers and job centres as well as on the internet. Get on to the relevant trade associations and ask who the movers and shakers are. You may just find the small pond you've been looking for all along.

Temping
The flexible choice

Many people still have rather sniffy attitudes to temping, believing it's just a way of keeping off the dole, practising your skills, or raising funds so you can take a year out and travel. But the truth is that flexible working is becoming a more prominent feature of corporate life. The temporary jobs market is bigger than ever and the image of temporary work is improving markedly. Nowadays, many people temp because they want to, not because they have to.

Temporary working allows you access to a huge variety of careers and employers. It can give you more control over your career than a permanent job – good temps are able to sell their services to the highest bidder. You're paid on an hourly basis so you're likely to be better off than your peers in permanent positions, and you won't necessarily have to work a standard 40-hour week. Temping also allows you to learn new skills and gain experience in many different working environments.

Temping is not just a way of grouting over the cracks in your CV. It's an ideal way to find out what sort of company you want to work for and the type of job you want to do – which might not be obvious from an hour-long interview and a tour of the office coffee machines. Remember, it's far easier to get a job if you're already in work. You might even end up working in a field that you hadn't contemplated before.

Many organisations use temporary staff for relatively high-level appointments – to undertake project management for government departments, for example, or to write corporate documents, and these are jobs that require extensive experience. These contracts last from a couple of days to six or nine months.

There's no one type of person who does temporary work: people who are between jobs, people who are bored with their current jobs, or those who just want to test the water before committing themselves. But don't let temping become a way of life. You could get used to moving from company to company and, before you know it, that's all you've done. Some employers prefer to see substantial experience in one job on your CV, especially at the beginning of your career. If you've temped for several years, they might think you're unable to settle. Nor will temping suit everyone. If you're shy and don't find it easy to manage change, form new relationships or quickly adapt to new cultures, it could destroy your confidence. But here are some tips for making the most of it.

Look for an agency that specialises in the kind of work you'd like to do
Most agencies specialise in an industry or sector. Look at the classified pages

of relevant trade magazines for your chosen sector. Compile a list of agencies and go through them one by one.

Know what you want and let your agency know
Be specific about the kind of work you're looking for and what you will and won't do. Don't be bullied into accepting a job you don't really want because your agency wants to make a sale. Let your agency work for you.

Don't underestimate your worth
Don't think that because you're a temp you should be paid less than the going rate for the permanent job. Negotiate your pay with your agency. Despite what they may claim, they may be in a position to tweak their commission and offer you more.

Learn how to work the agencies
Remember that they are in the business of selling. The more clients they place, the more commission they get. Don't be afraid to let agency y know that you're being paid x amount more by agency z for the same job they are trying to sell you.

Work through one or two agencies
Register with as many as possible but try and build a relationship with one or two that have found you regular work. Keep in contact with your chosen few and call in at least once a week to find out what jobs are going.

Go for a number of mid-term placements within the same sector
Your CV will look much better with three mid-term jobs rather than six short-term ones. And before you know it you will have built up a useful portfolio of experience and contacts. It's easier to convince an employer of your employability if you can show that you've stuck at something for a reasonable period of time.

Make sure each job enhances your skills base
This should be a combination of soft transferable skills, like time management and adaptability, and hard skills like knowing how to use a specialised computer package.

Get a job description
Permanent staff may be tempted to use you as a general dogsbody and have you do everything from the filing and faxing to the three times a day tea run. Don't do it! Insist on a job description before or at the start of a placement so you know what you're there for. Don't be afraid to remind a boss who

insists on treating you like a permanent staff member without the benefits that you're a temp. Remember, you work for your agency, not the company.

Work your way up
Increase your pay with each new placement. As you become more skilled you should be in a position to command more cash. Remember to put money away.

Seize the day!
A temporary placement through an agency at your dream company could turn out to be a foot in the door to that elusive permanent job. Most companies advertise positions internally first and usually as a temp you're able to go for these roles. This is your chance to sell yourself, make yourself indispensable and secure your own desk space, and maybe even a plaque on the door.

Volunteering
Good for the soul and the CV

Volunteering is, essentially, just working for free. It might be in the aid of a good cause, or that good cause could be a little closer to home – you. But why would any self-respecting, intelligent, well-qualified job-hunter want to work hard for nothing, when there are decent, salaried jobs to be had?

For one thing, while voluntary work may be good for the soul, it's also a cracking way of getting some decent contacts. In some sectors of employment, such as the media or broadcasting, you have little alternative if you want to make contacts and get a job. If you're trying to break into an area such as social work, counselling or probation, you may need substantial work experience in order to make an application for a professional training programme. And voluntary work is the best way in. In these sectors you're likely to get structured work experience through organisations such as CSV (Community Service Volunteers), who will offer allowances, accommodation and support.

You might want to do voluntary work for your own personal, moral reasons, because you think it's a good thing to do or you want to give something back to society. But remember, there is no money at all in voluntary work. If you don't plan ahead and develop good financial management skills, you'll end up in a frightening amount of debt. It might mean that you have to forgo some of the pleasures that your salaried friends are enjoying (a social life, new clothes, meals out), or that, horror or horrors, you'll have to live at home with your parents for a while. It's up to you to decide whether a short-term sacrifice is worth it for your long-term career or personal satisfaction.

A good starting point is to contact your local volunteer bureau or the regional branch of a national charity to find out what experience they're looking for (your phone directory will have a section on community and voluntary work). If you're interested in a particular cause or charity, you should make direct contact with the national office of the relevant organisation. Do thorough research just as if you were looking for permanent work. Find out about the structure of the organisation you're interested in and treat your application seriously. Don't take a job because you're afraid of letting someone down: match your skills to a job and find out what they can offer you.

In highly competitive, non-charitable sectors, such as the media, there are no set rules, but avoiding exploitation requires careful planning. Never answer a job advertisement and tell them you'll do the job for free: slavery may have been abolished but they'll take you up on it. It's better to send a speculative letter asking for work experience – and then make yourself indispensable.

Whatever organisation you work for, you need to be upfront. Volunteering is a two-way street. You're giving your time for free, so you need to tell your employer exactly what you want to get from the job, whether it's a particular skill or just personal satisfaction. As a volunteer you're in a position of power: if you're not happy you can vote with your feet.

Just because you've worked for nothing doesn't mean that you have to apologise for yourself. You haven't wasted your time (though you probably won't be your bank manager's favourite client): you've gained important skills and experience that any decent employer will value. When you go for job interviews, treat voluntary work just like paid employment. Don't play down unpaid work. Identify the skills you've developed which have market value and sell them.

More... on voluntary work

National Council for Voluntary Organisations
Regent's Wharf
8 All Saints Street
London N1 9RL
(t) 020 7713 6161
(↗) www.ncvo-vol.org.uk

Working for a Charity
NCVO
Regent's Wharf
8 All Saints Street
London N1 9RL
(t) 020 7520 2512
(↗) www.wfac.org.uk

Online reading
Community Service Volunteers www.csv.org.uk
Do-It! www.doit.org.uk
Idealist www.idealist.org

Through the ranks
Work your way up

Stories of managing directors who started out as the office junior are either the stuff of careers advice legend or a cliche, depending on your view. Cliche or not, most job-hunters today are not going to be signed up by the employer of their dreams but can still get the job they want, with a little patience.

Only a minority of the graduates who enter the job market each year are signed up by major blue-chip recruiters. Increasingly graduates are taking first jobs that were traditionally done by non-graduates and are then trying to move up the ladder from there. So don't be snooty about taking that secretarial position if it's in a company you really want to be with. It can be fruitful in certain people-based industries such as sales, PR, advertising and media, though you may have to be willing to retrain. Companies will often only advertise a position internally so once you are on the inside you'll be there to see it. Look for companies that are known to promote internally, then keep asking for more demanding work and make it plain to employers you are looking for more. But if you aren't being heard and you think you've been suckered into a dead-end job, don't just sit there. Be prepared to switch jobs if the prospects of promotion seem slow. You're there to progress and if that isn't happening, switch horses at the first opportunity.

The service sector
McJobs

Being absolutely honest, which of the following two phrases would you prefer to say out loud in front of someone you fancy? "I work in publishing, based in Covent Garden, though I'm often abroad on book tours", or "I work for Asda, managing fresh produce at our Bolton superstore, though I sometimes cover on the cold meats counter." Thought so.

We are a nation of job snobs who prefer to work in industries that are perceived as high-status and glamorous. We tend to ignore sectors such as service, hospitality and retail even though they increasingly offer attractive training and development opportunities to graduates and non-graduates alike.

The pervading image of the service sector is, of course, the dead-end hell of the McJob. It's an industry that's associated with poor pay, unskilled work and few prospects, so it's not surprising that ambitious job-hunters haven't been queuing to slither up the greasy pole at their local drive-thru. However, given the rapid expansion of service-sector companies and the need for skilled staff to manage that growth, it might be wise to think again.

Training in the service sector typically runs for one to three years, with off-site seminars, on-the-job training, mentors, buddies, appraisals, career-development plans and funded study towards professional qualifications once initial training is completed. During training, new recruits are given substantial responsibility for managing people and departments while having constant support from senior staff.

With starting salaries running at between £18,000 and £23,000 and benefits including private healthcare, subsidised restaurants and gym membership, staff discounts and share-schemes, from a purely financial viewpoint, service sector graduate jobs are not to be sneezed at. What's more, many companies in the service sector offer the chance to try out a variety of roles, allowing people to discover where their talents can flourish best.

The family firm
Calling the boss "Dad"

If you don't fancy working for a huge, impersonal company then perhaps the family business is a good idea. You'd be working with people you know, and with an assured career path (hopefully) there would be no need to worry about careers and applying for jobs; more importantly, you'd be keeping the family name in the business.

But before you jump at the chance of being the "& Son" or "& Daughter" on the sign outside, make sure it is what you want. Many, many, many's the time that family pressure has pushed someone into a job they feel they ought to do, rather than one they want to do. And once in there, the pressure is on to work harder than many of your peers. After all, it's the family name you're working for, not some faceless corporation. So while your mates are out carousing you may be feeling compelled to stay at your desk, going the extra miles.

Even if it is what you want, the problems might not stop there. You've known the business since you were little. You know how it works, and you know how it can work better. You've got plans – but those plans could cause resentment if they change the working habits of a generation of your own family or of family retainers who used to babysit you. In a business you're tied to emotionally, every decision you take has the possibility of wider implications than if you were at your desk at Blank Blank plc.

OK, you've thought through all that and you've decided the family business is for you. Assuming you're a graduate, is it better to join the family business straight from university? After all, if you're sure that's what you want, why waste time working for someone else? Or is it better to get work experience elsewhere first? The answer is almost always to get experience elsewhere first. That way, you'll know how other businesses work and you'll be able to see whether the family firm is run by a bunch of eccentrics or is based on sound principles. You can also prove yourself and so leap the hurdle of resentment when you do come "home", dispelling notions that you've just waltzed in with no qualifications and no knowledge. Taking a job in the outside world first means you can learn how to fail and make mistakes. You've done some study at the university of life and you now have something more to offer than just a DNA match.

But tread carefully: entering the family business can be a fraught business. Success and failure are written larger when shared with your nearest and dearest. Work conversations can be entwined with Sunday lunch, and family arguments may spill over into the boardroom. But at least you know you care.

Postgraduate study
Staying at school

Deciding whether to do a postgraduate course used to be a casual affair. You'd finish your degree, have a quick chat with the professor in his pipesmoke-filled room and it was all settled. But as the number of graduates wanting to prolong their stay in academia has grown, so has the number of courses on offer, and there are now literally thousands to choose from. Selecting the right course for you requires a bit more thought than it used to. The first thing you should ask yourself is, why are you thinking of undertaking a postgraduate course, and how is its completion going to help you in the long term?

You have to ask yourself whether the course you are contemplating is really going to broaden and deepen your experience in the eyes of a potential employer. Most postgraduate courses are very different from first degrees and you are no longer simply being lectured at. A good reason to embark on one is to learn how to manage yourself properly and to gain the critical thinking skills that will hopefully set you apart from someone who has done a normal degree. However, if you are simply doing a postgraduate course to put off the inevitable entry into the job market, you are probably not making the best use of your time.

Assuming that you have a valid rationale behind your choice of course, the next thing to consider is location. While it's very tempting to stay in the same town where you did your first degree because you have friends and accommodation there, moving to a new institution, and even another country, can be beneficial. Remember that you are trying to broaden and deepen your experience – a new university will bring with it new people, offering a new perspective and new ideas. It's worth asking whether you will gain that by staying at the same institution in which you are already studying.

To find out whether a course fulfils these criteria it's essential to talk to as many people as possible. It's not just a case of reading the syllabus on the internet. You've got to talk to the course leader to find out what makes him or her tick. Because the number of applicants is far fewer than for degree courses, most course leaders are happy to take enquiries from potential applicants – for most, their course is a matter of pride to them. It is also worth contacting ex-students to find out if the course delivered what it promised, both in terms of content and positive outcome on their employability.

Funding is another major issue. Given the amounts of money involved, postgraduate study is not for the faint-hearted, and graduates need to take a long hard look at the course and their circumstances before starting another round of study.

If you're considering postgraduate study, ask yourself these questions:

- How important is this course for your life aims, and how will it enhance your future career prospects?

- Having chosen your specialist subject area, do you really want or need to study this subject in so much depth?

- Can you get to where you want to be without studying full-time for a further year? Can the course be done part-time while you are working?

- Do you really want to spend the next year or several years of your life studying? Is it worth the cost in terms of both time and money?

- How good is your chosen institution, and are its qualifications well respected?

- Who are the academic staff and what are their research interests? Is anyone working in the specific field in which you might write your dissertation?

- Do former students have a good track record once they leave?

■ Life and work

You've got your first pay cheque. Congratulations! Enjoy it while it lasts... which won't be long.

Managing your salary
You're all grown up now

Once you become an earner, it's time to put away childish things (combat trousers and snakebite and black) and replace them with the trappings of adulthood (suits and good wines). The problem is doing it on a starting salary. No one warns you about the expenses of working life. You've got to buy a working wardrobe and finance after-work drinks and meals. Not to mention that in order to actually earn your salary, you've got to get to work, which means forking out for train or bus fares, or petrol money.

Suddenly, your monthly pay cheque looks less like a winning lottery ticket and more like the miserable scrap of printed paper that it is. The good news is you've got a choice. You can either Spend! Spend! Spend! and be in debt till you're 65. Or you can be sensible.

Sensible may not be sexy, but it works. The key to surviving on a starting salary is budgeting. It's all too easy to run out of money before the month is up, so you need to know exactly how much you have to live on and how much your bills, rent, student loans, council tax and so on will cost. Once you know, you can put the money aside. Then, if you're really clever, take out the exact amount of cash you've allowed yourself for each week and live on it. Seeing it physically disappear will make you more aware of your spending habits.

Many companies offer season ticket loans as a perk. If yours is one of them, take them up on it. You'll save a substantial amount on travelling costs. Remember though, that they're treated as a benefit in kind, which means you'll pay slightly more tax. You could also cut back on needless spending by bringing in homemade sandwiches and drinks. Avoid ready-cooked meals for one – they're not economical. If you're really organised, try cooking up dishes at the weekend, then separating them into portions and freezing them for consumption later in the week.

Building a working wardrobe can be difficult at the start of your career. Many companies are taking a more relaxed attitude to dressing, but in some professions (law, accountancy) you either get suited up or booted out. Either get a job as an artist's model, work only on dress-down Fridays, or learn to shop carefully.

The temptation is to put everything on the credit card. But if you do that, it's all too easy to make debt a habit. Choose a few good investment pieces and if you have no choice but to get them on credit, look for cards with low interest rates. It's a perverse fact that the more credit you have, the more you can get. If you're someone for whom credit spells danger you might be better off with a loan. Loans are easier to manage than credit cards. You know exactly how much you'll have to pay each month and will have a set date to pay it off by. If you do have a credit card, you can ask for the limit to be reduced, so you don't find yourself on a slippery slope to more debt.

There's no shame in being less well-off than your more senior (and higher salaried) colleagues. Don't be the first person to jump in and offer to buy a round of drinks: offer to buy your own, or even suggest starting up a kitty for social occasions. Often, team social events happen at set times of the year, such as Christmas. This means you can plan for them and save some money in advance. As for leaving collections, put in what you can afford when the envelope comes round, irrespective of other people's contributions. You're not a charity.

Living on a starting salary is hard, but making a few sacrifices at the start of your career is worth it in the long term. One day, you'll be able to live the life of Riley (nice car, nice house, nice holidays), while your less careful peers will still be living like students.

Six steps to clearing debt
Time to get out of that hole

If you've got several thousand pounds of debt against your name, how exactly do you start to repay it? And is it possible to escape from the red without being reduced to a social outcast who can only afford to stay at home, existing on TV, own-brand baked beans and one bottle of Blue Nun a week? It is difficult, but you can claw your way out of debt and still have a life. Just not such an extravagant one. For a while at least.

STEP ONE Admit that you're in a bit of mess. And then figure out just how much of a mess. Collect all your financial details together. Figure out who you owe money to, how much you owe them, and how overdue it is. This is by far the hardest part. Most of us have a tendency to be ostriches. But if you want to regain control of your finances, you do have to take your head out of the sand.

STEP TWO Work out your most important creditors – the ones who can impose the harshest sanctions on you for not paying. For example, if you don't pay your mortgage or rent, you can be evicted; if you don't pay your council tax, you can be put in prison; and if you don't pay your fuel bills your supply can be cut off. Other creditors, like credit card companies, can only sue you in the county court for non-payment.

STEP THREE Make your debts easier to pay off. Try renegotiating the payment terms. If you go to them, creditors are usually quite willing to accommodate you. It's in their interest to do so. Also try consolidating your debts. Instead of having several creditors to contend with, some of them applying top-whack penalties, it may be more cost-efficient to take out a single loan to pay everyone else off all at once. As for credit card debt, look at switching banks. Instead of paying 18–20% interest, under an introductory offer you could be paying nothing. As always, shop around for the best deal and read the fine print.

STEP FOUR Take stock of your outgoings. Yes, it sounds boring. Yes, it sounds time-consuming. It is. But there is no way round it. You just can't see how to save money unless you first know where you're spending it.

STEP FIVE Tighten your belt. But don't overdo it. It is possible to economise without causing too much discomfort. You won't have to cut out all of your pleasures, but you will have to trim some of them. And you will have to keep them in trim until you've seen off your creditors.

STEP SIX Don't panic. You've got a job now. If you're in a hole, that at least means you have the shovel in your hands to dig your way out of it. Things are looking up.

4

Day by day

How to find a job in a month

We all know Rome wasn't built in a day. But it was built one brick at a time. Finding the right job won't happen in 24 hours, but if you put enough of the bricks in place, you'll eventually build the career you want.

Week 1 **Finding a focus**

Week 2 **Finding the right words**

Week 3 **Finding your voice**

Week 4 **Finding another way**

■ Week 1 **Finding a focus**

Day 1 **Setting goals**

One thought We're all supposed to have goals, right? Your mum and dad, careers advisers and best mates say you should have them, so go on – write them down. What you want to have achieved and a deadline for achieving them. And don't just limit them to career goals. Write down what your personal goals are too.

Now take your list, roll it up tightly, and stick it in your bookcase. Don't think of going back to it for at least a year.

Lists are great ideas and goals can be great motivators. But they can also be huge burdens, millstones around your neck. They can depress you and slow you down: the distance from here to there seems so big you lie frozen in bed. Demoralised. Writing down a list of goals is valuable because it gives you focus. Dig out the list each time you feel you're losing focus. Otherwise, keep it out of sight.

One task Introduce structure to your days. Job-hunting is a full-time job. Although it is tempting to exploit your free time, don't start going fishing midweek or sleeping late. Get up at your usual hour, shower, eat breakfast and go to "work". The trick is to spend time every weekday working towards finding a job.

One question What's the one goal from my list that is easiest to attain right now?

One to read *Playing to Win: 10 Steps to Achieving Your Goals* by Karren Brady (Capstone Publishing)

Day 2 **Discovering strengths and weaknesses**

One thought There's much to be admired about people who overcome weaknesses to achieve some kind of goal they've set themselves. And there are plenty of self-help guides and coaches that will show you how to turn weaknesses into strengths.

But strengths and weaknesses are also a signpost to the kind of work you are likely to enjoy most. That's not to say we shouldn't try to address our weaknesses. Lack of self-esteem and confidence are debilitating in any sphere of life and need sorting out. But don't stress about them.

By acknowledging your strengths and weaknesses you acknowledge what you can do and what you can do well. Follow the signposts to the right job and your strengths will grow stronger and your weaknesses weaker.

One task Write down half-a-dozen things you've achieved in your life so far. Around each, scribble as much detail as you can remember about how you achieved those things. Then extract from your notes the key strengths you displayed during those times. Are all of these strengths listed on your CV? They should be.

One question What situations do you find most stressful?

One to read *Now, Discover Your Strengths* by Marcus Buckingham and Donald Clifton (Pocket Books)

Day 3 **Exploring options**

One thought The number of opportunities open to you and the wealth of jobs you could do is mind-bogglingly immense. The more you read careers guides like this one, the tougher the decision can seem. How on earth are you supposed to narrow your options down?

Think cheese. Think buying cheese at the deli counter in Tesco. Looking up and down that chilled cabinet, you see hundreds of chesses. All of them look good (when you're hungry). But how will they taste? There's only one way to find out. Try one. And so, little by little, you find the cheese that suits your palate.

Finding the right job is much the same. Yes, you can follow all the advice we give you in this guide and land a job. Great – but that doesn't mean that you will or should be in that job for life. Just as people move on from cheddar to something a little more exotic, you may find yourself switching to a new company, taking on new responsibilities, or maybe changing career path altogether.

Don't be scared of making mistakes. Ignore people who fret "How will this look on your CV?" There's no such thing as a wrong career move – each move is a step closer to the perfect cheese.

One task You're more likely to enjoy your work if you're doing something that you value. Most big companies have mission statements that encapsulate their values in a few words. Write down your mission statement – in less than a dozen words.

One question Who do you know that talks about their work with excitement and enthusiasm?

One to read *What Should I Do with My Life?* by Po Bronson (Ballantine Books)

Day 4 **Job snobs**

One thought We all dream of having the perfect job, doing the kind of work we'd love to do, earning the kind of money we'd like to make and enjoying the sort of status it would give us.

Some people will tell you not to settle for just anything, to hold out until the perfect job comes along. You might be waiting a long time. If you've worked extensively in a particular sector for a long period of time, then yes, you'll have a good feel for the kind of work that best suits you. But if you haven't got that experience, be careful about dismissing jobs that you deem unworthy of your talent.

There are many job snobs out there, and too many job-hunters worry about how they would answer the "So what do you do?" question at parties. Don't confuse high standards with procrastination. And don't knock a job until you've tried it.

One task Take an online personality test to begin exploring some of the jobs you might be best suited to. You could be in for a surprise. Try the one at www.reed.co.uk/careertools/SelfAssessments.aspx

One question Think of the jobs your friends have: which would you refuse to do, and why?

One to read *IQ and Psychometric Tests: Assess Your Personality, Aptitude and Intelligence* by Philip Carter (Kogan Page)

Week 1

Day 5 **Seeking advice**

One thought Job-hunting can be a lonely
experience, so why not share your highs and
lows with friends or family you respect?
Keeping them informed will help you
articulate and rationalise your progress
(or lack of it).

Good friends and family can also be an
invaluable source of advice. They won't always
understand the exact challenges you face, nor
the specific details of the jobs, sectors or
employers that you're targeting. But they know
a heck of a lot about you, about your plus and
minus points, your temperament, your values
and priorities.

Listen to their advice with an open mind.
Some of it may be of little value. But they
might just pinpoint something in your strategy
or attitude that you've missed or dismissed.

One task Ask one good friend or close family
member to act as your job-hunting mentor
and commit to giving them a weekly progress
report.

One question What was the last piece of
advice someone gave you? And what was the
last piece of advice you acted upon?

One to read *Shut Up and Listen!: The Truth
About How to Communicate at Work* by Cary
Cooper and Theo Theobald (Kogan Page)

■ Week 2 **Finding the right words**

Day 1 **Challenging CVs**

One thought You could pay someone to prepare your CV for you; after all, there are plenty of agencies and print shops in the small ads willing to take your money.

But is that really what you want? To hand over responsibility for the most important document in your job-hunting campaign to a complete stranger? If you approach CV writing with a negative attitude, of course it'll be a bore. But if you see your CV as a challenge – a two-sheet opportunity to win over employers with the key facts about your life and achievements – you'll find it less of a chore.

Elsewhere in this book you'll find all the practical advice you need to structure and style a CV for maximum impact. All you need to do is add some passion. And a stranger in a print shop can't do that for you.

One task Give your CV to a friend who has experience of recruiting and ask them for their honest opinion on how it reads.

One question Do you do enough to talk up your achievements and talents? If not, why do you find it difficult?

One to read *The Perfect Pitch: How to Sell Yourself for Today's Job Market* by David Andrusia (Warner Books)

Day 2 **No second-guessing**

One thought Writing your CV will help you realise how much you have to say about yourself. You may struggle to fit it all on to two sides of A4. What should you take out? What should stay in? And what image will employers have of you from reading it?

While it's important to rejig and tailor your CV to each job application, you can't predict how any employer will view your CV. Much of the recruiting process is subjective and each employer comes to a pile of CVs with different assumptions, impressions and ideas. So stop trying to second-guess the employer and don't fret about what's on your CV and what's not. If you've done your best, that's enough.

One task Inject a little verve into your CV by using as many "action verbs" as you can. Why say you "began" or "started" something when you could have "built", "conceived", "constructed", "created", "devised", "established", "launched" or "piloted" it?

One question You are a unique "product" – does your CV work hard enough to sell that product to the employers you're targeting?

One to read *Successful CVs in a Week* by Steve Morris and Graham Willcocks (Hodder Arnold)

Week 2

Day 3 **Covering letters**

One thought Job-hunting can sometimes feel like using a very large lumphammer to crack a very small walnut. Posting or emailing what seems like hundreds of CVs, covering letters and application forms just to try and land one job.

While you might set out on your job-hunting journey with the best of intentions, it can be tempting to slacken off as the days roll by. Sloppiness creeps in: typos start appearing, addresses get misspelled and the gender of the person you're writing to bends from Mr to Mrs.

You can bet your life these are the very mistakes that employers will spot, particularly in covering letters. Job-hunters spend an eternity refining their CVs, but tend to rush off covering letters with little thought. However, if you pay enough attention to details such as the recruiter's name, address and job title, and maybe even refer to something you've learned about their department or responsibilities, they'll be more likely to show you the same respect.

One task Have you been using the same template for all your covering letters? Delete it today and write a fresh one.

One question What sloppy job-hunting habits do you need to kick?

One to read *101 Best Cover Letters* by Jay Block and Michael Betrus (Schaum)

Day 4 **Job applications**

One thought If there's one thing that bugs recruiters more than anything else it's job-hunters who haven't bothered to find out anything about the organisation to which they're applying.

Crazy. Each time you complete and return a job application form, you're effectively saying to the employer "I want to spend the next few years of my life with you." But are you sure? Have you done all the research you possibly can on that organisation to know that a) it's the kind of place you'd be happy working in and b) you have the skills, personality and aptitudes necessary to work there?

Employers can tell immediately from reading application forms whether or not you've done that kind of homework. And there are no excuses: the information is out there, in recruitment brochures, websites and careers directories or at careers fairs and company presentations. You wouldn't propose marriage to a stranger – why should getting hitched to an employer be any different?

One task Subscribe to the leading trade magazine in the sector that you want to enter. The knowledge you'll gain about individual employers in that industry will be invaluable at this stage, not to mention for interviews at a later date.

One question Are you confident that you've researched all the relevant employers in the sector you'd like to enter?

One to read *CVs and Job Applications* by Judith Leigh, John Seely and Beatrice Baumgartner-Cohen (Oxford University Press)

Week 2

Day 5 **Spec letters**

One thought Many of the jobs we explore in this book can't be accessed via standard graduate entry programmes or application forms. And you may never see your dream job advertised in the newspapers. Friends and family may have warned you how difficult it is to get into a particular sector or how stiff the competition is just to get unpaid work experience.

Yet there are people out there doing the kind of work you want to do. If you genuinely believe you have the skills, personality and aptitude to work successfully in such a role, don't let well-meaning friends or family talk you out of sending off a speculative letter and CV to your target companies. Yes, the job you want may be wanted by thousands of other people, but your enthusiasm, energy and persistence can set you apart. And who would you rather recruit – someone who is merely answering an ad, or someone who has a passion for the job?

One task Depending on the sector you're trying to enter, think about other marketing materials (not gimmicks) you could send to accompany your CV and spec letter that would reinforce the key messages you want to give prospective employers.

One question What are the jobs you've ruled out just because you think they're too hard to get?

One to read *The Ultimate Job Search Letters Book* by Martin Yate (Kogan Page)

■ Week 3 **Finding your voice**

Day 1 **Passing tests**

One thought Most of us hope that we've sat our last ever test at school, college or university, but many employers still feel the need to subject job applicants to a battery of personality, competency and ability tests.

It can be easy to lose perspective before a test, and convince yourself that your whole career rests on whether you score well or not. But remember that it's OK to be nervous – you certainly won't be the only candidate feeling tense. And don't spend time after the test beating yourself up for every question you think you answered incorrectly.

Employers are looking at the total package in front of them and won't judge you solely on the results of any one test. In many instances, they simply use tests to confirm what they'll learn from you later at interview. So take a deep breath, pick up your pen and just let the test happen.

One task Most tests demand that you answer a large number of questions in a short period of time. Why not practise by setting yourself the challenge of completing a puzzle each day, in a set length of time – the newspaper crossword for example.

One question Have you a tried and tested method of controlling your nerves?

One to read *Passing Psychometric Tests* by Andrea Shavick (How To Books)

Day 2 **Group therapies**

One thought For almost completely sadistic reasons, some recruiters enjoy putting job applicants together in the same room, setting them a task and then watching them as they tear each other apart.

It's as close to Big Brother voyeurism as you'd want to get and can make you feel more than a little insecure and hostile to the other candidates. But don't let your negative feelings surface. Remember that this is a test and recruiters will be watching that you listen as much as you talk, that you respect others' opinions even if you don't agree with them, and that you help the group stay focused on the end result. By concentrating on helping the group to succeed, you'll set yourself apart.

One task Observe yourself during a group conversation today. Make a mental note of how you contribute and how well you listen, respond and move the conversation forward.

One question Do your friends say you're a good listener?

One to read *How to Win Friends and Influence People* by Dale Carnegie (Hutchinson)

Day 3 **Impression management**

One thought It shouldn't but it does – how you look at an interview matters. But not for the reason you might think.

Yes, wearing the right suit will make an interviewer sit up, take notice and listen to you with respect. Dress shabbily and you'll have to work much harder just to get to the starting line. How you dress won't win you a job on its own, but it can be an obstacle.

But the real reason appearance matters is that if you've made an effort to look the part, you'll feel good too and carry an air of confidence into the interview. And when you exude confidence, it might just give the interviewer the confidence to recruit you.

One task You don't have to dress like a stiff: smart clothes can be simple and comfortable too. Do an audit of your wardrobe today and invest where necessary.

One question What do your friends say about the way you dress?

One to read *Walking Tall: Key Steps to Total Image Impact* by Lesley Everett (Lesley Everett)

Day 4 **More interviews**

One thought Don't expect your first interview to be a success. Like riding a bike, skateboarding or tightrope walking, you can expect a few falls, cuts and bruises before you're happy with your interview technique.

View each interview as part of the learning process, as a practice for the next one. Instead of spending hours fretting about how you screwed an interview up, take 10 minutes to write down what you think you did right, and what you could have done better. Then forget about the interview and move on.

Some people apply for jobs they don't really want, just to get in some extra interview practice. That's just downright weird, but the more interview experience you clock up, the greater the chances of you landing the job you really want.

One task Describing your achievements is pivotal to success in any interview. Prepare for your next interview by summarising each of your key achievements into OARs: overview (the problem or situation that faced you); actions (all the steps you took in response); and results (concrete evidence of what happened next).

One question Do you dread job interviews, or look forward to them as an opportunity to sell yourself?

One to read *Handling Tough Job Interviews* by Julie-Ann Amos (How To Books)

Week 3

Day 5 **Handling rejection**

....

One thought So you didn't get the job. What
now? A few days of self-pity, self-loathing and
general self-debasement?

Get a grip. The recruiter didn't reject you
because you are any less a man or woman than
the successful candidate. Interviewers often
recruit people who are similar to them in
personality, temperament or outlook. While
you might think a rejection letter is a reflection
on you, it's more likely to be a reflection of the
interviewer.

That's not to denigrate recruiters.
Organisations need workers who can fit the
culture they've created. What it means is that
while you weren't the right fit for that job, your
chances of getting the next job you apply for
have in no way diminished. Never dwell on the
job that got away.

....

One task Is there one rejection that still bugs
you? Ring up the organisation today and ask
for some detailed feedback on why your
application was rejected.

....

One question How do you respond to
criticism or negative feedback?

....

One to read *The Bounce Back Quotient* by
Linda Nash (Prism Publications)

■ Week 4 Finding another way

Day 1 Cold calling

One thought The jobs that are advertised in newspapers represent only the tip of the iceberg. The majority of vacancies are never advertised: there's a "hidden jobs" market of vacancies that are only advertised internally, outsourced to headhunters or filled via an existing employee's referral or through speculative approaches.

If the thought of ringing a complete stranger and asking them for a job doesn't scare you, you're probably bluffing. But it's one way of accessing these hidden jobs. Successful cold calling requires a great deal of research and targeting. But remember that you're likely to increase the odds of success by targeting fast-growing small and medium-sized enterprises that find the cost of advertising jobs prohibitive. Almost two-thirds of the country's employers fall into this category – rich pickings for job-hunters who have done their homework.

One task Begin to build a database of smaller employers that might need your services, including details of the key decision-makers.

One question Have you considered achieving your career objectives with a smaller employer?

One to read *Complete Idiot's Guide to Cold Calling* by Keith Rosen (Alpha Books)

Day 2 Networks work

One thought If you think networking means muscling in on uptight cocktail parties or "pressing the flesh" over a couple of canapes, think again.

You're already at the heart of the most powerful network: your circle of family and friends. Employers would much rather recruit people they've been recommended than try to guess a person's ability to do a job from their CV. And the people around you are networked – even if they don't realise it. Maybe your best friend doesn't know anyone in management consultancy, but her dad might. You'll never know if you don't ask.

Not every contact you make through networking is going to offer you a job, but they might be able to point you in the right direction. Strike up enough of these conversations, and anything could happen.

One task Supplement your personal networks by contacting relevant trade associations to see if they host professional networking events.

One question How much do you know about what your friends and their families do for a living?

One to read *The Ultimate Guide to Successful Networking* by Carole Stone (Vermilion)

Week 4

Day 3 **Volunteering**

One thought Employers are looking for people who come to them already equipped with soft skills such as team-building and negotiation. Volunteering for charities and other not-for-profit organisations can be an ideal way of obtaining those skills.

Even if it's for a couple of hours a week – listening to children read in schools, clearing up a beach or working a shift in a charity shop – voluntary work can add extra depth to a CV. There are plenty of volunteering opportunities on your doorstep. But if you decide to volunteer abroad you'll experience a different country and culture. You might come back with a new language to boot.

One task Start trawling these websites for some ideas. It's best if you look for something for which you have a passion or a real concern.
- **Community Service Volunteers** www.csv.org.uk
- **Community Service Volunteers Environment** www.csvenvironment.org.uk
- **Idealist** www.idealist.org

One question Don't fancy what's on offer? Why not flex your entrepreneurial muscles and set up something yourself?

One to read *The Back Door Guide to Short-term Job Adventures* by Michael Landes (Ten Speed Press)

Day 4 **Careers events**

One thought Email and the internet have made job-hunting an increasingly impersonal activity, so maybe it's time to use a method that will enable employers to appreciate your personality.

Careers fairs offer a unique opportunity for candidates to meet employers face to face on neutral ground. Most are targeted at graduates and held at universities or large venues like the NEC in Birmingham or ExCeL in London. But in general they're open to anyone and in most cases they're free.

It's a very time-efficient form of job-hunting. In just one day you can meet more than 30, 40, maybe 50 different employers who are all looking for staff. And since an increasing number of fairs are focused on individual industry sectors, you can be sure that many of the positions on offer will match with your preferences.

One task Find a careers fair near you by checking out the listings at www.prospects.ac.uk.

One question How well do you listen? Careers fairs are learning opportunities and listening to what the employer representatives have to say is as important as impressing them with your knowledge.

One to read *Seven-Second Marketing: How to Use Memory Hooks to Make You Instantly Stand Out in a Crowd* by Ivan R Misner (Gilmour Drummond Publishing)

Week 4

Day 5 **Entry level**

One thought Some industries are harder to crack than others and to get the job you want may require doing two years or more of less glamorous, more menial work than you're qualified to do. This will be more likely in the so-called creative industries like advertising or broadcasting. But take heart: there are plenty of case studies of successful people who started their careers making the tea. The important thing is to get in on the ground floor with the right employer.

And it doesn't have to be two years of boredom. It's possible to learn from even the dullest of tasks. If you're photocopying, you can learn about the company by reading the documents. If delivering mail, you get to meet people and find out what they do. You can turn most jobs around.

One task Start lowering your sights. Look beyond the job description and salary in the classified advertisements for entry-level opportunities that will get your foot on the career ladder.

One question Is pride an obstacle in your career? Are you worried about what your friends will say if you take a "crap" job in order to get your foot in the door? It's your career, not theirs!

One to read *The Only Way Is Up: From Office Slave to High Flyer* by Christine White (Metro Publishing)

Glossary

Access course – a route into higher education aimed at adult learners or people from under-represented groups. Access courses cover study skills and a broad subject area, such as teaching or science. They are linked to a university, but are more likely to be taught in an FE college.

Accreditation of prior learning (APL) – a means of awarding credit to learning that has occurred in the past, such as academic or professional achievement. Nice to know it wasn't wasted.

Accredited course of training – a course recognised as giving proper training and qualification by a professional body.

Associated Board (music) – an international body governing theory and practical examinations in music.

BA/BA hons – bachelor of arts. The usual qualification after a three-year degree course (see Degree).

Blue-chip company – a well-established company with a good trading record, whose returns are usually large and considered reliable. Blue-chip can also refer to the stock of such a company.

British Council – the UK's organisation for overseas educational and cultural relations. It can offer information on educational exchange schemes and studying and teaching English abroad or in the UK.

BTEC, BTEC/SQA higher national certificate or diploma – qualifications validated by the Business and Technical Education Council, and, in Scotland, the Scottish Qualifications Authority.

Code of conduct – guidelines that one or more organisations agree to follow. Also referred to as "voluntary code" or "code of practice", it typically outlines service standards and ethical principles that you can expect in dealings with a company subscribing to the code.

Continuous professional development (CPD) – the process of maintaining, improving and broadening professional knowledge and skills.

County Council – the elected governing body of a county.

Credit accumulation transfer scheme (Cats) – an accreditation scheme for students, in particular mature students and those from non-traditional backgrounds. Credit can be given for previous learning: people who have already studied to HND level, on a degree programme or for relevant professional qualifications may be able to transfer credits when they start a new degree.

Cultural Heritage National Training Organisation – the official training body for the heritage industry.

Degree – most undergraduates in England work towards an honours degree such as a bachelor of arts (BA) or bachelor of science (BSc), which is awarded after the equivalent of three years of full-time university-level study. In Scotland, it's generally four years.

Diploma of higher education – awarded by some universities after two years of undergraduate-level study.

District/Borough council – the elected governing body of a district or council.

ESP – English for specific purposes. English taught to those who come from a non-English-speaking background and geared to specific ends, for example Medical English or Business English.

Ethics – the practice of applying a code of conduct based on moral principles to day-to-day actions to balance what is fair to individuals or organisations and what is right for society.

Foundation degree – a two-year university or college course set to replace the higher national diploma (HND).

Freelance – a mode of working where an individual sells their services to various organisations without having a contract of employment.

Greenwashing – glossing over a firm's more nefarious activities for the sake of its public image.

GNVQ – general national vocational qualification. An alternative to GCSE, each is related to a broad area of work.

GCSE – General Certificate of Secondary Education. Awarded in England and Wales after public examinations at the age of 16. Eight to 12 subjects are generally studied and individually assessed. GCSEs can also be a stepping stone to further qualifications, such as A-levels and BTEC HNCs.

Health and Safety Executive – official body responsible for regulation of almost all risks to health and safety arising from work activity in Britain.

Health Professions Council – the regulator set up to protect the health and wellbeing of people who use the services of the following registered health professionals: art therapists, biomedical scientists, chiropodists/podiatrists, clinical scientists, dieticians, occupational therapists, operating department practitioners, orthoptists, paramedics, physiotherapists, prostheticists and orthotists, radiographers, and speech and language therapists.

Higher education college – educational institution principally concerned with the provision of one or both of the following: a) full-time education suitable for persons over compulsory school age who are not yet nineteen, b) courses of further or higher education.

HND (HNC/HND) – higher national diploma. A diploma given for vocational training that prepares the student for a career in a particular area. The HNC, or higher national certificate, is also a vocational qualification. HNCs require 12 credits and usually take one year to complete whereas to achieve the more advanced qualification of HND will usually take two years and 30 credits. These credits can also be used towards gaining a full degree. In England and Wales it is called a BTEC HND or BTEC HNC.

Independent schools – defined by the Education Act 2002 as any school not maintained by a Local Education Authority (LEA) or a non-maintained special school. They provide full-time education for five or more pupils of compulsory school age, or one or more pupils with a statement of special educational needs or who is in public care.

Internship – a programme of supervised practical training for a student or recent graduate, particularly in the medical profession.

ITT course – initial teacher training course. The first stage of training to teach, usually undertaken as a PGCE at a university or college, with school placements as part of the training programme. ITT prepares trainees for qualified teacher status, the qualification necessary for those who wish to teach in state-maintained schools.

Local authority – an administrative unit of local government.

MA – master of arts. Postgraduate qualification awarded after additional study involving original research and analysis.

MBA – master of business administration. Postgraduate business course offered by business schools throughout Europe and the US. They are usually one- or two-year full-time courses, and companies often sponsor employees.

Maintained school – a community, foundation or voluntary school or a community or foundation special school.

MBTI – Myers–Briggs type indicator. A personality and behaviour test used by many firms in the recruitment process. The test analyses behavioural and temperamental preferences in order to build up a profile of the subject. Firms then use this to assess the suitability of potential recruits.

Metropolitan council – the elected governing body of a metropolitan area.

Milk round – the annual round of visits made by large companies to universities and colleges aimed at graduate recruitment.

MPhil – master of philosophy. Postgraduate qualification awarded following additional study involving a substantial amount of original research and analysis in a subject not previously studied.

MSc – master of science. Postgraduate qualification awarded after additional study involving original research and analysis.

National governing body coaching qualifications – sport-specific qualifications offered by the national governing body of the relevant sport.

Networking – the activity of building and maintaining contacts in your chosen field.

Olaf (online application form) – the term for the forms used when making online job applications, now favoured by some industries.

Outsourcing – the practice of moving business functions to a separate supplier.

PGCE – postgraduate certificate in education. A course of initial teacher training for graduates and those with equivalent level qualifications, which leads to recognition of qualified teacher status (QTS). Normally the course duration is a year.

PhD – doctor of philosophy. Title awarded to a student having published and presented a dissertation or thesis usually taking four years.

Pitch – in this context a presentation given to a client to sell a product or service, or the skills of a job-hunter.

Placement – a period of practical experience, normally away from the university, in a school, hospital, company, voluntary agency or other similar organisation, which may be assessed.

Portfolio – a collection of work that documents a student's educational performance and employment experiences over time, or a collection of securities held by an investor.

Postgraduate courses/qualifications – study or certification undertaken after a first degree.

Private school – A school controlled by an individual or agency other than a government entity, which is usually supported primarily by other than public funds, and the operation of whose programme rests with someone other than publicly elected or appointed officials.

Private sector – the part of the economy consisting of business, companies and professionals who trade products and services for income and profit.

Professional institution – body governing a profession and concerned with the accreditation of individuals, continuous professional development, and codes of ethics, conduct and standards.

Psychometric testing – method of assessing an individual's psychological makeup in variables such as intelligence, aptitude, and personality traits.

Public sector – consists of the national government, local government, government-owned or controlled corporations and government monetary institutions.

Qualified teacher status (QTS) – the professional status needed to teach in state-maintained schools in England and Wales. Normally awarded after successful completion of an initial teacher training (ITT) course and the skills tests.

Regulator – official body responsible for representing the interests of consumers and overseeing industrial compliance with legislation concerning standards, competitiveness etc.

Sandwich course – some courses offer a "sandwich year" of a placement in industry or the workplace. It usually takes place in the third year of university and is more common in certain universities and on science or technology-based or vocational courses.

Sourcing – activities related to locating and pricing a given product or service.

Soft skills – skills needed to perform jobs where job requirements are defined in terms of expected outcomes, but the process(es) to achieve the outcomes vary widely. Usually an area of performance that does not have a definite beginning and end (such as counselling, supervising, managing).

Sponsorship – it is possible to be sponsored by business or an organisation, the armed forces perhaps, which would give you money during your time at university in the expectation of employing you in the holidays and/or on graduation. You get their cash, but they'll want something back. Sponsorship is more common in vocational subjects such as engineering and business.

Tefl – teaching English as a foreign language. An internationally recognised qualification.

Tesol – teaching English to speakers of other languages. Although this term is sometimes used to mean the same as TEFL, it is also teaching aimed specifically at non-native English speakers living in English-speaking countries, for example refugees and first generation immigrants. Tesol teaching in this country is usually government-funded.

Tesl – teaching English as a second language. Generally taught in countries such as Nigeria and India where English is spoken as a second language – either for communication, administration or in diplomatic circles where several languages coexist.

Thinktank – an organisation which undertakes research to order and reports on the findings.

Ucas tariff – a points system used to give achievements a numerical score so that they can be assessed for entry to higher education. It establishes agreed equivalents between different types of qualifications (HND, Baccalaureates, and so on) and provides comparisons between applicants with different types and volumes of achievement. For most of you, the final grades for your A-levels or highers will counts towards your score. If the score is good enough, you get a place at university. The Ucas website has a tariff calculator, which can help you do the maths: www.ucas.ac.uk

Unitary councils – provide all the services within their administrative boundaries.

Vocational – of or in relation to a vocation or occupation; especially providing or undergoing training in special skills.

VSO – Voluntary Service Overseas. An international development charity which works through volunteers.

Work experience – a learning activity in which a student attends an approved workplace. May or may not involve the performance of actual jobs of commercial value and is usually unpaid.

Work placement – a period of unpaid experience with an employer undertaken to satisfy the requirements of a course of study.

Index

I

interview tests, 277–86, 314
  see also assessment days; group tests;
    IQ and aptitude tests; in-tray
    exercises; personality tests;
    psychometric tests; Swot analysis;
    teamwork exercises
interviews, 262–76, 315
  body language, 264–5
  dress, 264
  expenses, 271
  jokes, 272–3
  multiple, 270
  questions, 265–70
  quiz, 274–6
  research, 262–3
  techniques, 232, 233
  timing, 263
  see also interview tests
in-tray exercises, 277
investment analyst, 99, 100
investment banker, 99, 100
IQ and aptitude tests, 281–2
ISPAL (The Institute for Sport, Parks and
    Leisure), 49, 200, 201
ITN, 163
ITT (initial teacher training), 59

J
job advertisements, 224–6, 230, 294
job clubs, 232–3
job descriptions, 296–7
job-hunting, 1–3, 223–39, 307–19
  advice and support, 17, 231–3, 251,
    310, 311
  decision-making, 289–90
  follow-up, 229, 234
  newspapers, 223–4, 234
  research, 228, 248–9, 255, 262–3,
    291, 312
  structured, 228, 289, 308
  see also career changes; careers fairs;
    cold calling; CVs; inside
    information; job advertisements;
    job clubs; networking; recruitment
    consultants; letters, speculative;
    trade magazines and journals
job snobs, 299, 309
journalism, 13, 19, 25, 26, 158–64, 166–7
  broadcast, 161–4
  print, 158–61

journalist, 159, 160
  broadcast, 161–2, 163
  freelance, 18
  online, 163

K
keywords, 250
  see also buzzwords

L
land agent, 174
Landscape Design Trust, 176
Landscape Institute, 176
law costs draftsman, 143, 145
law, 6, 142–8
Law Society, 146, 147
Law Society of Scotland, 145, 146
leadership, 28–30
learning mentor, 58, 59
leaving jobs, 17
  see also sackings
legal executive, 143–4, 145
leisure attendant, 198, 200
leisure manager, 198, 200
leisure services development officer,
    198–9, 200
letters
  covering, 254, 255–6, 258, 259, 312
  rejection, 288–9
  speculative, 227–9, 232, 254–7, 313
licensed conveyancer, 144, 145
lifeguard, 199
local government, 105–8, 191
Local Government Employers, 107
logistics manager, 204, 205
London College of Fashion, 90
London Fire and Emergency Planning
    Authority, 220
London Investment Banking
    Association, 101

M
Management Consultancies Association,
    150
management consultancy, 6, 19, 32,
    149–52
manufacturing, 153–7
Market Research Society, 39